Migrants, Credit and Climate

# African Social
# Studies Series

VOLUME 12

# Migrants, Credit and Climate

## The Gambian Groundnut Trade, 1834–1934

*by*

Kenneth Swindell and Alieu Jeng

BRILL

LEIDEN · BOSTON

2006

This book is printed on acid-free paper.

Library of Congress Cataloging-in-Publication Data

Swindell, Kenneth.
  Migrants, credit, and climate : the Gambian groundnut trade, 1834–1934 /
by Kenneth Swindell and Alieu Jeng.
    p. cm. — (African social studies series, ISSN 1568-1203 ;  v. 12)
  Includes bibliographical references and index.
  ISBN-13: 978-90-04-14059-2
  ISBN-10: 90-04-14059-X (pbk. : alk. paper)
    1. Peanut industry—Gambia—History. I. Jeng, Alieu. II. Title. III. Series.

HD9235.P32G257 2006
382'.41336809665109034—dc22                                      2006047566

ISSN    1568-1203
ISBN-13: 978 90 04 14059 2
ISBN-10: 90 04 14059 X

Printed in the Netherlands

CONTENTS

# ACKNOWLEDGEMENTS

This book has been in gestation for a long time: it began in 1975 with doctoral research by Dr Alieu Jeng and ended with further archival research in England and The Gambia conducted by Dr K. Swindell. Dr Jeng's work was generously funded by the Commonwealth Scholarship Committee, The Gambian Government and Mr John Cadbury, while Dr Swindell received support from The British Academy: both authors gratefully acknowledge the financial assistance and support of the University of Birmingham. The illustrations were produced by Mr Harry Buglass of The Department of Archaeology and Antiquity.

The staff of the Banjul Archives was extremely helpful in according quick access to documents, as well as drawing attention to items that might have escaped our notice.

We would also thank those elderly Gambians who gave of their time and experience, and who made a valuable contribution through their oral testimonies.

# LIST OF ABBREVIATIONS

| | |
|---|---|
| BA | Banjul Archives, The Gambia |
| CO | Colonial Office |
| Conf. D | Confidential Dispatch |
| Conf. M | Confidential Minute |
| CS | Colonial Secretary |
| Encl | Enclosure |
| FO | Foreign Office |
| GNA | Gambian National Archives, Banjul |
| PRO | Public Record Office |
| RHL | Rhodes House Library, Oxford |
| SS | Secretary of State for the Colonies |
| TC | Travelling Commissioner |

# LIST OF FIGURES

# MEASUREMENTS, WEIGHTS AND MONETARY VALUES

During the period covered by this text all measurements and weights were Imperial. The following are metric equivalents: 1 inch is 25.4 millimetres; 1 bushel is 36.4 litres; 1 hundredweight (cwt) is 50.80 kilograms; 1 ton is 1.016 tonnes. Monetary values are pounds sterling, shillings and pence, with 20 shillings per pound and 12 pence per shilling. The shilling is equivalent to 5 pence in the present British decimal system.

# INTRODUCTION

From the 15th century onwards the peoples of West Africa were increasingly drawn into trading with Europeans, who vied with each other for control of the exports from this region. First the trade in gold, hides, ivory and gum arabic, then in the 17th and 18th centuries the Atlantic slave trade, which was replaced in the 19th century by the export of agricultural staples. The decline and abolition of the Atlantic slave trade in West Africa, and its replacement by legitimate trade have raised a number of issues about their implications for West African polities and societies. These issues include discussions about the political economies of the metropoles, free trade, the shifting balance of power between Africans and Europeans, crises of political and economic adaptation, together with partition and colonial administration. The Gambia was one of the first areas where commercial export agriculture took root, and the period from 1834–1934 covered in the following chapters embraces most of the issues surrounding the transformation of West Africa from a predominantly slave exporting region, to one exporting tropical produce. This was a commercial transformation that preceded partition, and one which was extended under colonial rule. Export crops and imported trade goods created revenues that were a central plank in the colonial economies, underpinning one of the inner dramas of colonialism, finding the means to pay for itself. Therefore, it seems appropriate to begin with an introductory review of these issues before discussing the Gambian groundnut trade in detail.

The abolition of the slave trade has been the subject of various interpretations. In market-economic terms the demise of the trade is held to have been inevitable, as it became marginal to the process of industrialization and urbanization in Europe. Austen has suggested that the anti-slavery movement was both a critique and affirmation of capitalism.[1] Slavery was the product of capitalism, yet it represented an archaic institution, the opposite of modernity and the antithesis of the social economic order of 19th century Europe with

---

[1] Austen, R.A., 1987, *African Economic History*. London: James Currey, ch. 5.

its emphasis on individual liberty and the nuclear family. It has also
been asserted that abolition and the burgeoning of legitimate trade,
supported by a British presence, was part of the vision of a world
economic transformation espoused by abolitionists, ideologues and
public servants. The philanthropic lobby believed that a British presence was justified in terms of forging links among Christianity,
Commerce and Civilization, a belief that possibly included a need
for role opposites to buttress their moral and theological certainties.
On the other hand, merchants and financial interests in the metropoles had a different view, based on profitability and opening-up new
niches for investment as the slave trade declined.

The Africa trade was consonant with Victorian attitudes as the
British regarded themselves as pioneers of commerce, industry and
progress, as well as leaders of civilization. In early and mid-Victorian
Britain there was not just a belief in the power of industry, but also
a belief in the ability to improve the human condition everywhere.
Expansion overseas was best achieved through private enterprise, free
trade and freedom from the shackles of state interference. In 1842
Palmerston opined that, "commerce may go freely forth, leading civilization with one hand and peace with the other to render mankind
happier, wiser, better", a sentiment which has some resonance for
the neo-liberals of the 21st century.[2] And later in 1867, John Stuart
Mill wrote of nations and races on the ladder of progress according
to their degree of freedom and enterprise: inevitably the British were
at the top while at the bottom were the 'aborigines' who had yet
to progress from the family and the tribe to the making of a state.[3]
Nonetheless it was imperative that the slave trader in Africa be
removed, and the Dark Continent be enlightened and brought into
the world economy. Not that freedom was a God-given-right, but it
had to be achieved through individual effort and hard work in the
'enterprise culture'.

Cain and Hopkins have argued that the end of the Atlantic slave
trade and the rise of 'legitimate' commerce and imperialism were
an integral part of the larger restructuring of the international economy during the early 19th century, a process spearheaded by Britain

---

[2] Robinson, R. and J. Gallagher, 1981, *Africa and the Victorians: the Official Mind of Imperialism*. London: MacMillan, Second Edition, p. 35.
[3] Mill, Stuart J., 1867, *Considerations on Representative Government*. London: People's Edition, p. 26.

who wished to extend the British model of free trade.[4] By the end
of the 18th century the Caribbean was a declining market for slaves,
while events in the European metropoles and North America were
influential too, but Cain and Hopkins eschew industrialization as the
motive power behind British expansion. Instead they posit different
phases of 'Gentlemanly Capitalism', that is the power of moneyed
interests to shape policy; an interest rooted in the 18th century class
of rentier capitalists who first became involved in commercial agriculture, and then embraced the City interest and the financial sector,
the two being welded together by shared values and culture. After
the Napoleonic Wars there was a restructuring of the international
economy and the moneyed interest essentially managed the increasingly important National Debt, while free trade emerged to placate
the taxpayers and increase customs duties. Thus cheap government
and free trade were not simply a product of industrialization breaking the 'old corruption' and a declining aristocracy. The free trade
of 1840–60 and the legislation that supported it was as much a tri-
umph for the City as industry, and it was the City that financed
and gave credit for the new areas of expansion. Overseas expansion
also became linked with strategic considerations, political stability at
home, and the need to bolster the metropole against America and
France after their respective Revolutions and wars against England.

However, some of those in government in the early 19th century
were cautious about the costs of a British presence in Africa, and
arguably African trade was relatively marginal to the British economy compared with trade in the Americas and Asia. Exports to
Britain from African possessions (excluding Egypt and South Africa)
in 1865–9 amounted to some £1.0 million rising to £2.0 million in
1890–94, compared with £20 million and £32 million for India during the same periods.[5] Nonetheless, African trade was important to
particular companies and specific industries. For example, merchants
collected oil palm and groundnuts from African producers to meet
the rising European demand for oils and fats to produce soap,
candles, cooking oils and lubricants. Groundnuts were found to be
especially good for soap-making, as well as being a cheap substitute
for olive oil, the latter being of importance in opening-up the French
market.

---

[4] Cain, P.J. and A.G. Hopkins, 1993, *British Imperialism*. London: Longman.
[5] Robinson and Gallagher, 1981, op. cit., p. 6.

And, if West Africa was economically marginal to British interests, and neither an area of White settlement nor an important area
of mineral exploitation, it was still part of the larger design of British
free trade. The colonies and protectorates which eventually emerged
by the end of the century were virtually self-supporting, requiring
minimal financial support, and benefited from new shipping technology which had been improved and cheapened. However, the rise
and development of the Gambian groundnut trade shows that notwithstanding the ideals of the philanthropists, and the often grudging
support of the government, it was merchant capital and credit backed
by the banks which effectively transformed African rural economies
in the early 19th century. The means were generally peaceful, although
insidious, and from time to time merchants met with considerable
economic resistance from African producers. In the Gambia during
the early 19th century the merchants and traders were the' foot soldiers' of British expansion, whose operations stretched beyond the
limited colonial enclaves.

But what were the social and political implications of the transition from the Atlantic slave trade to legitimate trade? The development of new crops in West Africa, such as oil palm and groundnuts
to replace the lost trade in slaves comprised a period of economic
uncertainty and one of experimentation, while there were profound
differences between the Atlantic slave trade and legitimate trade.[6]
Importantly legitimate trade in agricultural produce did not depend
on plantations; instead household producers became the core of the
production process. Under the new conditions of agricultural production returns to labour were tied to annual harvests and the regular export of produce, while a new European merchant class gradually
replaced the Atlantic trade monopolies and limited circle of entrepreneurs. Also, the costs of entry into legitimate trade were less,
while the volume and range of imported goods increased and were
socially and geographically distributed throughout West Africa.

The transition to legitimate trade has been viewed by some as
creating a crisis of political authority; for example Hopkins argued
the Yoruba palm oil industry led to warfare and plunder by chiefs

---

[6] See R. Law (ed.), 1995, *From Slave Trade to Legitimate Commerce: the Commercial
Transition in Nineteenth century West Africa*, Cambridge: CUP. Also, Cain and Hopkins,
1993, op. cit.

to maintain their incomes, ultimately leading to British annexation and partition.[7] Further disruption followed when producer-merchant relations were badly affected by the Great Depression of 1873–96. A similar argument has been advanced by Klein for Senegambia, where he believes the widespread involvement of the peasantry in the groundnut trade overthrew the old political order, and led to the Muslim wars from the 1850s onwards. Klein asserts that the slave trade strengthened the élites, whereas the peanut trade put money and guns into the hands of the peasants'.[8] Military chiefs could control the slave trade, but not legitimate trade. In essence both Hopkins and Klein believe the modern history of West Africa begins with legitimate trade. A rather different interpretation for the western savannas derives from assertions of a southward shift of the Sahara from the late 18th century onwards: this affected resources and caused political upheavals as well as the disruption of internal and external slave trading.[9] Other views suggest that either the Atlantic Slave trade was of marginal significance for African societies, or ruling élites maintained their positions and incomes because they were able to dominate the new legitimate trade. Indeed, the strength and continuity of African polities was not being weakened to allow European penetration; they were sufficiently strong to require military intervention for their overthrow.[10] Thus modern history begins with military conquest and partition.

Out of these contrasting opinions has emerged a consensus for the need to distinguish between coastal middlemen states, and the interior states. Arguably trading units on the coast were structurally changed less by the ending of the Atlantic slave trade than production units inland; for example, the Old Calabar élites controlled the new trade in Palm Oil, while the crisis of political adaptation for élites in areas such as eastern Senegambia may have been problematic.[11]

---

[7] Hopkins, A.G., 1968, 'Economic Imperialism in West Africa: Lagos, 1880–92', *Econ.Hist. Rev.*, 21, 580–606.

[8] Klein, M., 1972, 'Social and Economic Factors in the Muslim Revolutions in Senegambia', *Journal of African History*, 13, 419–41.

[9] Webb, J.A., 1995, *Desert Frontier: Ecological and Economic Change along the Western Sahel, 1600–1850*. Madison: University of Wisconsin Press. See also, G. Brooks, 1992, *Landlords and Strangers. Boulder: Westview Press.*

[10] See D. Eltis, 1987, *Economic growth and the Ending of the Transatlantic Slave Trade.* Oxford: OUP. Also, Austen, 1987, op. cit.

[11] Law, 1995, op. cit., Introduction.

A further modification of the adaptation argument lies in the suggestion that a periodization of the development of legitimate trade is required. With reference to the Palm Oil trade, Manning has pointed to an early period when élites were in control of the trade, followed by the middle decades of the 19th century when prices soared and free competition allowed the upward social mobility of small producers, and the late 19th century when stagnant prices tended to consolidate the power of the foreign traders.[12]

In some parts of West Africa the Atlantic slave trade lingered on until the mid-19th century, while the internal Saharan trade was probably expanded; both continued as a means of supporting rulers and merchants. With respect to internal slave trading several scenarios have been suggested. For example, in some instances legitimate trade stimulated the internal market for slaves, as they became sources of labour for new crops that offered some compensation to slave owners.[13] Alternatively, it has been claimed that in the interior there was an increase in regional slave trading to offset losses of the Atlantic trade.[14] Elsewhere chiefs withdrew from the slave trade, as happened in Asante where increased trading in kola nuts northwards and gold southwards compensated for lost income.[15] Different outcomes and strategies of adaptation depended on geographical circumstances, the prices of slaves, agricultural commodities, and importantly the relative profitability of the slave trade versus legitimate trade. Prices of slaves may have fallen after abolition because of gluts in supply, which also may have occurred (or been exacerbated) through increased capture as a result of *jihads* in the interior. Probably slave prices in real terms did not collapse until the 1850s; in the meantime when prices of palm oil and groundnut were good, the relative profit on slaves declined and many were set to work on growing the new export crops, or commercial food crops.[16] Exact comparisons are difficult because of the necessity for a range of data, not just prices, but costs of feeding, collecting, marketing and transport of slaves and produce.

---

[12] Ibid.
[13] Ibid.
[14] MacDougall, E.A., 1995, 'In search of a desert-edge perspective: the Sahara-Sahel and the Atlantic Trade, c.1815–1890'. In Law (ed) 1995, op. cit., 215–24.
[15] Law, 1995, op. cit., Introduction.
[16] Ibid.

What does seem to be evident is that the Atlantic slave trade was monopolized by a small number of large entrepreneurs, who included, or were backed by military and political chiefs, whereas legitimate trade was open to the generality of the population. Formerly, large-scale operations were important for slave trading, but there was no comparative advantage of size in the agricultural export trade. The evidence concerning the shift from the Atlantic slave trade to legitimate trade, and the crisis of adaptation shows there were considerable geographic and historic specificities. These reflect differences between weak and strong states, interior and coastal locations and the crops concerned. Some areas experienced a smooth transition, others less so.

The Gambia had its own trajectory of change and adaptation, which was shaped by forces peculiar to this area, as well as those common to other parts of West Africa. Local Gambian chiefs were largely brokers and intermediaries between suppliers and buyers in the Atlantic slave trade, which was in decline in the late 18th century and stopped rather abruptly after 1807 due to the British presence. However, legitimate trade, which had been carried on in parallel with the slave trade flourished after abolition before the groundnut trade took-off. Furthermore, the transition to groundnut farming was materially assisted by the long established social and commercial networks which supported the Atlantic slave trade, as well as legitimate exports. Arguably, the Atlantic slave trade was grafted onto an already flourishing commercial and internal slave trading economy, and it may have been less central to the economies of the Gambia and upper Senegal valleys than other parts of West Africa. However, in lower Senegal and Gambia, the Atlantic slave trade had an important impact on internal slavery: local servile populations were vital for the trade's operation as they produced grain to provision slaves in transit.[17] In turn it was these grain-producing areas which became the groundnut producing regions, with the north bank of the river Gambia forming the historic core of the Senegambian groundnut basin. In general the initial transition to legitimate trade in The Gambia was a smooth one, but producer-merchant relations deteriorated as the century progressed: after the Great Depression groundnut

---

[17] Searing, J.F., 1993, *West African Slavery and Atlantic Commerce: The Senegal Atlantic Valley*. Cambridge: CUP.

prices and market demand fluctuated, while producer terms of trade worsened.

There were also 'crises of adaptation' for millions of new peasant producers, as well as for their rulers. Legitimate trade certainly brought about immense changes in the domestic economy of West Africa, but the link to world commodity markets and climatic uncertainties in some areas increased the vulnerability of domestic producers, especially their levels of indebtedness. New crops, new economic and social relations shaped and re-shaped the lives of millions of African farmers, impinging on the internal authority of households, gender relations and labour mobility which created new domestic conflicts. It has also been suggested that the introduction of new crops disturbed food production, which in some instances made African farmers more vulnerable to drought, especially in the savannas.[18]

In addition to arguments about social and political adaptation after the ending of the slave trade, the mechanics of the expansion of the new export trade have been the subject of some debate. One of the most popular liberal economic explanations is encapsulated in Myint's vent for surplus theory propounded in the 1950s.[19] It does not include crises of political authority and social disruption; rather it is rooted in classical international trade theory and the power of the market and comparative advantage to create opportunities for marketable surpluses. In the context of West Africa it is based on three central assumptions: first, the large increase in exports was achieved without an increase in population, second, export crop expansion took place without any significant reduction in the amount of land and time spent in the production of goods and services in the domestic economy, and third, that expansion occurred without the introduction of new or improved technology. Therefore, the phenomenal growth in exports was achieved principally by the increased use of land and labour, both of which were underutilized until a suitable

---

[18] See for example, R.W. Franke and B.H. Chasin, 1980, *Seeds of Famine: Ecological Destruction and the Development Dilemma in the West African Sahel.* Monclair New Jersey: Allenhead Osmund.

[19] Myint, Hla, 1958, 'The "Classical" Theory of International Trade and the Under-developed Countries', *Econ.Journal* LXVII, 317–337. 1977, 'Adam Smith's Theory of International Trade and the Perception of Economic Development' *Economica*, 44(175), 231–248. Also, see J. Tosh, 1980, 'The Cash Crop Revolution in Tropical Africa', *African Affairs*, vol. 79, pp. 79–94. A summary is also given in A.G. Hopkins, 1973, *An Economic History of West Africa.* Longman: London.

opening (the vent) was supplied. In particular in under populated areas such as West Africa, under employment of labour occurs because of a lack of demand for its potential output. From these basic assumptions others follow. For example, the development of export crops begins with farmers as unspecialized export crop producers combining subsistence with export production; subsequently specialization deepens as some farmers find export crop production a more rewarding venture, and they rely on other farmers for their food supplies. Other subsidiary assumptions include the notion that export production is self-financing as producers employ family labour, and utilize traditional tools and have free access to land. Indeed, so successfully and cheaply did Africans respond and adjust to legitimate commerce, only minimal local investment was required of Europeans.

Central to the Myint thesis is the proposition that international trade provides the effective demand for the production of export crops, and this is the stimulus which makes the farmer utilize surplus resources. The market demand for exports also has a knock-on effect in that it stimulates improved internal transport and external transport arrangements, which further accelerate export crop development. Finally, the availability of imported consumer goods hitherto inaccessible provides another incentive for the producer. Thus export crop production and imported incentive goods are a net increment to production and consumption in the domestic economy, with leisure being increasingly forgone.

The Myint thesis has been attacked from various quarters, either with reservations or rejection, based on readings of the West African evidence that lead to alternative theories. For example, while Myint argues international trade and the role of merchants were important, the theory ignores indigenous capital and African traders and agents, as well as the power of merchant credit. Also, in some instances religion provided a context: in Senegal the groundnut industry as it developed after 1860 was increasingly influenced by the power of the Islamic brotherhood known as the Mourides.[20] But a more general reservation applicable to all the export zones of West Africa is that the vent for surplus theory misconstrues, or ignores the essential role of migration and labour mobility. Local population

---

[20] O'Brien, D.B. Cruise, 1971, *The Mourides of Senegal: The Political Organization of an Islamic Brotherhood.* Oxford: Clarendon Press.

densities were not always sufficient to initiate and expand the export trade under labour intensive farming systems, or able to provided sufficient labour at critical moments in the cultivation cycle. As we shall show, it was not just the stock of labour that mattered, but the flow and timing of inputs. In addition there were conflicts between food supply and export crops, especially in the case of groundnuts, where unlike tree crops both are cultivated annually within a short wet season.

But labour migration in West Africa was not just about labour inputs and wages; it was also about the spreading of innovations. In the Gold Coast as Hill has demonstrated, the spread of cocoa farming in the south between 1890 and 1930 involved the large-scale migration of farmers into scarcely inhabited forests.[21] These pioneer farmers bought land in northwestern and western Akwapim using money from the palm oil trade, together with money accumulated by travelling carpenters. Thus one economic crop contributed to the development of another. In order to buy land cheaply groups of farmers acquired blocs of land, which later they subdivided among themselves; then they re-invested cocoa profits in further plots to which they moved, leaving the original ones to be managed by family members who used hired labour. After 1900 the demand for hired labour increased: labourers were initially annual contract workers, then sharecroppers, and after 1960 wage labour became more common.[22] In the 1960s some 800,000 men annually came into the cocoa areas, principally as seasonal circulatory migrants, who were crucial to the operation of the cocoa industry.[23]

In southwest Nigeria the cocoa industry also relied on indigenous investments, which reflected the long established involvement of the Yoruba in external commerce. In particular the timing and rate of the adoption can be related to opportunities within the region itself. The growth of the industry was triggered by the ending of the Yoruba wars in the late 19th century and the involvement of ex-soldiers, while migration and a process of capital formation and investment in land led to the spread of cocoa farming. The rate of investment

[21] Hill, P., 1963, *The Migrant Cocoa Farmers of Southern Ghana*. Cambridge: CUP.
[22] Van Hear, N., 1982, *Northern Labour and Development of Capitalist Agriculture in Ghana*. Ph.D. thesis, University of Birmingham.
[23] Cordell, D.J. Gregory and V. Piché, 1996, *Hoe and Wage: A Social History of a Circular Migration System in West Africa*. Boulder: Westview Press.

was only partially related to world prices, it also depended on fore-
gone opportunities and local costs since hired labour was used from
the outset. As in the Gold Coast capital formation took place outside the market through kin, family and other networks, while both
land and labour became commoditized, Berry argues this did not
lead to full-blown capitalist relations of production: land was not
scarce which limited the exploitive powers of larger farmers, and
labourers with access to land could negotiate reasonable terms from
employers.[24]

In Northern Nigeria the British were intent on the introduction
of cotton in the 1900s, as the North became the latest in a long
line of source areas, which would save the Lancashire textile industry. The hopes of the cotton growers were harnessed to Lugard's
determination to extend the railway northwards, and in 1912 the
railway reached Kano. But the railway assisted the spread of groundnuts rather than cotton. Cotton never really succeeded in the North
as supplies were readily absorbed by a competitive local textile industry, while cotton cultivation seriously clashed with millet production
and could not be inter-cropped like groundnuts. Northern Nigeria
became the most important groundnut producer in British West
Africa, although this was largely a 20th century development, and
it had not overtaken The Gambia until the 1930s. Several authors
notably Hogendorn and Shenton have discussed the groundnut industry of Northern Nigeria.[25] The former places great emphasis on the
commercial acumen of Hausa traders who were important buyers
and intermediaries between local farmers and the firms, together
with the maximizing behaviour of a multitude of small producers,
who responded to the relatively good prices and the goods they could
buy with the proceeds of their harvests.

Shenton however stresses the wider structural forces that influenced
the groundnut trade, and the concentration of merchant capital in
Northern Nigeria. For example, 1900–11 was a period of stagnation
in Western Europe, and in Britain of falling real wages: one prosaic
response of the working class was to eat margarine rather than dearer

---

[24] Berry, S.S., 1975, *Cocoa, Custom and Socio-Economic Change in Rural Western Nigeria.*
Oxford: Clarendon Press.
[25] For contrasting views see J.S. Hogendorn, 1978, *Nigerian Groundnut Exports.* Zaria
and Ibadan: Ahmadu Bello University and OUP. R. Shenton, 1986, *The Development
of Capitalism in Northern Nigeria.* London: James Currey.

butter. By 1910 the production of margarine had been boosted by the hydrogenization process, whereby liquid vegetable oils could be cheaply converted into margarine. The expansion of groundnuts in Northern Nigeria was assured finally once the railway had broken the transport monopoly of the Niger Company, and Elder Dempster by 1912 had reduced its freight rates to Liverpool. In Shenton's view "the railway was the last link in the chain of conquest, occupation and taxation which was to bind Northern Nigeria to the international economy".[26] In The Gambia the river was the major transport axis that linked the region to the international economy, but well before colonial rule.

Radical analyses have stressed the relatively poor terms of trade enjoyed by African farmers, and at times this was a problem for Gambian groundnut farmers. Producers had to face the uncertainty of prices from year to year, and they had little information about the world commodity market, while there were periods when the merchants fixed prices. Other misgivings about international trade theories have focused on the role of indirect and direct coercion by Europeans, especially after the introduction of new currencies and colonial taxes in the late 19th century and the creation of economic dependency. Taxation it is argued pushed local producers into the export economy, while in the economically marginal interiors labour migration was stimulated by the need to pay taxes in coin. But the groundnut trade in Senegambia began in the 1830s well before formal colonial rule; therefore the emergence of the groundnut trade and the various cycles it went through require a different perspective— at least in the early stages, especially the role of merchant capital, credit and migrant workers. This book takes up some of these ideas about the development of the West African export trade in the context of Gambian groundnuts, and explores the social and economic adjustments that were required of producers. It also seeks to qualify or amend some of the major issues, as well as opening-up other lines of inquiry. We believe that notwithstanding the importance of the international market the Gambian groundnut trade from its inception was significantly shaped by merchant credit, migration, climate and food supply.

---

[26] Shenton, op. cit., 1986, pp. 81–3.

By the end of the 19th century all the established export crop zones relied heavily on the recruitment of seasonal labour from the commercially less developed interior.[27] And, the Gambian ground-nut trade in the first instance flourished through the pioneering efforts of African traders and migrant farmers, especially the Soninke. These migrant farmers were coming into The Gambia from the 1840s onwards, and the groundnut trade initiated one of the earliest migrant labour systems in West Africa. The trade progressed in tandem with increased flows of migrants drawn from a wide area. By the early 20th century a substantial boost was given to labour migration, which was due less to taxation and more the result of the erosion of domestic slavery. But because the Gambian migrant labour contract required hosts to feed their workers, rice was imported and distributed by merchants on credit as the number of migrants rose, as well as during periods of poor rainfall. After 1857 when the trade became more specialized food imports became crucial. By the early 20th century the British Administration had also become involved in the distribution of rice on credit: food became a policy instrument to underpin the groundnut trade locally as less food crops were grown, and as a means of securing a continued flow of migrant workers. In effect the Gambia had become a migrant driven economy. Contrary to the Myint thesis food importing was necessary and The Gambia stands as one of the earliest West African examples of large-scale international food importing, not to satisfy an expanding urban population, but to facilitate changes in the rural economy. Throughout British West Africa the colonial authorities were concerned about food supplies and food policies, which were riddled with doubts and uncertainties about the appropriateness and effectiveness.[28]

The politics of food distribution, together with the development of the groundnut trade in general cannot be considered in an ecological vacuum, and one of the problems of the vent for surplus thesis (as well as crisis of adaptation arguments) is the limited discussion of the environment and crop ecology vis-à-vis land and labour. In

---

[27] Swindell, K. 1996, 'People on the Move in West Africa: From Pre-Colonial Polities to independent States'. In R. Cohen (ed.), *The Cambridge Survey of Migration*. Cambridge: CUP.

[28] Guyer, J.I., 1991, *British Colonial and Post-Colonial food Regulation with Reference to Nigeria: An Essays in Formal Sector Anthropology*. Working Papers in African Studies, No. 158. African Studies Center, Boston University.

recent years there has emerged a realization that the European conquest of Africa and the expansion of trade coincided with a series of environmental disasters. Environmental contingencies are important themes in the groundnut industry, because droughts, floods and pestilence periodically affected both groundnuts, and food, either separately or together; a distinction which could be very important. Often it was the *timing* of such environmental disturbances and their persistence vis-à-vis the fluctuations in world groundnut prices which was critical. For example, it was relatively easy to counter the effect of low rainfall on food crops, by importing food as long as groundnut prices were good: if they were not, then greater consideration had to be given to rice distribution on credit. Thus environmental and economic fluctuations were not discrete entities, but closely linked.

The Gambian groundnut trade was shaped by a number of forces: some were structural, others contingent. Of some significance in the Gambian case were the boundaries that resulted from partition at the end of the 19th century. Africa's political boundaries were arbitrary creations that re-structured African polities, and after independence many new states were territorially anomalous and unsustainable, while border trading rendered the idea of economies contained by geopolitical boundaries as untenable. These boundaries are arguably the most enduring consequences of colonial rule, and since their inception, they have created areas of tension, and have become contented terrains. None more so than The Gambia, a sliver of land either side of a major river inserted into Senegal. From the late 19th century onwards the boundary had both negative and positive effects on the groundnut trade: differences in market prices, monetary systems and taxation, as well as political conditions affected the flows of produce and imported goods. After partition Africans believed boundaries were to keep Europeans apart, not Africans, and subsequently their ability to shift produce across borders became the means of showing their contempt and distrust towards merchants and rulers, while the movements of people have been prodigious. The boundary question and Gambia's geographical disposition in West Africa assumed greater proportions for the colonial administration as the 20th century developed, when they realized its full implications.

Europeans not only divided up the continent, they also brought with them their own intellectual baggage and beliefs about Africans and Africa, which were influenced variously by the Universalist assumptions of post-Enlightenment thinking, the evolutionary ideas

of Darwin, and the development of social Darwinism. Some early
Commissioners and District Officers were perceptive, albeit amateur
observers, but soon the Empire became a grand experimental labo-
ratory for the emerging band of experts in the natural sciences. By
the late 1920s it is apparent that the expert scientific advisor was
someone of increasing influence, and the latter part of this book
explores the creation of the Gambian Agricultural Department,
together with the first experimental irrigation and mixed farming
schemes. Such schemes were seen as a rational means of curing local
food shortages due to natural hazards, as well as rescuing the economy from massive food importing which reached dizzy heights after
the First World War. It is also apparent that by 1917 there was the
awareness among the Gambian administrators that the climate might
be deteriorating, and that the relentless expansion of groundnuts and
the bush clearing it entailed might have adverse ecological consequences. Such deliberations on climatic change pre-figure the debates
on the Sudan-Sahel, which were to follow in the 1970s and 1980s.

In the 1900s the attitudes of administrators and technical experts
in the metropoles and the colonies were part of a developing political culture and discourse about the role of Empire and its management. Repertoires of ideas and policies were developed often with
a view to their transferability among several overseas possessions. For
example it is interesting to see the attempts to transfer to Africa
experiences and ideas formulated in Asia, something which is still
extant in contemporary development thinking. And, among those
who carried out colonial rule there were competing agendas for the
use of power and influence: there were differing visions of authority
and responsibility, as well as a gap between the ideal and the actual.[29]

Since the 1980s there has been a growing interest in African business history and relations between business and government. Instru-
mentalist views of a compliant colonial state serving the interests of
capital and business have been challenged, while the view that the
colonial state was a relatively autonomous interventionist body has
also been attacked. A number of studies negate the idea that both
state and business were monolithic entities; rather they represented
a diversity of interests which led to conflicts and compromises, with
their own particular historic and geographic specificities according

---

[29] See special edition of the American Ethnologist, 1989, vol. 16 (4).

to the particular period and colony.[30] At times the state was a mediator, at times openly interventionist, at times it backed particular interests, and our understanding of The Gambia is broadly consonant with this view. However, while not actively supporting the merchants, the Gambian government often did so by default; the sheer weight of merchant interest was at times overwhelming in a small colony so dependent on the revenues from a single export. The methods whereby the several interests voiced their views and advanced their cases varied: the merchants used their Chambers of Commerce in The Gambia and England as lobbies, the colonial state passed Ordinances, the producers resorted to 'hold-ups' and took produce across the border. As for an agricultural policy, the Administration largely managed without one and reacted to the repeated crises in the groundnut industry on an *ad hoc* basis.

The first four chapters of this book focus on the development of groundnut production from the 1830s into the opening years of the 20th century. The early part of this period saw the adaptation to the ending of the Atlantic slave trade and a shift from a range of legitimate exports to an increasing concentration on groundnut production, supported by locally produced foodstuffs. Later, expanded production became increasingly specialized and dependent on migrant workers and food imports, while after the Great Depression of the 1870s a shift occurred in the balance of power between merchants and African producers. But. The Gambia never became a monoculture in the full sense of the word, and local farming systems showed remarkable resilience and adaptation to the rising demand for groundnuts. By the late 19th century the British had established the Protectorate along the river, and introduced new forms of political control, which affected local producers as well as European merchants and their agents.

The last two chapters of the book are principally concerned with a nexus of political, economic and environmental events that shaped The Gambia from 1913–1934. Great changes occurred over a short period, when a cluster of events impinged on The Gambia, some of which were global in origin, some metropolitan, some African and

---

[30] Olukoju, A., 1995, 'Anatomy of Business Government Relations: Fiscal Policy and Mercantile Pressure Group Activity in Nigeria, 1916–1933', *African Studies Review*, vol. 38 (1), pp. 23–50.

others specifically Gambian. During 1913 there occurred one of the most serious droughts ever recorded in Africa, and in 1918 the Influenza pandemic swept the continent, while locally the 1917 cattle plague and the 1918 floods were disastrous for many Gambians. These natural calamities occurred within the context of the larger structural upheavals in Europe associated with the Great War of 1914–18. The War and its aftermath set in train profound changes within European society, while in Africa it was an economic threshold beyond which life for farmers became increasingly difficult. After a brief postwar boom there was a disastrous slump in commodity prices in 1920–21 leading to a credit crisis.[31] Another local issue in 1922, which shook this small colony was de-monetization (precipitated by the War), which bore heavily on a majority of Gambians and exposed the incompetence of the government and the opportunism of the merchants. A revival of trade occurred from 1922–29, which was accompanied by an improvement in the net barter and net income terms of trade, but this was partly offset by the large amounts of debt accumulated by producers, and price-fixing by the merchants After 1929, the Depression years in Europe meant a further downward slide of the net barter and net income terms of trade, and Gambians were left in no doubt about the vagaries of world commodity markets.

From 1870 onwards, Gambian groundnut producers along with many other West African farmers experienced a 'roller coaster' economy, which became very bumpy, and by 1930 had run out of impetus. The Second World War eventually led to an upturn, but this lies beyond the scope of this book. The events from 1913–1933 had a profound effect on the Gambian people, while the attitudes, perceptions and policies of the colonial administrators underwent changes too. One significant policy initiative was the creation of the Department of Agriculture. Unfortunately the years of trade depression from 1929 to 1933 and the Second World War deflected attempts to change Gambian agriculture, especially plans to introduce irrigated farming. Notwithstanding these delays, the future trends in Gambian agriculture were mapped-out in the 1920s and 1930s, and the notions

---

[31] Martin, S.M., 1989, 'The Long Depression: West African Export Producers and the World Economy, 1914–45' in I. Brown (ed.), *The Economies of Africa and Asia in the Inter-War Depression*. London: Routledge.

and ideas that were developed during this period are central to an understanding of agricultural policies carried out in post-war and post-independence Gambia. Of particular and general interest is the historiography of the irrigation schemes.

Although this book is focused on the historical development of the groundnut trade, there are a number of issues that have a resonance with contemporary concerns. Food importing of rice and wheat attracted the attention of governments, planners and academics during the 1970s, as well as the management of 'boom' and 'slump' economies. For example, of particular concern was the high level of food imports in Nigeria during the oil-boom and the effect on local agriculture. Yet food imports have a much longer history in The Gambia, where the difficulties of food distribution and its impact on the rural economy in the early 20th century may have some parallels with the modern distribution of food-aid.

The contentious issue of food crops versus export crops which was debated in The Gambia in the early 20th century re-appeared during the 1980s, as the IMF and the World Bank have insisted that poorer countries in the Third World should use their comparative advantage in the production of tropical export crops, and if necessary import foodstuffs. The evidence from The Gambia indicates that when prices are erratic or depressed, and coupled with the contingency of either natural disasters or political disturbance, then farmers can be economically exposed and indebtedness results. Currently the slow improvement achieved by the adoption of the New Economics in some parts of Africa is put down to climatic disasters, but The Gambian evidence shows the isolation of climate as an independent variable is highly suspect. On another but related front, the nature and ecological wisdom of African farming systems was a prevalent theme in the 1980s, and continues to attract attention.[32] But arguably there were some early intimations of this debate in The Gambia during the early years of the 20th century. As for the irrigation schemes in The Gambia, they demonstrate that any real understanding of them and their current difficulties must be rooted in at least some comprehension of how they were conceived and developed.

---

[32] See for example P. Richards, 1985, *Indigenous Agricultural Revolution*. London: Hutchinson.

When reading the archives in Banjul and London on which this book is principally based, at times one has an intriguing sense of "plus ca change, plus la meme chose", or of the continuous re-invention of the wheel. Perhaps all government ministers, experts and policy makers should be confined to the archives for a time before being released to impose their policies on a long suffering, but no longer unsuspecting rural populace. And, perhaps they should be obliged to uncover the alternative oral histories of rural peoples, in the hope of deriving a number of perspectives on the past that will lead to a 'useable' history to assist the process of rural development. However, to be cynical, there is no real incentive for planners and politicians to engage in such activities: drawing a line under previous experience and performance is the *sine qua non* of getting a contract, or building a successful political platform—both for donors and African governments.

The Gambia is a very small West African country that does not receive wide attention and study, but it has a long and well-documented history. And, groundnuts provided one of the earliest commodities in the West African export trade that led to the development of one of the earliest migrant labour systems. It is also important to understand that in the past, as in the present, the social and economic 'catchment' of the river extends many hundreds of miles into the surrounding countryside beyond the Gambia's boundaries into what are now known as Senegal, The Republic of Guinea, Guinea Bissau and Mali. Historically the Gambian groundnut trade preceded that of Senegal, although until partition their development was closely linked, and eventually by the 1900s the Senegalese trade was more than twice that of The Gambia. In conclusion, the development of the Gambian groundnut trade and the social, economic and physical milieux in which it as situated deserves to be written, as it comprises a hitherto unexplored but historically important part of the development of legitimate trade in West Africa. It also provides a vignette, which illuminates both regional and global issues, before, and during colonial rule.

# CHAPTER ONE

# THE GAMBIAN GROUNDNUT TRADE, 1834–1893: THE EMERGENCE OF AN AGRICULTURAL EXPORT ECONOMY

During the early 19th century European control of The Gambia was limited to the British enclaves of St. Mary's Island (later Bathurst), the Ceded Mile, Fort James, British Kombo, MacCarthy Island and the French fort at Albreda. (Fig. 1.1) The British presence derived from the suppression of the Atlantic slave trade, first through naval squadrons operating from Freetown, and then the establishment of Bathurst in 1816 on St Mary's island at the mouth of the river. Subsequently the naval squadrons and the soldiers posted at the forts were used to intervene in local affairs, which provided a basic sanction in support of British traders prior to partition. However, the colonial possessions and squadrons along the West African coast were not without their critics who attacked them as expensive and unnecessary, yet few of those in power could afford to be seen as 'soft' on the slave trade.[1]

Senegambia's contribution to the Atlantic slave trade peaked during the 1740s, and by the end of century the river Gambia was not a major supplier of slaves compared with other parts of the coast. By 1806 the operations of the anti-slave trade squadrons were effective because they could easily patrol the geographically fortuitous narrows at the mouth of the river, and while the slave trade continued elsewhere, it did so because it was less well policed. Some slave trading continued on the river at the French fort at Albreda, and between Gambia and Sierra Leone, especially at the mouth of the Casamance. In 1828 British merchants and the Administrator of The Gambia complained about the French buying slaves at Albreda and in Casamance and taking them to Gorée.[2] The complaint was less motivated by humanitarian concerns, and more by the fact that French

---

[1] Austen, R.A., 1987, *African Economic History*. London: James Currey, ch. 5.
[2] Blue Book, 1829.

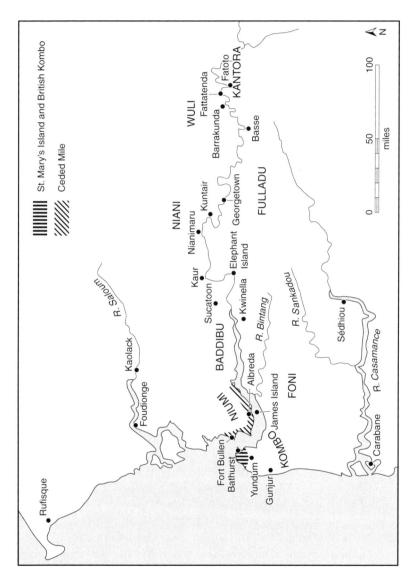

Fig. 1.1: *Principal African polities and areas under European control, along the Gambia circa 1843*

slave trading was attracting African merchants from the interior and
diverting the gold and hide trade from The Gambia.

After 1807 the Atlantic slave trade along the Gambia had virtually collapsed, except at Albreda, and by 1810 slaves were no longer
the principal export. Exports were dominated by beeswax, hides,
timber, gum, gold and ivory, which were long established items of
legitimate trade: in 1816 beeswax amounted to some 41% of total
exports by value, followed by hides (14%), teak (13%) and gum arabic (10%).[3] Legitimate trade had continued alongside the Atlantic
slave trade, but by the late 1820s it had assumed a higher profile,
and the British were making treaties with the up-river kingdom of
Wuli to try and divert the gum trade from Galam in upper Senegal
towards The Gambia.[4] In 1829 Hutton, the Administrator acting
without London's approval, (which eventually led to his dismissal)
agreed to pay nominal annual gratuities to local rulers, as part of a
deal with the merchants who were to send £7,600 of trade goods
to open-up trading posts at Fattatenda. By 1833 Hutton believed it
was necessary to "encourage commerce and the growth of rice, hemp,
indigo and cotton: settle the captured Negroes on the banks of The
Gambia: take off the oppressive duties on wax and other articles,
increase the fortification of Barra Point. . . . and The Gambia will in
a very short time be more valuable than all our other Settlements
in Africa put together".[5] Hutton's plea for cotton was to be a recurrent one in his successor's reports, while his mention of rice referred
to the export in 1822 of 22 tons of paddy rice to London; later in
1829 rice was also exported to the West Indies.

Although there was a diverse legitimate trade out of The Gambia
in the early 19th century, the ending of the Atlantic slave trade
brought a period of economic uncertainty for both merchants and
producers. Beeswax, hides and gum were subject to sharp fluctuations
in supply and were not as valuable as slaves, and while they represented a diversity of goods, they were less easy to handle, store and
transport. In such circumstances the emergence of the groundnut
trade was particularly propitious in the context of changed economic
conditions. Hutton's enthusiastic account of 1833 actually overlooked

[3] Ibid.
[4] CO 87/2, Hutton to SS, May 18th 1829.
[5] CO 87/9, Hutton to Hay, 4th March 1833.

the 100 baskets of groundnuts which had been exported to the West
Indies in 1830, which were valued at £10 16s 8d, while in 1834
213 baskets worth £21 16s 3d were exported to London. In 1835,
a mere 47 tons of nuts were exported, a total which rapidly rose to
1,211 tons in 1840, and 2,608 tons by 1842.[6]

Throughout West Africa, the ending of the Atlantic trade and the
development of legitimate trade required social, economic and political adaptation, which had specific trajectories in different locations.
In this chapter the analysis of the development of Gambian groundnut exports is divided into two periods, 1834–1857, and 1858–1890,
which represent different phases of adaptation and development. The
first period saw a relatively unspecialized groundnut trade with limited internal disturbance or producer-trader conflicts, a sufficiency of
local food, and with the exception of 1848–49, exports increased
steadily. Adaptation and change were relatively smooth: the groundnut trade was facilitated by the established commercial networks of
the western savannas, as well as being advanced by the activities of
the merchants, especially the French. This was a region where the
ways of merchant capital and markets were well understood, at least
by the political and commercial élites. After 1857, specialization
occurred, food importing became a necessity to support the groundnut industry, and political and economic disruption affected the trade
through disturbances caused by producer hold-ups, Islamic wars,
market conditions and climatic variability. Nonetheless, despite these
difficulties, merchant activity intensified with the assistance of a widespread network of African sub-traders and agents who advanced
goods on credit against next season's groundnut crop. However, after
1870 the economic downturn of the Great Depression led to low
groundnut prices and indebtedness. The second period of the groundnut industry was much more turbulent politically and economically, and a threshold was reached in 1893 with partition and the
imposition of British colonial rule through the establishment of the
Protectorate.

---

[6] Blue Book, 1834.

*The pre-specialization period of groundnut production 1834–1857*

*The conditions for adaptation and change*

Soninke and Mandinka traders heavily influenced the slave trade and legitimate trade along the Gambia, and it must be emphasized at the outset that conditions in the interior were of some consequence for the river and its peoples. The Soninke are a branch of Mande speaking West Africans, who inhabit the upper reaches of the Senegal valley and spread into present day Mali and Mauritania. (Fig. 1.2) In The Gambia they are known as the Serahuli. This group comprises the core of the Jula (also known as Marka), the itinerant long distance merchants who historically dominated trading in the Western Sudan and Sahel, and whose activities spread towards the coasts. The nodal position occupied by the Soninke between the desert and upper Niger valley was the locus of a commercial culture, which traded slaves and grain, for salt, gum and horses from the pastoral Beydan and Futanke on the desert margins, while slaves and cotton came from the south. To the east, slaves and grain were supplied to the gold fields of Bambuk and Bure.[7] Also, the Soninke were skilled upland and wetland farmers, and their heartland was one of surplus grain production (sorghum, millet and maize) heavily dependent on slave labour, which was also vital to other forms of trading and transportation.

The role of the Soninke as suppliers of slaves to the goldfields and the desert side economy, together with their own prodigious use of them is why they became the partners with European slave traders in Senegambia. Thus the Atlantic slave trade was grafted onto an already sophisticated network of commercial exchange and internal slave trading, with the Atlantic slave trade providing an opportunity for its expansion and access to European goods. As part of the slave trade to the coast, Soninke merchants rented farms from locals in lower Senegal on which slaves worked to produce their own food while awaiting sale and transportation. Furthermore, along the coast and river the slaves of local chiefs also worked on commercial grain

---

[7] Manchuelle, F., 1997, *Willing Migrants: Soninke Labor Diasporas, 1848–1960*. Athens: Ohio University Press.

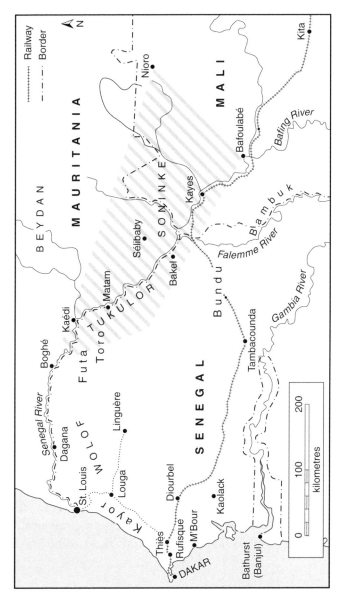

Fig. 1.2: *The Soninke and the western Sudan–Sahel. Adapted from F. Manchuelle, 1997*

farms that supplied the European ships and settlements.[8] Arguably the Atlantic slave trade was but one component of a wide commercial network, and its demise, while important, was of less significance than elsewhere.

The Soninke were not the only traders in the lower Gambia, as Mandinka from the upper Niger valley (also referred to as Jula), together with Fulbe created commercial outposts in lower Gambia, for example in the small kingdom of Niumi (also known as Barra). From the 14th century onwards the coastal saltpans around Niumi were the source of a thriving trade, as salt was taken up-river into the interior via Kantora; in addition Niumi also provided grain for the factories and ships operating the Atlantic slave trade. (Fig. 1.1)[9]

In Searing's view the groundnut trade in Senegal first emerged in those areas where commercial grain farming was an integral part of the slave trade, and where locally owned slaves, especially of chiefs were used in commercial grain cultivation.[10] This analysis can usefully be applied to the Gambia river; for example the, European factories purchased locally produced grain, especially rice, and captives awaiting transportation were set to work on grain farms around the factories.[11] Niumi supplied the Royal Africa Company with corn in 17th century for its garrison and waiting ships, while as late as the 1740s European agents were buying grains.[12] French maps of The Gambia river in the mid-18th century note that the kingdoms of Barra and Barsalli provided the greater part of the rice consumed by the European factories. (Fig. 1.3) Further up-stream Kaur located in Baddibu, was the chief town along the entire river, as it was the chief market place for traders from Bambuk. Thus the kingdoms of Niumi and Baddibu, located on the north bank of the Gambia had a substantial mercantile hinterland and flourishing commercial agriculture by the late 18th century.

---

[8] Ibid. See also J.F. Searing, 1993, *West African Slavery and Atlantic Commerce, The Senegal Atlantic Valley* 1800–1960. Cambridge: CUP.

[9] Wright, D.R., 1997, *The World and a Very Small Place in Africa*. M.E. Sharpe: New York

[10] Searing, 1993, op. cit.

[11] On the provisioning of factories, see F. Moore, 1730, *Travels into the Interior Parts of Africa*. London, pp. 22–23. On slaves working farms around factories see Mungo Park, Travels in the Interior of Africa. Edinburgh: Nimmor, Hay and Mitchell, edition, 1896, pp. 23 and 295.

[12] Wright, 1997, op. cit.

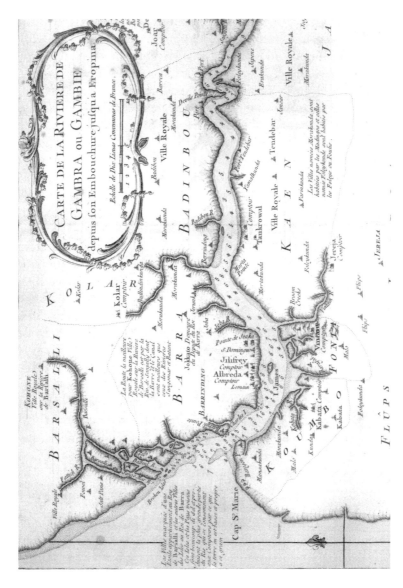

Fig. 1.3: *Polities and settlements along the lower Gambia River, mid 18th-century*

These petty kingdoms along the north bank had centralized Islamic political structures whose rulers had acted as brokers between Soninke slave caravans from the interior, and the European merchants and ships' captains to whom they also supplied grain, and importantly from whom they exacted tolls. Also, they provided some slaves themselves for the Atlantic trade by taking captives from the south bank of the river. Albreda and Juffure in Niumi were long established centres for the export of slaves; the local use of slaves was concentrated here, while they continued as slave markets until the 1860s when the local Soninke-Marabout wars increased the supply of captives.[13] Slavery in general, together with agrestic servitude continued until the colonial authorities attempted to introduce abolition in the late 19th century.

If one accepts there was a correlation between the emergence of commercial groundnut farming, slave trading, commercial grain farming and trading, it is not surprising that the earliest areas of groundnut cultivation for export along the Gambia appears to have been in Niumi and Baddibu. Although there are no records of groundnut sales from specific locations, accounts of the gubernatorial tours (especially for 1861) show that specialized groundnut cultivation had first taken hold in Niumi, Baddibu, Saloum and Wuli. Oral histories collected in the 1970s corroborate this, and also suggest that groundnuts were already an established subsidiary food crop in the early 1800s before commercial famining had taken hold. Thus, by the early 19th century local North Bank chiefs were using their slaves to produce groundnuts destined for Europe, which replaced the lost grain and slave trade with European merchants and slave shippers. Until 1857, slaves were most likely to be in the households of chiefs: in particular they were concentrated around Albreda, Juffure, and the Kombos south of Bathurst.[14] Admittedly, the use of slaves for groundnut farming may not have been widespread, but agrestic servitude was an early component in the process of adaptation to legitimate trade. As for the south bank of the river, groundnut cultivation was limited; Foni was principally a rice and corn growing area on which the specialized groundnut areas became increasingly dependent for foodstuffs, which we discuss later in Chapter Three. Further

---

[13] CO 87/87, D'Arcy to Blackall, 15th November 1866.
[14] Local fieldwork.

east the Fula were only secondarily farmers, as they were nomadic clients of the Mandinka, and they were not united as an independent entity comprising the Fulladus, until the Fula uprising under Alpha Mollo in 1867.

An evaluation of the adaptation to legitimate trade requires calculations of relative profitability of the slave trade and legitimate trade, which is difficult, and embraces several factors. The evidence is often circumstantial, but it is worth noting that in 1828 male slaves were selling in the Casamance river to the south of the Gambia for £14 17s 0d, while the f.o.b. price for groundnuts averaged £12 0s 0d per ton from 1834 to 1857.[15] An active male could produce roughly one ton of groundnuts per season, which suggests a relatively good annual return to agricultural labour, compared with a once for all sale of a worker. Governor MacDonnell commented in 1848, that the groundnut trade had the effect of inducing native proprietors of slaves to retain them for the fruit of their labours, instead of being anxious to dispose of them when an opportunity arose, or could be created.[16] Writing of the Casamance in 1856, Bertrand Bocandé provides corroboration of MacDonnell accounts of 1848 and 1851, when he observed that the ending of the trade in slaves provided an incentive for erstwhile owners and traders to develop new enterprises, which they found in the cultivation of groundnuts.[17] Elsewhere, in Sierra Leone on the north side of the Freetown estuary, chiefs of the Bullom area were using slaves to produce rice for the Freetown market, and one declared that each earned him over and above the cost of their subsistence, about £7 10s annually, whereas the average selling prices was only £10.[18] And in the late 19th century, the Soninke used slaves brought back from trading expeditions as farm labourers, which they viewed as a profitable re-investment as it took only three years to produce enough surplus grain to buy one more slave.[19] The cases cited from The Gambia,

---

[15] CO 87/2, Findlay to SS, 12th March 1829. Findlay reported slaves selling at $70, that is silver Maria Theresa dollars, which exchanged at approximately 4s 0d per dollar.

[16] CO 87/43 Annual Report 1848, MacDonnell to Gray, 21st June 1848.

[17] Bertrand-Bocandé, E., *Les résources que présentent dans leur état actuel les comptoirs français établis sur les bords de la Casamance Carabane et Sédhiou.* Extrait de la Revue Coloniale. Encl. in C0 87/3, 12th July 1861.

[18] See Introduction in R. Law (ed.), 1995, *From Slave Trade to Legitimate Commerce: the commercial transition in nineteenth century West Africa.* Cambridge: CUP.

[19] Manchuelle, 1997, op. cit.

Sierra Leone and upper Senegal suggest that chiefs retaining their slaves rather than exporting them made greater profits.

The chiefdoms and kingdoms of the lower Gambia not only profited from grain sales to the European slavers, but also they exacted shipping tolls: the traditional 'master of the river' was the *mansa* of Niumi, whose north bank domain historically controlled the entrance to the Gambia. Initially the British allowed the tolls to continue after setting-up Bathurst on the south bank, but after 1817 the Bathurst merchants were less than keen to follow the old trading patterns, and under pressure Grant the Administrator instructed them to pay only half the amount demanded. Relations with Niumi deteriorated, and because of French influence at Albreda the British pressed for the ceding of a strip of the Niumi coastline to defend and control the river entrance.[20] (Fig. 1.1) After some resistance and a show of force by the British, Niumi agreed to cede one mile from the shore inland in return for quarterly payments of £87. 0s 0d, as well as agreeing to the establishment of Fort Bullen at Barra Point. (Fig. 1.1) Further trouble erupted and another show of force finally settled the issue in 1832.[21]

The ending of the Atlantic slave trade and British intervention meant Niumi and Baddibu had lost trade and revenue, which arguably heightened the importance of their engaging in the new groundnut trade. Elsewhere along the Gambia, local chiefs located beyond immediate British influence were able to maintain and extend tolls and taxes as the groundnut trade developed, which to some extent compensated for losses on slave trading. Unlike some parts of West Africa, Gambian chiefs could effectively collect tolls and rents from Europeans, African traders and the growing band of migrant farmers associated with groundnut farming because collection was relatively easy. Trading and farming were concentrated at specific points, namely the wharves around which, and from which groundnuts were grown and exported. The collection of taxes by local rulers, together with government annuities continued until the 1890s when new forms of taxation were introduced by the British.

The concentration of early groundnut cultivation along the river and around the wharves was advantageous as it reduced transportation costs. Elsewhere some new export crops were expensive to transport

[20] Wright, 1997, op. cit.
[21] Ibid.

using pack animals or human porterage, compared with self-transporting
slaves. For example, in the palm belt of the Niger delta, head loading or using canoes to deliver to the ports was not cheap.[22] And,
along the Gambia the use of river transport was materially assisted
by a special group of migrant workers. After the British left Gorée
as part of the post-Napoleonic war settlement to establish bases at
Bathurst and MacCarthy Island, they were followed by an important
group of *habitant* merchants from Senegal, together with artisans and
former slaves. Of particular importance were the *laptots,* an occupa-
tional class of mariners (many of whom were Soninke), who established the river-boat system to transport groundnuts to the ocean
going ships at the mouth of the Gambia.[23] The connection between
Bathurst and Gorée by this group eventually led to the spread of
the groundnut industry back to the lower Senegal after abolition
there in 1848.

The transition to groundnut cultivation along the north bank of
the river appears to have been quick, with limited disruption and
losses to local rulers formerly involved in the Atlantic slave trade,
which was already past its peak. In the first half of the 19th century groundnut prices were steady, and the terms of trade good for
producers, whose transport costs were low. The emergence of Niumi
and Baddibu as the earliest groundnut producing areas could be
interpreted as being consonant with them having lost most as the
slave trade collapsed, and they were suited to commercial farming
because of their earlier involvement in commercial grain cultivation.
But importantly land was sufficiently in surplus not only to accommodate chiefs, but to other members of local communities, as well
as migrants. It seems that initially the most likely losers after the
abolition of the slave trade were the Soninke merchants who brought
slaves from the interior, and indeed the Senegal valley experienced
some economic uncertainty in the early 19th century, especially after
the temporary loss of St. Louis to the British, while the French were
also conscious of their loss of Caribbean sugar estates in Dominica.
A succession of French Governors tried to establish agricultural
'colonies' along the Senegal valley, assisted by merchants such as
Marc Maurel.[24] And, as we discuss below, the enthusiasm and acu-

---

[22] Law, 1995, op. cit.
[23] Searing, 1993, op. cit.
[24] Manchuelle, 1997, op. cit., ch. 2.

men of Maurel and his fellow traders spilled over into The Gambia where they became the mercantile core of the groundnut trade.

However, the situation for the Soninke in the upper Senegal valley was not so bad, as the expansion of the French textile industry stimulated a temporary revival of the gum trade (at this time was the single most important source of gum in the world), while the regional slave trade also continued. Gum was collected from acacias along the desert margins by the Beydan and traded with the *métis traitants* of St. Louis. The trade, centred on Galam (Upper Senegal) boomed after 1830 when the French introduced free trade, which opened the market to non-French purchasers (hence the importance of the Gambian gum trade for the British). The result was a fourfold increase in trade and an outbreak of 'gum fever', which raised the demand for grain from the Soninke, and thereby increased the demand for slaves.[25] Thus the ending of the Atlantic slave trade was smoothed for the Soninke through the temporarily revived gum trade. But the Soninke were long established mercantile entrepreneurs, and they were quick to seize the opportunities offered by the groundnut trade along the Gambia, where they hitherto had traded slaves. Many Soninke became pioneer migrant groundnut farmers, who secured land from the rulers and chiefs of Niumi and Baddibu. While local chiefs moved into the groundnut farming, the presence of a large number of Soninke migrant farmers became pivotal to the development and expansion of the groundnut trade. Their involvement in the groundnuut trade at an early stage is also arguably an important part of the Soninke adaptation to the ending of the Atlantic slave trade. Their role, and the question of migrant labour in general are discussed in some detail in the next chapter.

Finally, the commercial networks and linkages between the coast and the interior were also important for the spread of *arachis hypogea*, the variety of groundnut exported from Senegambia. There is no pre-European evidence of *arachis* in Africa, (there are numerous pre-Columbian accounts of it in South America), and the first mention of it in West Africa was by Bosman in 1705, when he discriminated between *voandzeia* and *arachis*.[26] *Voandzeia subterranea* is an indigenous groundnut, known as Bambara nuts (*guerte bambara*), which was and

---

[25] Ibid.
[26] Péhaut, Y. 1992, L'arachide en Afrique occidentale, *Cah.d'Outre Mer* (45), 179–180.

is still grown in the interior, although it never entered the export trade. However, *voandzeia*, may have indirectly assisted the spread of *arachis* as it served as an ethno-botanical equivalent.

The variety of groundnuts, *arachis hypogaea* was introduced into Central and West Africa from South America by the Portuguese in the 16th century. The introduction was through small gardens planted around Portuguese coastal settlements, and of particular importance were those along the Angolan coast, the islands of Cape Verde, Sao Tomé and Principe. These islands were important nodes on the trade routes for the movement of goods, and slaves. It was here that the merchants of the interior, the Jula of the upper Niger and Senegal basins, and the Hausa of the central Sudan met European traders, to whom they brought henna, indigo, ginger and sugar cane, while they returned to the savannas with manioc, maize, and importantly groundnuts. Thus the diffusion of *arachis* into the interior proceeded through a collaborative effort by African merchants and the Portuguese.

The European explorers of the 18th and 19th centuries confirm the cultivation of *arachis* in the interior along the upper Senegal and Niger valleys, where it was used as a local foodstuff, while one European observer in the 18th century also commented on its use as horse fodder.[27] On the other hand there are few accounts of ground-nuts in lower Senegambia: the first descriptions for Sine Saloum were in 1822, just before the first exports from Bathurst in 1834. Thus in the early 19th century groundnuts were being grown principally in the interior, while their spread into lower Gambia reflects European demand, and as we shall show later through the Soninke, who pro-vided a surge of pioneer migrant groundnut farmers from the upper Senegal and Niger valleys. In effect the early 19th century saw the transition of *arachis* from a secondary food crop and source of fodder grown in the interior, to a major export crop grown along the rivers and coastal margins.

## *The Anglo-French Connection*

The export of groundnuts in increasing quantities proved to be a striking development in the first half of the nineteenth century, which was to transform production and exchange along the banks of the

---

[27] Bowditch, T.E., 1835, *Excursions in Madiero and Porto Santo*, London, pp. 211, 156. Because chiefs used the tops as fodder, groundnuts were not taxed through a tithe, like millet, which may have been an additional incentive for small farmer cultivation.

Gambia river. And, not only along the Gambia, because by the 1850s commercial groundnut cultivation had spread to neighbouring areas of French influence in the lower Senegal valley and, especially in the Casamance. Although the French were not as active as the British over abolition (and their missionary impulse was weaker), French officials combined with merchant interest to establish a French sphere of influence and create an economic base in Senegambia commensurate with the demands of the oilseed industry in the metropole.

After 1817 a new breed of resident French merchants, chiefly from Bordeaux, appeared in lower Senegambia who gradually supplanted the old Atlantic trading monopolies and the *habitants* who had controlled the trade of the valley. And although the groundnut trade did not take-off in the lower Senegal valley until after 1850, having been preceded by a flourish in the gum arabic export trade, as early as 1827 the Governor Baron Roger was pressing the agricultural potential of this area.[28] One problem in France was the inability of the olive oil industry to meet the rising demand for vegetable oil, and despite the heavy protection of olive oil merchants were looking for alternatives. In 1838–39 the Marseille and Nantes Chambers of Commerce were pressing the government for lighter duties on oilseeds from West Africa.

In 1840 the reduction of French tariffs on imported oil seeds, which had been designed to protect the olive oil industry, was a significant event for the Gambian groundnut trade.[29] However, the reduction only applied to French vessels, and the oil processors in Nantes and Marseille were still protected by the retention of tariffs on groundnut oil. Thus at an early stage a broad metropolitan-satellite relationship of dependency was established whereby Senegambia provided raw materials for French milling interests. Although the very first export of nuts from the Gambia was by a British firm, Forster and Smith of London, the French dominated the Gambian groundnut trade until the First World War, broken by a brief period from 1837–41, when a majority of nuts went to America until the industry there was protected by tariffs to encourage groundnut farming in the southern states.[30] As early as the 1830s the French firms

---

[28] Villard, A., 1943, *Histoire de Sénégal*. Dakar.

[29] Schnapper, B. 1961, *La politique et le commerce française dans le golfe de Guinée de 1838–1870*. Paris.

[30] Brooks, G.E., 1975, 'Peanuts and Colonialism; consequences of the commercialization of peanuts in West Africa, 1830–70', *Journal of Afr. Hist.* XVI (1), 29–54.

of Peyrissac, Hilaire Maurel and Hubert Prom were trying to persuade Gambian chiefs to encourage groundnut production, a strategy
they later repeated in the early 1840s in the Jolof and Cayor regions
of Senegal.[31] The French firms were crucial to the development of
the groundnut trade and the export of nuts, while the British were
more involved with the importing of trade goods.

After 1843 the production of groundnuts for export accelerated
and became a serious economic enterprise: the money economy along
the river expanded, local farmers and migrants from the interior
entered into export crop production, and by 1857 13,544 tons were
exported. (Figs. 1.4, 1.5) But it is important to recognize that groundnuts were being produced on soil beyond the limits of British rule,
while at times groundnuts produced in French spheres of influence
entered the Gambian groundnut trade. In The Gambia, the formal

Fig. 1.4: *Gambian groundnut exports: tonnage and values, 1844–1857*

| Year | Tonnage Exported* | Total Value (F O B) | | | Approx Price per ton (F O B) | | |
|---|---|---|---|---|---|---|---|
| | | £ | s | d | £ | s | d |
| 1844 | 3,426 | 43,583 | 14 | 0 | 12 | 14 | 6 |
| 1845 | 4,027 | 52,270 | 2 | 0 | 12 | 19 | 6 |
| 1846 | 5,597 | 74,636 | 18 | 0 | 13 | 6 | 6 |
| 1847 | 8,237 | 99,938 | 16 | 0 | 12 | 2 | 6 |
| 1848 | 8,637 | 103,778 | 0 | 0 | 12 | 0 | 0 |
| 1849 | 4,327 | 51,923 | 0 | 0 | 12 | 0 | 0 |
| 1850 | 6,478 | | | | | | |
| 1851 | 11,095 | 133,133 | 0 | 0 | 12 | 0 | 0 |
| 1852 | 10,908 | | | | | | |
| 1853 | 11,226 | | | | | | |
| 1854 | 9,162 | | | | | | |
| 1855 | 12,485 | | | | | | |
| 1856 | 10,875 | 131,908 | 4 | 8 | 12 | 2 | 6 |
| 1857 | 13,554 | 162,649 | 0 | 0 | 12 | 0 | 0 |

\* Figures rounded to the nearest ton.

*Source*: CO 90/31, see also BA, Class 54, piece no. 157, Groundnut Trade Statistics

---

[31] Graham, G.S. 1956. 'The Ascendancy of the Sailing Ship', 1850–85. *Econ.History Rev.* 74–78.

Fig. 1.5: *Gambian groundnut exports (tons) 1844–1857*

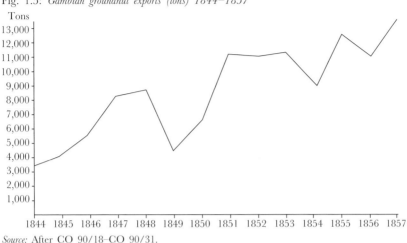

*Source:* After CO 90/18–CO 90/31.

British presence in 1850 was still confined to the small enclaves of Bathurst, Fort James, Kombo and MacCarthy Island. So what was the role of the colonial government in encouraging the export trade? This question does not form part of the Myint thesis, and the radical critiques of the 1970s attacked this neglect and were particularly emphatic about the interventions of colonial regimes, which assisted the penetration of merchant capital and the extraction of surpluses, as well as the unequal terms of trade. However, in The Gambia British colonial government was restricted to its limited holdings, although the river was physically controlled by Bathurst, strategically sited at its mouth, together with Fort Bullen and the Ceded Mile.

Apart from controlling the river entrance and collecting duties on shipping, the direct colonial involvement amounted to little more than the encouragement of farming through a government sponsored groundnut farm, worked in the late 1830s by 'liberated Africans' to supplement their major occupation as brick makers at Lamin a few kilometers from Bathurst.[32] In addition, the Wesleyan mission on MacCarthy Island ran a model farm, which produced rice, corn and groundnuts.[33] In the adjacent French territories, a parallel intervention took the form of trying to cement scattered trading populations

---

[32] CO 87/21, Ingram to Marquis of Normandy, 30th Oct. 1839.
[33] CO 87/24, Huntley to Russell, 22nd April 1840.

on the rivers into a plantation economy, but by 1831 the experiment had been abandoned.[34] In essence such activities were peripheral to the main thrust of the groundnut industry, which was driven by merchant interest and local participation. In The Gambia, the liberated Africans found more important niches as clerks, book-keepers, and messengers to the business firms.[35] The failure of the Wesleyan model farm supports the general view that the missionary effort to modernize the African economy met with little success: Africans wanted trade goods, including firearms and liquor, items not on the missionary agenda.[36] Consequently, the churches failed to convert the barbarity of the slave trade into a modern work ethic, yet missionaries were successful in the coastal enclaves in producing a class of educated creoles. However, missionary interests continued to form a powerful lobby in England in the 19th century, when the African continent became increasingly important as it became apparent that the churches' impact in India was likely to be minimal.

During the early 19th century there were no imposts on groundnut exports, and the financing of British possessions came from levies on imported goods together with a tonnage duty on vessels, which excluded the French trading post at Albreda.[37] In 1849 the British sought to restrict foreign firms, confining the French to Bathurst and Albreda, which allowed British merchants to open trading posts all along the river. Yet France was the principal market for nuts, where a duty of 20 francs per ton was levied on foreign vessels, which allowed the French firms to continue as the principal shippers of groundnuts.[38] Thus, the intervention of 1849 was aimed at counterbalancing French influence by placing the internal collection of nuts in British hands. The French connection became a particular case for concern in 1848–49, when the Revolution there disrupted trade and shipping, and substantial amounts of nuts were left in the hands of the shippers. This was an early warning to Gambian producers of the vicissitudes of the world market.

---

[34] Newbury, C.W. and A.S. Kanya Forstner, 1969, 'French Policy and the Origins of the Scramble for Africa', *Journal of Afr. Hist.*, X, 253–76.
[35] Whitford, J., 1879, *Trading Life in Western and Central Africa*. London: Frank Cass 2nd edition, 1967.
[36] Austen, R.A., 1987, op. cit.
[37] CO 87/45, McDonnell to Gray, 6th June 1849.
[38] Ibid.

Relations with the French reached an important turning point in 1857 with the formulation of the Anglo French Convention. Under the Convention the British gave up their rights to engage in the gum trade at Portendic, while in return the French closed their factory at Albreda and ceded the settlement to Britain.[39] This meant that all French ships entering the river were subject to British control and levies, but in addition, and much to the annoyance of the British merchants, the 1849 restrictions on French trading posts along the river were removed. At a stroke the river Gambia was opened-up as a free trading zone for all nations. The British merchants already had petitioned the Governor earlier in 1853 about their fears that English imports were being undercut by French firms, as well as emphasizing the disadvantages they faced in France due to the 20 franc levy on foreign ships.[40] The British government in London was unmoved, both in 1853 and 1857, remaining faithful to the principle of free trade and the belief competition would be beneficial.[41] Certainly the groundnut trade had flourished up to this point and tonnages increased from 2,608 tons in 1843, to 13,554 in 1857; an increase of 400%.

Meanwhile a French presence and commercial influence had been established in Casamance immediately to the south of Bathurst. A central figure here was Bertrand Bocandé, the Resident at Carabane, whose detailed reports give comparative information on the European presence and the emergence of the groundnut trade during the 1850s.[42] Bocandé was a man of various talents not just confined to administration, which he carried out with a mixture of mediation and force. Unlike his British counterparts he was an entrepreneur, a passionate entomologist, linguist and ethnologist, who was exiled from from France and ended up in Casamance.[43] Bocandé was a principal actor in Governor Faidherbe's strategy of establishing French control within a triangle linking Bamako, Senegal and Gambia, and he

---

[39] Hargreaves, J.D., 1963, *Prelude to the Partition of West Africa*. London: Papermac, p. 24.

[40] CO 87/64, 'A True Copy of the Memorandum from the Merchants and Liberated Africans of the British Settlements on the River Gambia', 11th June 1853 to Newcastle, in O'Connor to Labouchere, 30th May 1857.

[41] CO 87/64, O'Connor to Labouchere, 31st May 1857.

[42] Bocandé, 1856, op. cit.

[43] J.G. Débien and Y. Saint Martin, 1969. 'Emmanuel Bertrand-Bocandé (1812–1881) Un Nantais en Casamance.' *Bull de l'IFAN XXXI*, Ser. B. no. 1 pp. 279–308.

effectively secured lower Casamance by marginalizing the British and Portuguese interest and controlling the local populations.[44]

Bocandé's report of 1856 (bound into the Gambian Official Correspondence) is full of enthusiasm for the benefits that could accrue from the combined efforts of Commerce and Civilization, which justified the French presence.[45] He also believed that abolition of the Atlantic slave trade had profoundly changed local agriculture, and with Gallic zeal shaped by post-Enlightenment rationality, he urged the necessity of intelligent trading based on a sound knowledge of Casamance, which would bring Civilization to a people presently plunged into barbarity: thus commerce and the civilizing impulse should go hand in hand. His emphasis on this twofold task, "double travail" as he called it, is reminiscent of Lugard's later affirmation of a Dual Mandate. Bocandé also emphasized the changes in agriculture around Carabane and Sédhiou, which grew out of the rapid expansion of the groundnut trade. (Fig. 1.1) In 1852, 30,000 baskets were produced which had risen to 250,000 by 1857, which translates into 3250 tonnes. But this rosy picture was soon to be dimmed by conflicts between merchants and producers. After a good harvest in 1867 the Mandinka refused to sell groundnuts unless the buying measure was reduced in size. In part their demand was a means of taking revenge on the merchants, who had sold rice at exorbitant prices the previous season.[46] Some merchants reduced the size of the measure, but the Gorée merchants prohibited their agents from buying any produce for cash during 1868, a move deplored by the French governor Pinet-Laprade, as a local poll tax had just been implemented.

By January 1868 the 'no cash' rule was scrupulously observed everywhere, and in response the Mandinka and Serahuli refused to pay their debts contracted during the previous season. By May 1868 producers had to sell because of the approaching 'hungry season', but many migrant Serahuli and Mandinka sold their crop in The Gambia for cash. The 1869 trade year also proved disastrous, as there were outbreaks of violence and only 250,000 baskets were sold instead of 600,000. This 'hold-up' of produce in Casamance was significant because it pre-figured later disputes in The Gambia, as

---

[44] Faidherbe L., 1863. 'L'Avenir au Sahara et du Soudan', *Rev Maritime et Coloniale*, Tome 8 pp. 221–248.
[45] Bertrand Bocandé, 1856, op. cit.
[46] Ibid.

well as establishing a trend which became a feature of the Senegambian groundnut trade, that of producers crossing borders or spheres of influence, to take advantage of different commercial conditions and government policies. The French were well aware of the importance of the river Gambia as a major route way: Bathurst was a source of imported goods, and it provided a link between Casamance and the French bases at St. Louis and Gorée. It was the river that played a major role in The Gambia's rise to importance in the groundnut trade, as it provided a navigable trade axis penetrating the interior; the river facilitated the bringing of produce to ocean going ships, and it could be used to shift local food surpluses to the areas of groundnut specialization.

### The beginnings of specialization, 1857–1893

After the Convention of 1857 it was inevitable that competition along the river intensified, and French influence over the groundnut trade increased. Groundnuts began to dominate not only the finances of the British colony, but the domestic economy too, while production had spread to the Kombos and middle river (Jarra and Saloum). In 1857 groundnuts accounted for 87% by value of The Gambia's exports, and significantly food importing began to appear although Gambian farmers still integrated groundnuts with their food crops. A general shortage of food occurred in the villages of the productive North bank in 1857, which coincided with an unprecedented export of 13,554 tons of groundnuts, and the Governor was moved to write that "the greater prosperity of trade was not felt by natives, on account of their neglect of the rice and corn fields, and the consequent need for them to spend groundnut income on imported food".[47] The popularity of groundnuts was also influenced by the greater availability of imported goods. For example in 1847 it was reported that cotton goods imported into Bathurst had increased by 300% since 1842, and that much of the goods were of Manchester and Glasgow manufacture.[48] And in 1856 the Annual Report noted that the "improvements in Customs Revenue have been due to the greater importation of fancy goods of all kinds—particularly cotton manufactures, spirits,

---

[47] Annual Report, 1857.
[48] Annual Report 1847, encl. in Blue Book CO 87/41.

gunpowder and rifles, tobacco, sugar and salt".[49] Thus by 1857 it is
arguable that Gambia had become a specialist producer of groundnuts, in the sense it was integrated into the world trading economy
and subject to the law of comparative advantage, but although food
was being imported it had not become a monoculture.

*The groundnut trade and warfare*

During the second half of the 19th century The Gambian groundnut trade continued to expand, although troughs and peaks were
quite pronounced (figs. 1.6, 1.7), and in addition there were signs of
growing British intervention. Fluctuations in the amount of groundnuts produced arose from a number of factors, such as changing
world demand, poor rainfall years, pestilence and plague, and from
internal strife along the river associated with local political rivalries
and religious warfare. Interestingly, these conflicts attracted mercenaries, both Soninke and Mandinka from the interior, which is
another gloss on their involvement in The Gambia. For example, in
1853 O'Connor, the Governor was reporting local conflicts between
the King of Barra and the subordinate chiefdom of Jokadu, led by
Jwalior, who was seeking independence. Jokadu was both inspired
and assisted by the King of Baddibu, while O'Connor was concerned
that Barra was using Tillibunka (Mandinka) mercenaries, who took
employment as soldiers and then plundered the country for pay.[50]

Later in 1857 there were reports of trouble between the Serahuli
town of Ansumanu Jaggi led by Ansumani, and the King of Barra,
which was disrupting the groundnut trade and therefore necessitated
another tour by O'Connor. Previously the King of Barra had employed
Ansumani against his rival Jwalior, but now he refused to leave and
the king wanted to rid himself of this Serahuli mercenary. O'Connor
in his report described the Serahuli (Soninke) as, "leaving their distant country they ramble over different kingdoms, in event of war
sell their services to the highest bidder, in times of peace, farm, trade
and the crop season over return home with the proceeds of their
labour.[51] O'Connor's account is another testimony to the multiple
skills and activities of the Soninke within the Gambian region, and

[49] Annual Report 1856 encl. in Blue Book CO 90/30.
[50] CO 87/55, O'Connor to SS, 8th July 1853.
[51] CO 87/64, O'Connor to SS, 12th Jan. 1857.

Fig 1.6: *Gambian groundnut exports and public finance, 1858–92*

| Year | Groundnut | Tonnage | | | Groundnut Exports Value (F O B) £ | All Exports Total Value £ | Government Revenue £ | Government Expenditure £ |
|------|-----------|---|---|---|------|------|------|------|
| 1858 | 15,728 | 18 | 9 | 1 | 162,649 | 227,460 | 15,920 | 15,457 |
| 1859 | 8,593 | 1 | 3 | 0 | 188,736 | 210,764 | 15,599 | 16,962 |
| 1860 | 9,951 | 9 | 1 | 0 | 98,921 | 109,137 | 14,154 | 15,274 |
| 1861 | 12,632 | 10 | 0 | 0 | 129,909 | 136,837 | 16,162 | 16,492 |
| 1862 | 13,423 | 0 | 8 | 0 | 145,404 | 154,443 | 15,169 | 15,178 |
| 1863 | 10,294 | 4 | 8 | 3 | 129,988 | 141,673 | 17,263 | 19,325 |
| 1864 | 6,252 | 0 | 6 | 0 | | 148,157 | 17,204 | 17,662 |
| 1865 | 7,544 | 5 | 3 | 0 | | 138,693 | 14,758 | 17,151 |
| 1866 | 13,090 | 9 | 3 | 0 | | 158,368 | 19,079 | 17,681 |
| 1867 | 15,305 | 7 | 3 | 0 | | 214,389 | 22,415 | 18,664 |
| 1868 | 12,889 | 3 | 7 | 0 | 99,804 | 187,357 | 22,088 | 17,082 |
| 1869 | 7,417 | 5 | 6 | 0 | 94,010 | 109,312 | 15,518 | 20,236 |
| 1870 | 12,132 | 9 | 1 | 3 | 104,623 | 142,517 | 18,969 | 21,937 |
| 1871 | 13,351 | 0 | 1 | 7 | | 153,100 | 17,490 | 16,662 |
| 1872 | 10,149 | 3 | 1 | 1 | | 127,225 | 17,249 | 17,783 |
| 1873 | 9,800 | 12 | 1 | 0 | | 110,816 | 19,335 | 24,068 |
| 1874 | 16,790 | 4 | 8 | 0 | | 180,094 | 21,380 | 20,787 |
| 1875 | 13,313 | 4 | 5 | 1 | | 147,465 | 22,700 | 19,565 |
| 1876 | 9,986 | 0 | 0 | 0 | | 86,216 | 19,787 | 21,489 |
| 1877 | 15,939 | 0 | 0 | 0 | 111,572 | 125,051 | 26,585 | 21,381 |
| 1878 | 19,197 | 0 | 0 | 0 | 191,970 | 204,301 | 25,731 | 19,807 |
| 1879 | 22,890 | 0 | 0 | 0 | 183,122 | 207,364 | 28,505 | 20,639 |
| 1880 | 13,824 | 0 | 0 | 0 | 110,943 | 138,983 | 24,553 | 19,926 |
| 1881 | 16,958 | 0 | 0 | 0 | 118,711 | 140,423 | 24,451 | 22,116 |
| 1882 | 25,552 | 0 | 0 | 0 | 229,700 | 254,711 | 26,265 | 22,964 |
| 1883 | 23,094 | 3 | 0 | 2 | 170,164 | 209,120 | 28,952 | 23,982 |
| 1884 | 18,404 | 0 | 0 | 0 | 141,388 | 199,481 | 24,959 | 29,482 |
| 1885 | 12,354 | 0 | 0 | 0 | 87,108 | 119,388 | 20,236 | 26,595 |
| 1886 | 5,996 | 0 | 0 | 0 | 38,401 | 79,511 | 14,528 | 23,353 |
| 1887 | 2,986 | 0 | 0 | 0 | 26,001 | 86,933 | 13,377 | 23,920 |
| 1888 | 10,207 | | | | 74,877 | | 20,986 | 21,315 |
| 1889 | 19,636 | | | | 140,086 | | 26,281 | 21,566 |
| 1890 | 18,262 | | | | 129,817 | | 30,537 | 22,759 |
| 1891 | 19,702 | | | | | | 31,038 | 27,697 |
| 1892 | 21,218 | | | | | | 30,977 | 28,739 |

*Source:* Blue Books

he was certainly enthusiastic about them, judging them to be' intelligent and strong', largely because he used Serahuli troops in the Kombo War of 1855. O'Connor declared his intention of protecting them, and noted that some have settled in Bathurst and Cape St. Mary.[52] This relates to his reference in the Blue Book for 1856

---

[52] Ibid.

Fig. 1.7: *Gambian groundnut exports (tons), 1858–1892*

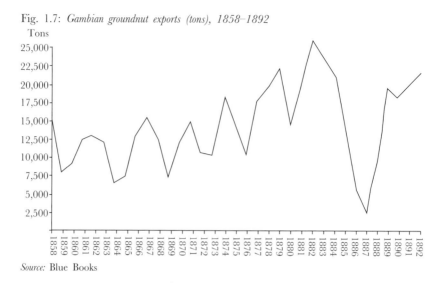

*Source:* Blue Books

to the settlement of 400 Serahuli in British Kombo, "a useless territory" ceded to the British in 1853, which O'Connor believed needed a thrifty population and therefore land had also been allocated to Syrians and pensioners of the West Indian regiment.[53]

The problem at Barra was that the King wouldn't settle with Ansumani, who by May 1857 was fighting his way accross the King's territory, but as things turned against Ansumani, he and 800 refugees arrived at the British fort at Barra seeking protection. Much as O'Connor liked Ansumani and the Serahuli, the Barra area of the north bank in Niumi was crucial to the groundnut trade, which was a focal point of production in the 1850s, and good relations with the King of Barra were essential. As O'Connor grandly proclaimed "Peace is the mainspring of Trade; the only real legitimate agent to spread civilization through Africa".[54] So Anusmani and 300 followers were taken up-river to Fattatenda, while the rest were scattered in Kombo in the hope of bringing it into cultivation, by which O'Connor meant groundnuts as the local Jola and Mandinka were primarily interested in rice cultivation. During his tour of 1857 O'Connor generally supported the presence of Serahuli, as he realized they were useful in the development of the groundnut trade:

---

[53] Blue Book, 1856.
[54] CO 87/64, O'Connor to SS, 14th May 1857.

they were good traders as well as farmers, and bought quantities of British imported goods.[55]

More important than these local conflicts were the Soninke-Marabout religious wars, which rumbled on from the1862 until 1894, and have been crudely characterized as hinging on the differences that divided strict Muslims, the Marabouts, from the more relaxed Soninkes who drank alcohol. Rather confusingly in this context 'Soninke' is not the same as the Soninke people. The Marabouts tended to be recruited from among patricians, such as village heads (*alkalos*), merchants, clerics and peasants, while the Soninke comprised the aristocracy and their retainers. The aristocracy had a more pragmatic and relaxed attitude towards Islam, which embraced traditional African practices such as divination. The general situation in Senegambia was one of long established tension between these groups, which arguably became exacerbated with the ending of the Atlantic slave trade, and the slow decay of the aristocracies, which was a feature of 19th century Senegambia. It has been suggested that abolition undercut the slave owning aristocratic classes, and boosted the power of merchants, clerics and peasants. In particular local merchants became increasingly involved with French firms engaged in the groundnut trade, who as we have noted were busy negotiating with village heads.[56]

Militant Islam in Senegambia crystallized around a Torodbe cleric from the Futa Toro, Umar Tal, who after a pilgrimage to Mecca in 1830 had become the head of the new Tijaniya brotherhood in West Africa. His reformist jihad started in the 1830s, and at his death in 1864 his influence extended as far as Timbuktu, and included large portions of Senegambia. The jihad and the sectarian differences were translated into outbreaks of local violence along The Gambia, centred on Gunjur in Kombo (1851), Baddibu and Niumi (mid-1860s) and the Fulladus (late 19th century).

The north bank disturbances were the more significant for the groundnut trade, where Umar's support was centred on Baddibu, through a Torodbe cleric Maba Diakhou. Maba's influence gradually increased, which prompted Soninke rulers, such as Demba Sonko of Niumi, to engage 'Tillibunka' (Mandinka) and 'Serahuli' (Soninke)

[55] Ibid.
[56] Searing, 1993, op. cit. See also Archer, F., 1964, *A History of The Gambia*. London: Routledge, Kegan Paul.

mercenaries to bolster their regimes.[57] In 1861 Maba led a successful jihad against the Soninke rulers of Baddibu, which sparked-off
further trouble in Niumi, assisted by Baddibu. Those under attack
suffered severely from the committed warring minorities, and the
Annual report of 1863 noted the desolation of corn growing districts
through fighting, while in February of the same year there were
reports of 2,000 Wolof and Serer refugees fleeing their homes in
Saloum seeking protection at the British fort at Barra Point, later
followed by another 700.[58] Eventually the British intervened in 1866,
with an armed force led by Governor D'Arcy to secure this strategic
area, which controlled the river entrance, as well as being an important groundnut producing area.

Klein has argued that sectarian wars and jihadism in Senegambia,
reflected the weakening of political and social structures, which resulted
from the ending of the Atlantic slave trade, and was symptomatic
of a crisis of adaptation.[59] Slave sales had been the means whereby
rulers had access to guns, liquor and luxury goods, which were used
to cement political alliances and secure the loyalty of their followers.
Of particular importance amongst the Wolof and Mandinka were
the *ceddo*, or warrior caste. As the Atlantic slave trade declined, the
*ceddo* increasingly pillaged farmers and traders, or became mercenaries to compensate for favours no longer forthcoming from their
patrons. In some instance, traditional chiefs either colluded with
them, or became their agents. Although the ending of the Atlantic
slave trade may have undercut the power of aristocracies in Senegambia, the situation along the Gambia was rather different. With
the partial exception of Niumi (whose coastline included the Ceded
mile), local rulers continued to exact customs and tolls. Furthermore,
the local slave trade continued as it was stimulated by the Soninke-
Marabout wars, and the chiefs now used slaves to cultivate groundnuts.

But certainly part of the transition from the Atlantic slave trade
to legitimate trade was a widening of the economic base to include
rural households, which gradually integrated them into the world
trading economy, giving them access to money and trade goods
(including guns) through their income from groundnuts. On the point

---

[57] Wright, 1996, op. cit.
[58] CO 87/76, 1863, D'Arcy to Newcastle, 11th September, 1863.
[59] Klein, M.A., 1972, "Social and Economic Factors in Muslim Revolution in
Senegambia", *Journal of African History*, XIII (3), 419–441.

of the purchase of arms, which is attested for example in accounts of 1871, it is important to emphasize that the vast majority of Gambian farmers were more interested in securing and defending their farms than engaging in the struggles between armed Soninkes and Marabouts.[60] The overwhelming majority of people were Soninkes subject to Muslim attack, and Curtin's statement that "most people in Senegambia were concerned most of the time about crops, not states holds good".[61] Marabout strongholds were restricted along the Gambia, and the view that maraboutism had a wide appeal for the mass of producers as the means of escaping their oppressors, appears to be at variance with local evidence.[62]

One of the problems of civil and religious disturbances was that although the British claimed control of 300 miles of the river, they accepted that the banks outside British settlements were under native jurisdiction.[63] And, especially up-stream of MacCarthy Island, the government afforded no protection to British commercial interest. The merchants and traders complained bitterly of the disruption to trade through these local wars and the financial losses at their stations.[64] Despite merchant deputations the British government was singularly unhelpful, as they had neither the means nor the finance to afford protection, and were supported in their stand by the Colonial Office.[65] Any sympathy the government might have shown was tempered by a belief that the merchants were at fault as they were importing and selling guns to the warring factions, as well as being involved in the proliferation in slave trading which the wars activated. On the other hand the French were not so reticent, and policies aimed at political domination and suppression were first articulated under Faidherbe who was Governor from 1854–61 and 1863–65.

---

[60] CO 87/101, Anton to Kennedy, March 3rd 1871. See also A.B. Ellis, 1878, *The Land of the Fetish*, London.

[61] Curtin, P.D., 1975, *Economic Change in Pre-Colonial Africa: Senegambia in the era of the Slave Trade*. Wisconsin Press, p. 13.

[62] See M.A. Klein, op. cit., 1972 and C. Quinn, 1972. *Mandingo Kingdoms of the Senegambia: Traditionalism, Islam and European Expansion*. Evanston: Northwestern Univ. Press.

[63] CO 87/87, D'Arcy to Blackall, 15th Nov. 1866.

[64] CO 87/102, A Deputation of the Merchant Community of Bathurst to Simpson, 4th June 1872.

[65] CO 87/118, Havelock to Kimberley, 24th Feb. 1882.

The effects of the wars on groundnut production and trade were considerable but paradoxical: they disrupted the groundnut trade, but increased the potential labour supply through the slaves captured. Disruption was evident especially in the last quarter of the 19th century, when groundnut exports declined from 18,404 tons in 1884 to 12,354 tons in 1885, and sank to a low of 2,986 tons in 1887. (Figs. 1.6, 1.7) Disturbances were particularly acute in Niumi and the Baddibus, the major centres of groundnut production. Finally, in 1887 the French mounted a military action on the North bank against the warring factions, who were threatening their sphere of influence in Sine Saloum, and as a result exports rose to 10,207 tons in 1888. The French action pushed the British towards quelling the warring factions, which ensured that the French did not expand into the upper river to quell the disturbance.[66]

It is clear that war-torn Niumi and Baddibu had a considerable impact on the groundnut trade, but there were other factors too. In l869 the opening of the Suez Canal brought Indian groundnuts to the Marseille market, which resulted in a decline in the prices of groundnuts in Senegal from 27.50 franc per kilo in 1867, to 15.00 francs in 1883.[67] Similar falls occurred in The Gambia. Thus the disruption to trade caused by civil and religious disturbances coincided with falling groundnut prices associated with alternative supplies coming into Europe from Asia. Furthermore, from the 1870s to the 1890s Europe experienced The Great Depression, which precipitated a general fall in commodity prices. Whatever the arguments about the true nature of the Depression, oil-seed prices were particularly affected, and the consequences were transmitted back to African producers through the merchants and traders.[68] The producers reacted through a series of hold-ups, which became a persistent feature of the groundnut trade, extending into the 20th century causing as much, if not more disruption, than the Soninke-Marabout wars.

*The Merchants, trading networks and credit*

From the outset European firms such as Peyrissac, Maurel and Prom were extremely active in persuading the *alkalos*, (village heads), to

---

[66] Annual Register 1887. The Times, 7th and 12th May and 3rd Nov. 1887.
[67] Adam, J., 1908. *L'Arachide Culture, Produits Commerce-Amélioration de la Production.* Paris.
[68] Saul, S.S., 1969, *The Myth of the Great Depression.* London: Macmillan.

encourage groundnut cultivation possibly as a means of replacing lost revenues from the former slave trade, which mirrored their own concerns about opening new commercial niches. Also, it was important that the *alkalos* and their people should see the groundnut trade as a means of accessing a range of European imported goods. In practice the operations of merchant capital involved extended chains of dealing, which embraced merchants, traders and indigenous middlemen, something which also obtained during the Atlantic trade, but which receives little attention in Myint's vent for surplus theory. However, he does stress the simultaneous activation of indigenous structures and the role of expatriates. Expatriate firms linked European demand and the Gambian desire for imported goods, but as the Gambian groundnut trade demonstrates, Africans were heavily, if subordinately, involved in groundnut buying and the trading of imported goods. As early as 1842 the Annual Report outlined the way the system worked. European merchants gave-out goods to agents in Bathurst, and in turn agents employed perhaps a hundred African sub-agents, or traders as they were called, who took quantities of trade goods and settled in villages as far as 300 miles from Bathurst.[69] The Annual Report for 1843 pointed to the two colonial enclaves of Bathurst and MacCarthy Island as the two great depots from which the traders dispersed into villages, where they paid the local chief an annual 'custom'.[70]

Traders in general operated in a variety of ways, using a mixture of cash, barter and credit; the latter being particularly important, but always at the centre of their dealings were groundnuts. They bartered trade goods for groundnuts, they advanced trade goods against a proportion of the next season's groundnut crop, they sold goods and bought groundnuts for cash. In addition they advanced seed nuts on credit at the beginning of the farming season; they advanced food against groundnuts; they sold food for cash and they made cash loans against repayment in groundnuts. The peak time for such trading was during the dry season after the harvest and sale of the groundnut crop. African sub-agents were especially important as they had the benefit of local knowledge; they could assess the risks, evaluate local growing conditions, and they were able to advance credit before the groundnut season which provided producers with

---

[69] CO 87/28, Annual Report 1842.
[70] CO 87/28, Annual Report 1843.

working capital. The merchant houses benefited considerably from African traders, as the risks of advancing credit were reduced, because only small amounts were in the hands of any one of many sub-agents, who were spread over wide areas that were risk prone for Europeans prior to pacification.

From the very beginning of the groundnut trade the advancement of credit through African agents was a highly successful means of incorporating rural producers into the world economy. What is not revealed in the official correspondence is who these African agents and sub-agents were. Were they local Gambians, or were there substantial numbers of Soninke and Mandinka, hitherto involved in moving slaves and goods between the coast and the interior? The presence of traders from the interior however is revealed in an account we referred to earlier, when O'Connor in 1857 dealt with disturbances along the river. At the trade port of Yanimarou, O'Connor found there were both Strange Farmers (migrant farmers), and Trade Strangers who were Tillibunkas (Mandinka), two of whom had been imprisoned and their goods seized.[71] It would appear that the presence of strangers was not always, welcome, but O'Connor had them released by King Sandikabar and brought them to Bathurst, where he "presented them before the chief men of the Serahuli and Tillibunkas, as well as Syrian traders", as a mark of British commitment to them and their importance to the trade along the river.[72]

Credit systems were certainly not new: credit, brokers and intermediaries were all part of the trade carried on by the Soninke and Mandinka which spanned the western savannas of West Africa, and linked them to the coast on the one hand, and the desert on the other. But the groundnut trade introduced new categories of creditor and debtor, which were more widespread and linked a multitude of household producers to European merchant houses and tied them into the circulation of international merchant capital. Elderly Mandinka informants are quite clear on these different categories, which are reflected in the Mandinka nomenclature. *N'donto kodolar* represents a loan of money or food from a 'brother' on which there is no interest: in addition a good muslim would lend to an honest man interest free. *Julabar n'donto kodolar* is a loan of a similar kind,

---

[71] CO 87/64, O'Connor to SS 12th Jan. 1857.
[72] Ibid.

but from a big-farmer or trader, where the interest is a private matter between lender and borrower and repayable over a year, or possibly as staged repayments with a certain amount of flexibility. But in a different category lies *Julabar n'donto kodolar mbejola tiola*, where interest is paid in groundnuts. For example, an advance of money would require re-payment, plus a stated number of bags of groundnuts. Such types of loan were overt ones associated with foreign traders, especially the Syrians and Lebanese whose importance increased during the 20th century.

In common with the other commercial crop regions of West Africa, the number of traders in The Gambia and the quantity of imported trade goods matched the increase in exports. Newbury has shown that the importing of various manufactured staples into West Africa from approximately 1810 to 1850 increased by factors of at least three, and in some cases fifty.[73] Imports of cotton piece goods showed big surges in 1836, 1850 and 1880, and although there were notable fluctuations, imports of 358,000 yards for 1812 had risen to 116,900,000 by 1880. As studies in Nigeria have shown, the large trading Companies made significantly greater profits on imported goods than the export produce they collected.[74] The importation of cotton piece goods into The Gambia increased in the 1840s and 1850s, and it was reported in 1847 that they had risen by 300% since 1842.[75] The 1840s and 1850s also saw the unprecedented importation of other manufactured staples, such as guns and gunpowder, rum, spirits and tobacco and in a period of unchanged tariffs, import duties increased from £6,231 7s 7d in 1840 to £21,103 4s 2d in 1857.[76] Such growth as this, was facilitated by European firms working in conjunction with their African agents.

Governor O'Connor in 1856 wrote of firms disposing of goods up to £90,000 in value, which was substantially more than half of the value of groundnut exports,[77] while in 1853 he also indicated that he knew of a young English merchant, "who in the summer of last year commenced business on his own account, and has up to

---

[73] Newbury, C.W., 1972, 'Credit in Early Nineteenth Century West African Trade', *Journal of African History* XIII (1), 81–95.
[74] Shenton, R., 1987, op. cit.
[75] CO 87/41, Annual Report 1847
[76] Blue Books, 1840, 1843, 1845, 1851, 1854 and 1857.
[77] Annual Report 1856, encl. in Blue Book 1856, CO 90/30.

the present time realized £1,700 on the small capital of £2,000".[78] And, for the first time O'Connor's report gives an inkling of the terms of trade; a bottle of trade rum value $4\frac{1}{2}$d was sufficient exchange for one bushel of groundnuts worth 2s 8d.[79] By the 1850s Gambia had become drawn into the mainstream of the international economy, and after the Anglo-French Convention of 1857, rivalry among the European merchants led to the extension of credit as the river was opened-up to free trade.

Between 1857 and 1863 four French firms became prominent in The Gambia, they were Maurel et Prom, Fermick, Barrières Frères and Maurel Frères: collectively they spearheaded the competition for groundnuts, and Maurel et Prom had established factories as far east as Damasansan near Elephant Island.[80] (Fig. 1.1) Governor D'Arcy noted the French firms trading methods in his dispatches to the Colonial Office, especially their use of coin, whereas the English merchants were firmly wedded to the use of barter.[81] The spread of currency in the mid-19th century, illustrates the power of merchant capital to monetize the economy for its own purposes in the pre-colonial era, but the struggle over barter trade shows it was not monolithic, and there were tensions within the business community. Also, indigenous monetary systems continued throughout the 19th century, and the local unit of exchange along the river was lengths of cotton cloth know as *pagns*. Monetary systems co-existed, much as labour systems co-existed, even within the same community; both exemplifying their compatibility with capitalist penetration which was far from homogenous or evenly spread.

Although different currencies were maintained along the river, it seems French firms were gaining the advantage as Gambian producers, and especially migrant farmers, preferred the 'dollar', by which was meant the silver five franc piece. The result was that imported trade goods (and the revenue on them) dropped considerably, while the importation of specie (exempt from duty) correspondingly increased as it became widely used along the river. The

---

[78] CO 87/63, O'Connor to Labouchere, 29th April 1856.
[79] Ibid.
[80] CO 87/84, D'Arcy to Cardwell, 25th Mar. 1866: A MacMillan, 1920, *Red Book of West Africa, Historical and Descriptive, Commercial and Industrial Facts, Figures and Resources*, Complied and Edited, London, p. 291.
[81] CO 87/69, D'Arcy to Newcastle, 24th May 1860: CO 87/71 D'Arcy to Newcastle, 24th July 1861.

duty of 4% on imported manufactured goods fetched £35,000 in 1858, but at the same rate yielded only £2,000 in 1860, while the amount of specie imported rose from £2,861 in 1857, to £19,103 in 1863, which gives some indication of the popularity of coin.[82] The government responded to falling revenues by the introduction of a direct tax on groundnut producers in British Kombo, in the form of a farm tax encapsulated in an Ordinance of 1864, which represented the first general tax on Gambian producers. Allotments of land containing one or more dwellings were taxed at 4s 0d per annum, and groundnut farms of over one acre at 8s 0d.[83] Taxes were now added to normal cash needs of producers in Kombo, and laid the basis for later taxation in the Protectorate in 1894.

The domestic economy also became increasingly monetized as coins spread to the local trading economy, not least for the purchase of slaves, many of who were being used to produce groundnuts. Governor D'Arcy in 1861 reported that he believed specie did not just stay in Bathurst, because it was also the currency of the internal slave trade along the river and the Rio Pongos: thus the circulation of specie was assisted by slave dealers.[84] In one sense the new money opened-up the economy as more domestic goods were purchased, but these 'goods' frequently were slaves used for groundnut production and thus were expenditures dependent on external commerce. At the same time, in French territories taxation was being introduced with more rigour, which prompted an influx of migrants into The Gambia, especially seasonal workers.

The new competition along the Gambia associated with the French firms and monetization initially seems to have improved producer prices, but it also encouraged the merchants' agents and their sub-agents to overbid each other and enhanced the pernicious system of credit.[85] Competition and credit advances also took their toll of smaller mercantile businesses, and between 1857 and 1863 seven closed with liabilities of between £50,000–60,000 to their home firms.[86] In Casamance during the 1860s the credit system was also well entrenched around the French post of Sédhiou. Terms were usually repayment

---

[82] Blue Books, 1857–63, BA Class 54, piece no. 157.
[83] CO87/79. An Ordinance to Collect a Revenue in British Kombo, 1864
[84] CO 87/69, D'Arcy to Newcastle, 19th June 1861
[85] CO 87/69, D'Arcy to Newcastle, 24th Oct. 1860.
[86] CO 87/69, D'Arcy to Newcastle, 19th January 1860.

of two bags of seeds after harvest for the one advanced before planting, while for food it was 10% of the harvest.[87] The introduction of
the credit system and its extension after 1857 can be seen as the
precursor to the chronic indebtedness which at times swept rural
Gambia, and which helped to insert farmers into the international
commodity markets. While the government was not averse to competition and the credit system, it was concerned about falling revenues as the volume of imported trade goods declined in the face
of specie, and it was equally concerned about the different attitudes
of French and British merchants, as the latter were continuing with
barter trade. So as well as taxing Kombo farms, the government
introduced a tax on groundnuts of one half penny per bushel exported,
as a means of redressing falling revenues and taxing French merchants who were largely exporters.[88]

*Producer resistance*

By the 1870s the river Gambia had become an important ground-
nut-exporting region, and farmers were increasingly concentrating
their efforts on the production of this crop. And although European
merchants, African traders and agents, together with Africans trading on their own account were at times united in their opposition
to the government, there were growing signs of a conflict of interest among them, as well as between them and the groundnut farmers. Farmers had become enmeshed in groundnut production principally
through the credit system, and specialization increased during the
1860s, but when the Great Depression in Europe took hold producers became acutely aware of the fluctuations in the prices they
received as a result of changing world demand. The result was the
initiation of *tong*, or hold-ups. Violence and insecurity along the river
increased not just because of the Soninke-Marabout wars, but also
because of producers' disillusionment with the prices they received.
The government and merchants could not control world prices, and
both tried to put this point to the producers, but without success.
On the other hand the government felt the merchants in the good
years made extremely handsome profits, while the producers benefited
only marginally.

---

[87] Vallon, A., 1862, 'La Casamance, Dépendence du Sénégal' *Rev. Maritime et
Coloniale*, tome VI (Oct. Dec.), 456–74.
[88] CO 87/69, D'Arcy to Newcastle, 24th October 1860.

Direct action by Gambian farmers against poor prices was first recorded in 1873, and reflected earlier attempts at resistance in French territory.[89] The groundnuts in The Gambia were generally bought by the bushel measure, but the trade bushel was a nominal one as its size changed from year to year. In 1873 the producers on the north bank at Sucatoon queried not the price of 1s 3d, but the size of the bushel.[90] Violence broke out when the traders refused to reduce the size of the bushel; Dodgin, a British born subject dealing with Maurel et Prom was attacked and wounded, and prevented from leaving with his goods after deciding 'enough was enough'.[91]

Possibly, the merchants' refusal to reduce the bushel size was a result of the duty on groundnuts entering France being raised in 1871–72.[92] However, the dispute between merchants and farmers had a particularly depressing effect on the smaller traders. These African agents trading on their own account were in effect brokers, and chronically indebted to the European merchants, who controlled the economy. An agent took goods on credit which were exchanged for a specified amount of groundnuts agreed upon in advance, while in turn they had sub-agents to help spread dealings with groundnut producers along the river. Importantly, the merchants arbitrarily fixed the exchange value of the goods to the agents, without regard to fluctuations in the supplies of groundnuts. Therefore, if for any reason groundnuts were in short supply after the harvest then agents were left with goods they had taken on credit: many were taken to court, and those found unable to pay their debts were given prison sentences. The merchants also played-off the agents one against the other: the same kind of goods were given out on different credit terms to their various agents, who competed among themselves as well as with the self-employed African traders for a groundnut crop that might be reduced by poor rainfall, civil strife or hold-ups. Thus aggressive competition led to cheating on measures, disputes between merchants and traders, as well as producer hold-ups, which contributed to discontent and violence.

In the buying seasons of 1884–86, a majority of producers in the Kombo, Jarra, Baddibu, Saloum and Niumi districts staged the most

---

[89] Roche, C., 1995, Histoire de la Casamance: Conquêt et résistance, 1850–1920, Paris: Éditions Karthala

[90] CO 87/104, Cooper to Harley, 26th Mar. 1873.

[91] CO 87/104, T. Brown, President The Gambia Chamber of Commerce to Cooper, 15th Feb. 1873.

[92] CO 87/104, Cooper to Harley, 28th May 1873.

effective *tong* to date. In 1884 they rejected the merchants offer of 1s 3d for the 16 × 16 inch bushel,[93] and in 1885 and 1886 rejected an offer of 1s 0d for the 14 × 14 inch bushel measure.[94] However, the migrant Strange Farmers ignored the *tong* and their considerable presence along the river undermined the actions of local producers. These migrants wanted to sell their produce and return home with money or trade goods, as their perception of prices and returns to their labour were of a different order from local farmers. Many of these migrant workers came from the upper Senegal and Niger valleys, where the groundnut and gum trade, and cotton cloth industries were collapsing in the 1880s. Falling world prices after the opening of Suez in 1869 discouraged merchant interest in these inland areas, dis-advantaged by high transport costs compared with the riverine enclave of the Gambia and lower Senegal. Gambians were bitter about migrant attitudes to *tong*, and while the British government admitted it could be imposed, they forbad interference with those who wanted to sell.[95]

The attitude of the British administration to these complaints about *tong*, was on the one hand one of indifference to the merchants, whom they believed to be avaricious, while on the other they protected the rights of producers to sell if they wished, and supported individual rights to counteract collective action. Government attitudes also smacked of what Robinson and Gallagher have described as, "those who governed still thought of themselves as arbiters above the tumult".[96] The British Administration of the time was largely drawn from the minor gentry and the professions, especially the armed forces, who considered themselves 'above trade'. But although they didn't like traders and middlemen, they knew they were essential to the economic workings of the territory they administered.

However, producers on the north bank who were in favour of *tong* adopted other means of resistance. In 1884 they took to their canoes and evacuated their groundnuts to Foudiougne on the River Saloum in Western Senegal. (Fig. 1.1) Here the same merchant houses trad-

---

[93] CO 87/126, Maloney to Rowe, 13th Oct. 1885: CO 87/127, Carter to Rowe, 22nd Jan. 1886.
[94] CO 87/126, Maloney to Rowe, 15th Oct. 1885.
[95] CO 87/126, Maloney to Rowe, 13th Oct. 1885: CO 87/127 Carter to Rowe, 22nd Jan. 1886: CO 87/130 Carter to Rowe 15th April 1887.
[96] Robinson and Gallagher, op. cit. 1981.

ing out of Bathurst paid 2s 0d cash per Imperial bushel. Thus in the mid-1880s groundnut farmers by-passed the credit system, and engaged in direct trade with the merchant houses to cope with falling prices and the economic crisis in the European market. Letters from the Bathurst merchants to the Governor indicated their concern over *tong* and, incidentally confirm that the producers were well entrenched in perpetual and heavy indebtedness to the merchants, their agents and traders.[97] One merchant, Thomas Chown complained that the nuts sent to Rufisque and Foudiougne "belonged to us, as we have, as our usual practice run huge current accounts with the natives".[98]

The Rufisque-Foudiougne bonanza soon came to an end, but producers along the river were still determined to impose *tong*. As a result the merchants decided to suspend the river trade in 1886. The government explained to London that the producers failed to understand falling prices was not a conspiracy on the part of merchants, but the depression of the European market.[99] In effect, dueing the 1880s the clamour for better prices, producer resistance and violence was a reflection of the poor purchasing power of groundnuts, exacerbated by taxes on imported consumer goods. The producers were buying Kola nuts taxed at 9%, salt 40%, sugar 30%, and tobacco 9%, which reduced their purchasing power further as groundnut prices fell, and meant real economic hardship for many Gambians.[100] Despite the Administrations reservations about the tax on imports, it did not deter the Colonial Office from insisting in 1887, that further taxation must be fully explored before any consideration could be given to Imperial aid.[101] As a result of this injunction, it was decided there was a need for an additional tax on imports, not subject to specific duties to make good the loss on groundnut exports. A new *ad valorem* tax of 5% was imposed as well as specific duties on rice, oils and palm wine.[102] The economic crisis of 1884 and the leaking of nuts into Senegal, led to a four-year period when expenditure exceeded revenue by between £4,423 and £10,543. Producers

---

[97] CO 87/126, Maloney to Rowe, 15th Oct. 1885.
[98] CO 87/128, Carter to Rowe, 22nd Jan. 1886.
[99] CO 87/130, Carter to Rowe, 15th April 1887.
[100] CO 87/128, SW to Meade, Minute no. 11085. 2nd June 1886.
[101] CO 87/131, SW to Meade, Minute no. 24800, 10th Dec. 1887.
[102] CO 87/131, Meade to Hutton, Minute no. H/25614, 27th Dec. 1887.

suffered, as they were now dependent on groundnuts, and were already experiencing the difficulties of specialization well before the partition and establishment of formal colonial rule along the river.

*Summary*

Although there were severe fluctuations in the groundnut trade, its establishment proceeded rapidly. From 1840 onwards, the transition from the external slave trade to the production and export of groundnuts took place in those areas which had been heavily involved in the Atlantic slave trade, and was achieved partly through a set of pre-conditions. Such pre-conditions are important in evaluating theories about adaptation after the ending of the Atlantic slave trade, as well as vent for surplus theory. First, the existence of commercial grain farming and trading areas associated with the Atlantic slave trade, second, the continuance of a long established legitimate trade which helped the transition to a groundnut economy, third activities of the new French merchants and traders who penetrated the rural areas, and fourth the use of slaves, and most importantly through the influx of pioneer migrant farmers (largely Soninke and Mandinka), who diffused grounuts of the *arachis* variety into lower Gambia. As the groundnut trade developed, more local producers were drawn into the trade; rural areas were transformed and African political systems and societies were incorporated into new European spheres of commerce, and were subject to the rigours of international markets. Up to 1850 the Europeans could shape trading patterns in Senegambia through agreement and consensus, but subsequently this changed, as the spread of groundnut cultivation among myriad rural households transformed social, political and religious structures.

After 1857 the groundnut economy along the Gambia river became more specialized, and although output showed an upward trend there were notable poor periods, for example when production was affected by the Islamic wars. Rice importing appeared, and by the 1860s the credit system was firmly established, while as the century progressed the economy became increasingly monetized. Indebtedness of producers became commonplace, and lower groundnut prices were reminders of the vicissitudes of the world market on which they depended. The variability of the climate and outbreaks of pestilence were also becoming apparent. The relations between merchants and producers deteriorated as world prices faltered, and provoked resistance from producers who instituted hold-ups, while merchants and their agents reacted by cheating over buying measures. Intervention by the British government was minimal, although it increasingly taxed exports and imported trade goods, which affected production and consumption along the river and its hinterland. The importance of merchants in the development of the groundnut trade was of the essence; but production could not have been achieved in such a lightly populated area without extra inputs of migrant labour, and it is to labour that we turn in the next chapter.

CHAPTER TWO

# MIGRANT FARMERS:
# SERAWOOLLIES AND TILLIBUNKAS

The cash crop revolution in West Africa may have proceeded with minimal technological innovation, but almost everywhere it did require an increased supply of farm labour.[1] Along the river Gambia population densities were low, there were no large urban centres such as those along the Niger, or in Hausaland, therefore seasonal and permanent migration were important means of increasing the local labour supply. Also, seasonal migrants generally were cheaper and more flexible, as employers were not responsible for the full reproduction of a temporary labour force on short contracts. By the same token smaller households could afford to boost their available labour by the addition of one or two seasonal workers. In particular, a sufficient and timely labour supply was important for the development of groundnuts and cotton in West Africa, because unlike tree crops, which are grown over years, they are grown annually during the wet season. These new export crops competed with food crops for agricultural labour, and while there may have been surplus land, the local labour supply soon became a constraint on the rapid expansion of the export trade.

As legitimate trade developed in West Africa there was a prodigious transfer of farm labour from the non-export crop areas, especially in the drier interior towards the areas where cocoa, coffee, palm produce, cotton and groundnuts were grown. By the early 20th century, some 2.0 million men were seasonal long distance migrants, who became part of the social and economic fabric of West Africa. Explanations and theories of these movements abound.[2] In the 1950s

---

[1] This was not unique: agrarian change occurred elsewhere, when existing technology such as field practices and livestock management were found to be compatible with alternative forms of control and access to land. See Parker, W.N. 1986,' Agrarian and Industrial Revolutions' in R. Porter and M. Teich (eds), *Revolution in History*. Cambridge: CUP.

[2] For a review of models of development see R. Peet and M.J. Watts, 1993, "Introduction: development theory and environment in an age of market triumphalism", *Economic Geography* 69, 227–253.

and 1960s equilibrium models were popular, with the emphasis on rational economic behaviour, 'target workers', and the respective 'push' and 'pull' of contrasting environments and their economic potential. By the 1970s such neo-liberal models were under attack from more radical analyses, which invoked the forces of international capital and colonial policies of taxation and monetization, as the means whereby migrant farmers were pushed into finding cash wages in the export crop areas. While such scenarios have some substance, they appear too crude for West Africa, and especially the ground-nut industry of Senegambia. For example, Manchuelle has explored the cultural and historic tendency of the Soninke to become labour migrants from the late 18th century into the present day, and sug-gests poverty and taxation were not sufficient conditions to explain their migratory movements.[3] In general, it is necessary to consider migration with reference to the historical trajectories and geograph-ical conditions of specific regional economies of West Africa, and their transformation after the abolition of the Atlantic slave trade prior to formal colonial rule. Theoretically, a useful distinction may be made between 'rate' and 'incidence' of migration: the former referring to general flows and the larger structural forces of inter-national and West African political economies, the latter referring to the motives and aspirations of individuals and groups who were drawn into labour migration.

It is also important to recognize that in common with land tenure and farming, African labour embraced (and still does) a plurality of structures and processes whereby different methods of recruiting, con-trolling and organizing labour co-existed, and which shifted in their relative importance seasonally, as well as over longer periods. For example, wage labour existed in the early 19th century but it was not widespread and was seasonal; today it has become commonplace in rural areas where it can extend across wet and dry seasons. Nor is the plurality of labour contracts incompatible with capitalist pen-etration, and radical analyses have taken this on board through con-structing the emergence of small commodity producers as constituted within capitalism, which does not necessarily lead to the widespread development of a landless proletariat who become wage labourers

---

[3] Manchuelle, F., 1997, *Willing Migrants: Soninke Labor Diasporas, 1848–1960*. Athens: Ohio University Press.

and migrants.[4] In 19th century Gambia, the groundnut trade relied on a labour force of African cultivators and transporters, who comprised chiefs, freemen, slaves, waged labourers, clerics, Islamic students, mercenaries and migratory workers, whose relative proportions shifted over time.

One of the problems of exploring labour systems in the 19th century is the absence of detailed information about labour inputs. Therefore, we propose to deal with the Gambian case beginning with more recent observations on farm labour, in order to explain why extra workers were needed to develop a successful cash crop revolution. If labour constraints in recent times have exerted a limit on production, it seems that they were likely to be just as important to the 19th century cultivation of export crops when population levels were much lower than at present.

*Labour and the groundnut cultivation cycle*

It is important to begin by clearing away some misunderstandings about African farm labour; misunderstandings which were common in the economic development models of the 1950s when economists began to examine the evolution of cash cropping, and the future development of African agriculture. For example, Myint's thesis first appeared in 1958, when the surplus labour scenario was an integral part of most economic development paradigms, and the received wisdom suggested the existence of a pool of surplus agricultural labour whose marginal productivity was zero. It was argued, that agriculture could accommodate to outward transfers of labour into the modernizing urban sector to the benefit of both industry and agriculture. This view was probably more relevant to Asia, and there seem to have been serious misunderstandings about the nature and organization of African labour-intensive cultivation systems, a view that to some extent has persisted.

In tropical Africa the growing season for rain-fed food and non-food crops is contained within a wet period which may be as short as six months: in The Gambia it usually extends from April to late October. And, it is important to appreciate that rainfall both within

---

[4] Cohen, R. 1988, *The New Helots*. Aldershot: Gower.

and between years may exhibit considerable variability, and farming tasks may have to be carried out with an urgency which requires sustained inputs over relatively short periods of a few days, followed by virtual inactivity. During the cultivation cycle serious labour bottlenecks may develop at the times when land is cleared and weeded.[5] For example, in savanna environments ridging and weeding are especially important compared with clearing low bush and grass, which is less labour intensive than in the forested areas. Farming of this kind is primarily labour intensive, and when units of production are centred on households, then, the ability to marshal sufficient labour inputs (albeit of short intensity) is of the essence. In other words it is the *flow*, not just the *stock* of labour that is crucial. Household models and observations from Senegal show that whereas 480 hours is the minimum labour input required to cultivate one hectare of groundnuts, some five-eighths of the labour time is expended on planting and cultivation, and for each day of delay in planting there is a 2% fall in yield.[6] On the other hand losses can occur at the end of the season during harvesting: if lifting is delayed after the rains the ground can harden quite quickly under the hot sun, and nuts stick in the soil unless they are pulled immediately. Thus bottlenecks can occur at planting, weeding and harvesting, and timing is of the essence. On the other hand, the timing of these tasks varies from year to year and from region to region, principally according to climatic variations.

Haswell's investigations in Genieri village in 1949 also underline the relationship between groundnut production, labour supply and the timing of labour inputs.[7] Haswell observed that the average time spent per acre varied between 256 and 278 hours, depending on the status of farmers and the quality of the land. But the effects of the timing of sowing and weeding were quite remarkable. On early sown and much weeded plots, yields were 663 lbs compared with 498 lbs on late sown but much weeded plots. In the case of early sown but little weeded plots, the yield was 478 lbs compared with 404 lbs for late sown and little weeded plots. These results show

[5] Swindell, K., 1985, *Farm Labour*. Cambridge: CUP.
[6] Van Haeverbeke, A., 1970, *Rémuneration de travail et commerce extérieur; essor d'une économie paysanne exportrice et termes de l'échange de producteurs d'arachide du Sénégal*. Louvain.
[7] Haswell, M.R., 1953, *Economics of Agriculture in a Savannah Village*, Colonial Research Studies, no. 8. London: HMSO.

that yields can be impaired by over one-third when sowing and weeding are mis-timed, or when weeding is reduced to a minimum. If farmers do mis-time operations, particularly weeding, then they have to exert greater efforts later to remove weeds at an advanced stage of growth. Thus, measurements in Genieri showed that the time required to produce 100 lbs of groundnuts displayed considerable latitude, and varied between 31 and 118 hours. Haswell concluded that from the farmers' point of view, the importance in devising some kind of production strategy was not so much in yields per acre cultivated, but the returns to labour. The observed variations in labour inputs and yields indicate the opportunities for additional income, at least for those who can mobilize sufficient workers at specific times. It is clear that the marginal productivity of labour can be very high at certain points in the cultivation cycle, and that farmers who are faced with a 'fixed' or reduced domestic labour supply during the cultivation cycle may have to look elsewhere for workers, if yields are to be improved, or more importantly maintained.

An adequate and suitably timed labour supply is vital for the successful production of groundnuts: we repeat there can be a serious conflict over the allocation of labour for commercial groundnut farming and food production, and the development and resolution of this conflict was important for the successful expansion of the Gambian groundnut trade. From what we know of conditions in the 19th century (as elsewhere in West Africa), labour rather than land was the chief constraint on production: it is necessary therefore to consider how labour was mobilized, managed and controlled, first to start-up the industry, and then to ensure that production continued to expand. On the one hand, this requires an assessment of social relations within Gambian domestic groups and villages on which local production became increasingly centred, and on the other, the conditions and regional labour resources of the western Sudan from which migrants were drawn.

We believe that from the 1830s to the late 1860s production primarily depended on the efforts of long distance pioneer-trader farmers from the interior, known as Strange Farmers (*navetanes* in Senegal), while migrant mariners, the *laptots* operated river transport. The Soninke from the upper Senegal valley were central to the migrant system, while methods of recruitment and organization of the workers were varied. At this time there was limited involvement of local farmers, who as we suggested in the last chapter were chiefs reliant on slave labour. Second, in the later 19th century while production still involved chiefs and pioneer migrants, the expansion of the groundnut trade required that many more small local farmers were involved, who needed the services of an increasing number of seasonal migrant workers. By the 1870s strangers were no longer wholly pioneer trader-migrant farmers; their numbers were swelled by itinerant Islamic students, and occasionally by mercenaries who were farming as well as fighting. Also, the economic conditions in the upper Senegal and Niger valleys had altered, which heightened the necessity for additional forms of employment through migration. And, as the migrant labour system became established, the contractual arrangements of employment narrowed to a preponderance of shared-time arrangements. By the end of the century the usefulness of extra migrant workers in The Gambia was widely appreciated as they seasonally assisted smaller domestic units to enter the groundnut trade, as they were convenient and relatively affordable. But migrant labour contracts posed new problems, such as the feeding of workers, and while local food farming was not abandoned, it was not sufficient to meet all the needs of locals and migrants, especially in times of environmental disturbance.

The role of migrants and the development of export crop farming was not unique to The Gambia: the re-organization or modification of domestic labour, together with the use of seasonal circulatory labour became a feature of legitimate trade in West Africa during the 19th century. And, so we turn first to the pioneer migrants who were key players in the transition of the Gambia river basin from an exporter of slaves and a heterogeneous collection of legitimate goods, into a specialized groundnut economy.

### *The development of the migrant labour system*

Historically the earliest migrant workers associated with the Gambian groundnut trade were the *laptots*, who pre-date the Strange Farmers. As we observed in the last chapter these men were African sailors, who manned the French river fleets along the Senegal from the 18th century onwards. They were primarily drawn from the Soninke in the upper Senegal valley and included Royals, as well as slaves (probably privileged ones) belonging to the métis *habitants* of St. Louis, who hired them out to French merchants with the wage being split between owner and slave.[8] The *laptots* were well paid, and their calling (which also included defending the river fleets) was regarded as an honourable one, as well as being profitable. As we have noted earlier, the *laptots* followed the French trading houses into The Gambia during the first half of the 19th century, and were important in the creation of the fleets of groundnut cutters which plied along the river.[9]

The earliest reports from the Gambian Administrator in 1829 indicate the greater portion of the inhabitants of St. Mary's were in fact slaves belonging to the French merchants in Gorée, who resided in the new British settlement, and worked as labourers and sailors (*laptots*). In addition the report mentions casual itinerant workers from the interior, while the permanent "British" population comprised a small number of liberated slaves and a few ex-soldiers of the West Indian Regiment and Royal Africa Corps.[10] The Administrator complained to the Secretary of State that the settlement was suffering from an export of earnings to French territories, as workers remitted a good proportion of their wages. As a result of his dispatch, the British government instructed the Governor of Sierra Leone to send 200 liberated slaves from Freetown to St. Mary's. Thus St. Mary's Island, which was the nucleus of Bathurst began as a migrant settlement, and had important ties with the historic coastal commercial trading networks, which complemented those between the interior and the coast.

The *laptots* were remarkable, as they represent an early-specialized wage labour system in Senegambia, primarily geared the merchant interest, but the cultivation of groundnuts for export required greater numbers. The Strange Farmers provided this additional workforce, and they became a vital element in the development of the groundnut trade. They also represent the oldest large-scale migrant labour system in West Africa, and like the groundnut trade it was a precolonial development. The first specific reference to the cultivation of groundnuts by long distance migrants was in the Annual Report of Governor MacDonnell in 1848,[11] although a later report of 1851

[8] Manchuelle, F., 1997, op. cit.
[9] Searing, J.F., 1993, *West African Slavery and Atlantic Commerce: The Senegal Atlantic Valley, 1800–1968.* Cambridge: CUP.
[10] CO 87/2, Findlay to SS, 1st May 1829.
[11] Annual Report, 1848.

indicates their presence in the 1830s and early 1840s.[12] According
to MacDonnell in 1848 groundnuts were being cultivated "not so
much by the inhabitants of the petty kingdoms along the river, but
by Tillibunkas and SeraWoollies coming from 500 to 600 miles from
the interior". Frequently they stayed for two or three years to enable
them to acquire imported trade goods, which could be taken back
into the Sudan.

In his 1851 report MacDonnell refers to the strangers paying their
landlords a share of the crop at the end of the season, together with
tribute to local chiefs, and in effect were 'renting' land.[13] But in a
dispatch of 1852, he also writes of migrants travelling towards the
river as part of trading caravans, who attached themselves to a
Gambian host and worked for him for between 2 and 4 days per
week in return for a a groundnut farm[14] Tillibunka, or Tillibo was
the local name given to Mandinka migrants, who came from the
upper reaches of the Niger valley around Keita, while the SeraWoollies,
also known as Serahulis or Sarakolle are now generally referred to
as the Soninke. Although long distance seasonal migrants were important, groundnut farming apparently involved some local movements
of labour. MacDonnell's report of 1851 also notes that "the farming mania took hold of liberated Africans and Jolloffs in Bathurst,
who "although they could earn one shilling per day in the town,
readily quit the Colony with the onset of the rains, hiring land from
the Mandingoes, to enable them to produce a crop of groundnuts
ready for sale at the end of the year".[15]

The importance of long distance migrants, especially the Soninke
is confirmed in a later report of 1860, when governor D'Arcy refers
to the SeraWoollies (whom he described as a nomadic tribe of
Mohammedan farmers from Senegambia), as being the principal cultivators of groundnuts along the borders of the river.[16] Repeating
MacDonnell's comments of 1851, the chief point of his observations
was that they were "less careful than local farmers, because they
threshed their nuts instead of hand-picking them in the manner of
local Jolloffs and liberated Africans", although he admits that locals

---

[12] CO 87/50, MacDonnell to Gray, 1st May 1851.
[13] Annual Report, 1851.
[14] CO 87/53, MacDonnell to Pakington, 12th July 1852.
[15] Ibid.
[16] CO 87/53, D'Arcy to SS, 24th July 1861.

had the services of their women, children, servants and domestic slaves to perform this task. Importantly, these comments give a clear indication of the several forms of labour, which were being mobilized in the early development of the groundnut trade.

The contention that in the early stages of the groundnut industry men were being drawn from a sizeable hinterland, extending over several thousand square miles, is also corroborated by French reports for the Casamance. Between 1840 and 1862 reports give details on strangers, and emphasize their importance in the development of the groundnut trade, as well as the existence of seasonal circulatory migration. In 1857 the French post of Sédhiou in Jola territory some 60 km south of Bathurst had a total population of 770, which included 114 Serahulli. It appears the French actively encouraged these migrants from the upper Senegal basin, by allowing them to occupy land (despite Mandinka protests) abandoned by 'Soninke' during the local Soninke-Marabout wars of the 1850s.[17] It is clear this was an attempt to settle temporary migrants, who came each year from the Bakel region in the upper Senegal valley to plant nuts which at the end of the season they exchanged for merchandise to take back home. The impact of pioneer groundnut farming was sufficiently striking for reports to note that the plains around Sédhiou were gradually being denuded of woodland.

In 1840 the French established the village of Dagorne just to the west of Sédhiou to receive black liberated soldiers,[18] however the bulk of them left because the village was under the control of the French Commandant, and having been freed they wanted to return to their traditional lifestyle rather than remaining under French tutelage. But as the soldiers left, the village was gradually taken over by temporary migrants. Another fortified village (Sumukunda) some 200 metres to the west of the port of Sédhiou was founded by Jules Rapet, a merchant who represented the House of Griffon. This palisaded village was inhabited by Mandinka and Serahuli, and when any of the latter arrived they were offered a house and land if they agreed to sell their groundnuts to Griffon. Other merchants objected, but to no effect, and both villages gradually became quarters of Sédhiou, while the Serahuli became the chief groundnut farmers around the town, and were largely responsible for raising exports

---

[17] Roche, C., 1985 edition, *Histoire de la Casamance*. Paris: Éditions Karthala.
[18] Ibid.

from 250,000 baskets in 855, to 600,000 in 1867. Vallon in 1862 estimated that each individual farmer produced an average of 190 baskets (equivalent to 2565 kg using the 1862 measure), and as of March, 454,545 baskets had been collected which meant approximately 2,390 ha were under cultivation around the town.[19]

It seems clear that the early groundnut trade had a strong association with migrant workers from the interior, who were pioneer farmers attracted to the twin foci of the north bank of the Gambia and the southern Casamance. This migrant stream pre-dates effective colonial rule of Senegambia, as well as the erosion of domestic slavery under colonialism which later in the early 20th century contributed to the burgeoning flow of migrant workers. Until around 1870 these migrants were the driving force in the spread of groundnut cultivation, and, as we noted in Chapter One along with the merchants they were integral to the spread of *arachis hypogea*. Furthermore, the evidence strongly suggests that in large measure the Strange Farmers represent a devolution from the historic Soninke and Mandinka trading networks linking the interior and the coast, which required adaptation to the curtailment of the Atlantic slave trade. Young men who had been part of slave trading caravans moved into wet season groundnut farming, which they could combine with dry season trading. Labour migration was another aspect of the adaptation to legitimate trade. and its replacement by legitimate commerce. But how were these migrants organized, and what were the conditions in the upper Senegal valley that led to the emergence of this area as a prime source of migrant farmers in The Gambia?

*Labour migration from the upper Senegal valley in the early 19th century*

Soninke society displayed considerable stratification: there were Royals, clerics, aristocrats, freemen (nobles), the poor, artisan castes, and a large slave population comprising between one third and one half the population. It was a society where status and class were not necessarily co-incident, and one where centralization waxed and waned, which meant clientage was extremely important.[20] Under

---

[19] Vallon, A., 1862, 'La Casamance Dépendence du Sénégal', *Revue Maritime et Coloniale*, VI, 456–74.
[20] Manchuelle, 1997, op. cit.

such conditions where centralized power might fluctuate, village society had to be robust and cohesive, but like the state there was competition for power and resources. Among the Soninke clientage and honour were related: honour was equivalent with wealth, influence and independence, yet paradoxically few could manage without some form of clientage, which required resources and payments. Also, like many African societies *rites de passage* were a necessary social event, and required surpluses in kind, or money for the exchange of gifts, such as bridewealth.

Acquisition of wealth came via war and booty, especially among the Royals and aristocrats who virtually behaved liked bandits. Wealth for other classes came through agriculture and trade, and the entry into trade could come through labour migration. And, for all who successfully accumulated money, slaves were a valuable source of labour, while additionally Royal slaves were soldiers and administrators. Among slaves there were important distinctions, other than those associated with their owners. What have been termed 'actual' slaves worked in their owners' households, where their masters fed them 6 mornings a week, and they fed themselves on 6 afternoons. Alternatively, there were those more akin to 'serfs,' who were married second-generation slaves; they worked 5 mornings per week for their owners, or in some instances paid an annual rent of 150 mudd of grain (a mudd is a measure equivalent to 2.25 kg of sorghum). In other instances the rent was two pieces of cloth. Male serfs were also allowed to go with trading caravans, and in the 19th century they went to the French commercial centres to work on the boats, as well as to The Gambia. It was this segment of the slave population, which became a particularly important source of labour migration into The Gambia.

The trading and farming activities of the Soninke were prodigious and of long standing. Dry season caravan movements of goods and slaves were common in the 18th and early 19th centuries, travelling as far as 1500 km from the upper Senegal valley. The caravans were made up of Jula (often the children of clerical families) who engaged in continuous accumulation, as well as young men who as farmer-traders might trade for one or two seasons. Such caravans had a mixture of participants; professionals, semi-professionals and casuals, who chiefly worked during the dry season which avoided the disadvantages of wet season travel, as well as the diversion of labour from farming.

Evidence collected by Mauny, especially on the Mandinka Jula, emphasizes the extent to which merchants were operating across the Sahara, as well as within the Sudan, and between the interior and the riverine coastlands. It was not unusual for men to join caravans for limited periods: as long as was needed to earn sufficient money for bridewealth, or a range of goods for consumption, or as trading capital.[21] The Gambia had been a principal axis of trade for many years prior to the groundnut trade: salt went up river, slaves were driven down to the coast for export via Bathurst, Fort James, St. Louis and Gorée. Fish, hides, beeswax and gold were other commodities transported between the lower Gambia and upper Niger basin. The use of slaves as porters was an additional advantage, and the accounts of Mungo Park frequently refer to "slave caravans (*coffles*), a business chiefly in the hands of SeraWoollies".[22] Slaves for the Atlantic market were used for transport westwards, because they could carry goods at no extra cost; after the sale of slaves, donkeys were used to transport return goods eastwards. Neither were merchants averse to setting slaves in transit to farming, while they waited to be taken on board ship or in the hope of realizing better prices, and this may have been equally the case with porters, thus reducing maintenance costs of the labour force. Indeed, Curtin draws attention to the advantages enjoyed by African merchants over their European counterparts through their ability to offset 'storage costs'.[23] According to Curtin, in the 1780s young men from Bundu working the coastal salt pans also planted millet nearby, as they attempted to maximise their earning capacities as trader-farmers.

Manchuelle has argued it was the ending of the Atlantic slave trade, especially in British areas such as The Gambia, which converted seasonal caravan workers into migrant groundnut farmers.[24] As we noted earlier The Gambia was part of the Soninke trading network, and in addition to supplying slaves and grain to the European trading posts, there was the attraction of maritime and estuarine salt, which was traded for gold in Bambuk. Reports from The Gambia, also indicate the importance of 'the Serahuli in the cattle trade. In

[21] Mauny, R., 1961, Tableau géographique de l'oest Africain au moyen age. Dakar p. 387.
[22] Park, M., 1878 edition, *Travels in the Interior of Africa performed in the years 1795, 1796 and 1797*. London, pp. 56–65.
[23] Curtin, P.D., 1975, *Economic Change in pre-Colonial Africa*. Wisconsin, pp. 168–73.
[24] Manchuelle, 1997, op. cit.

1854, O'Connor while on tour observed "in Saloum the extensive areas of grazing and the large herds of cattle driven to Bathurst via Barra as speculative ventures by Tillibunkas and Serahulis".[25] He noted the lagoon-like nature of Saloum and its salt-flats, which gave rise to a salt trade, as well as trade in corn, groundnuts, fish and pottery. Thus the Soninke trade networks embraced slave trading, commercial agriculture, salt extraction and cattle herding, all of which proceeded on a seasonal basis,that involved large-scale movements of people and goods between the coast and the interior.

Once the British had decided on the abolition of the Atlantic slave trade and European merchants encouraged groundnut cultivation, then former seasonal traders, especially farmer-traders and serfs, became seasonal farmers. It appears there were several methods of acquiring groundnut farms. Gambian sources suggest that at first individual migrants 'rented' land from local chiefs by paying tribute, which by 1890 amounted to three dollars (12s 0d), and gave a share of the crop to their hosts; alternatively, they gave labour time in return for land. Reports and accounts from Senegal indicate itinerant merchants hired, or used serfs to cultivate land they negotiated from local authorities, which allowed them to participate in the groundnut trade while continuing trading elsewhere.

Writing in 1856, Bocandé commented on the inhabitants from the interior who entered into the groundnut trade, and on the 'caravans de travailleurs', who came into the Casamance in the rainy season to cultivate groundnuts on land around the European forts.[26] Bocandé's report is interesting on two points. First, these were caravans coming in the rainy season, whereas caravanning was usually a dry season activity: this is an indication for the beginnings of what was to become a large scale movement of workers into Senegambia for the wet season farming of groundnuts. Second, the report contains an early reference to the system of 'labour rents', whereby migrants negotiated their stay with local hosts on the basis of a share of their time on the host's farm. However, (unlike the Gambian reports) he makes clear that initially the organization of migration was in the hands of merchants and traders from the interior. Merchants, both alone or

---

[25] CO 87/116, O'Connor to SS, 10th May 1854.
[26] Bocandé-Bertrand, E. 1856, *Les ressources que présentent dans leur état actuel les comptoirs français établis sur les bords de la Casamance.* Paris: Dupont. Encl in CO 87/3, 12th July 1861.

in association with chiefs assembled groups of free men and domestic slaves, and brought them into the groundnut areas. Presumably, this was a new venture to offset losses after the abolition of the Atlantic slave trade.

This account reinforces the notion that this process of labour mobilization for groundnut farming, devolved from the long established movement of slaves and goods from the interior to the coast. Bocandé noted that before groundnuts dominated trade in the 1850s, slaves carried beeswax and ivory to the coastal forts and factories, where the slaves were later sold. But by the 1850s slaves could no longer be regarded as one form of merchandise transporting another, and their owners had come to realize that their labour represented a considerable asset. The slaves referred to were used, or hired by the Jula, and were most likely to be second generation 'serfs' who gave 'rent in kind' to their masters, and who were allowed to join caravans. An inquiry into slavery in the cercle of Bakel in 1894 refers to trusted second-generation slaves working in "St. Louis, The Gambia and Kayes etc."[27] On their return they shared their earnings with their master, and importantly, often used their share to purchase their freedom.

Although it was quite feasible to grow groundnuts in the interior, the loads of produce the porters could carry in no way compensated the merchants or chiefs for the costs of feeding them en route: therefore the workers had to be brought to the most economic point of production. The caravan chiefs brought together the necessary labour to the place of production and the place of sale (as they did with slaves), which suggests the Jula by entering the groundnut trade replaced lost incomes from the slave trade without abandoning itinerant trading. The organization of caravans, or columns of labourers was also consonant with the need to travel in armed groups during the troubled times which obtained in Senegambia. The movement of migrants in protected groups was not uncommon in other parts of the Sudan; for example in Hausaland,[28] and they continued in Senegambia into the 20th century. Accounts given by migrant workers in the 1970s passing into and through The Gambia from

---

[27] ANS 13G 195, Desmarets, *Rapport sur la captivité dans la cercle de Bakel*, 26th mai 1894. Cited in Manchuelle, 1997.

[28] Swindell, K., 1984, 'Farmers, Traders and Labourers: dry season migration from northwest Nigeria 1900–1933', *Africa*, 54 (1), 1–19.

Senegal and Guinea, show that they used column leaders to negotiate laissez-passer, and to avoid border guards, as well as arranging
travel and feeding arrangements en route.

Gradually, Strange Farmers became entrenched in groundnut production, and as we have noted, Serahuli received preferential treatment from both French and British authorities who tried to encourage
their settlement.[29] The outflow of Soninke migrants into areas such
as The Gambia, Casamance, and as far as the Rio Grande of Guinea
was well established, and. while seasonal groundnut farming may
have compensated for losses in the Atlantic slave trade, it is interesting that these men initially were coming from an area of relative
prosperity, where the gum trade was still booming and the desert
side economy very active. Why migration was so attractive is probably explained by the good terms of trade that obtained for groundnut producers on the coast, at least until the 1870s, and the Strange
Farmer contract, which we discuss later. Our own figures for The
Gambia suggest that if a farmer could cultivate around one acre—
and migrants might have managed more—then an annual return of
one ton valued at £12 to £14 was possible. Figures provided by
Manchuelle based on modern production values provided by Pollet
and Winter, suggest that between one and two hectares could produce 100 to 130 francs per year, minus gifts and 'taxes' amounting
to about 75–102 francs.[30] This compared very well with the grain
farmer around Bakel, who after family consumption and other local
expenses might manage to sell between 20 and 23 francs of grain
per year. Much of the advantage enjoyed by the migrant in The
Gambia hinged on his being away from home, with limited expenses
and especially that part of the host-migrant contract which covered
the stranger's daily feeding. However, there remains the question of
who replaced the lost labour of the migrant, and the effect on home
grain production? The answer probably lies in the trade-off between
one less to feed at home, and the goods brought back which could
be bought at a discount on the coast.

---

[29] Annual Report, 1848 and Roche, 1985 op. cit.
[30] Pollet, E. and G. Winter, 1971, *La societé soninké (Diahunu, Mali)*. Brussels:
Université Libre de Bruxelles, Édition de l'Institut de Sociologie.

*A broadening of the migrant and producer base*

As the 19th century developed the social origins and motives of both migrants and local producers widened. An important strand, especially in Senegal, were Islamic students called *talibes*, who were also used locally as farm labourers.[31] The contractual basis of Islamic studentship was such that the *talibes* provided their teachers with farm labour, alms, and generally a substantial present at the end of their studies. Such presents could be acquired through general trading, and students were easily absorbed into commercial networks where merchants and traders generally were drawn from clerical families; thus trade networks and religious networks overlapped. But as the economic conditions of Senegambia changed, *talibes'* objectives could be met by a season's work on groundnut farms. D'Arcy's report of 1860, refers to the migrants as, "mohammeden" farmers, which could be taken to support this view.[32] It has been observed that one of the strengths of the Maraboutic faction in The Gambia was the ability of its Muslims followers to transcend ethnic differences and political boundaries, something which would have buttressed seasonal migration.

In The Gambia before 1860, the possibilities of residential koranic study was limited, as there were only a few pockets of Islamic teaching to which students were attracted. The majority of chiefs were Soninke, and resistant to a reformist Maraboutic Islam; they saw education as a threat to their authority. The important exceptions were Baddibu and Niumi, flourishing areas of Islamic teaching, and as we have shown these were the earliest areas of groundnut cultivation. But as the 19th century progressed Islam took a firmer hold, and by 1880 the Marabout leaders of the South Bank had formed a confederacy of chiefdoms, extending into Casamance, which provided an emergent focus for *talibes*, who became an important source of labour in the groundnut fields of their teachers.[33]

The students, who came to Gambian villages were aged between 8 and 40 years, and traditionally they passed on the alms they received to their teachers, as well as providing farm labour. The marabouts stressed the spiritual value of labour on the land, and as

[31] Manchuelle, 1989, op. cit.
[32] CO 87/53, D'Arcy to SS, 24th July 1861.
[33] Annual Report, 1888.

teaching was done early morning and late evening, the day was free
for agricultural work. In addition to student labour, marabouts might
receive workers, or a portion of crops from other compound heads,
which through such gifts hoped to gain spiritual enhancement and
social standing in the community. By the 1870s, some marabouts
were substantial farmers and were selling considerable quantities of
groundnuts to traders.[34] Marabout teachers had acquired, and were
able to mobilize and manage a well disciplined labour force held
together by an economic rationale based on spiritual aspirations.

The importance of Islamic institutions and *talibe* labour in Senegal
was materially advanced by the rise of the Mourides around Touba
in Senegal. The Mourides led by the founder of this Islamic brotherhood Ahmadu Bemba, effectively opened up the drier eastern regions
of Senegal from 1880 onwards.[35] With a committed work ethic, the
Mourides became a wealthy group and a powerful force in the expansion of groundnut cultivation in Senegal, who became clients of the
French and an integral part of the groundnut industry. By the 20th
century they had the power to influence French policy and when
necessary they coordinated producer resistance, which was a contrast to The Gambia where Islamic factions never exerted such a
powerful hold on the government. In general, the mobility of Muslim
freemen, and their integration into the new commercial networks of
the groundnut trade, encouraged the independence of rural peoples
after the ending of the Atlantic slave trade, and was part of a process
that loosened the hold of the élitist Soninke class.[36]

### Migrant farmers: contracts and obligations

The rising tide of migrants swelled the farm labour force along The
Gambia, but what were the advantages for local producers, and how
were migrants managed and controlled locally? We have already suggested the importance of extra labour to remove labour bottlenecks,

[34] CO 87/110, Berkeley to Gov. in Chief, 25th Jan. 1877. CO 87/126, Mahoney
to Rowe, 13th Oct. 1885.
[35] For accounts of the Mourides, see O'Brien, Donal B. Cruise, 1971, *The Mourides
of Senegal*. Oxford: Clarendon Press, and 1975, *Saints and politicians. Essays in the organization of Senegalese peasant society*. Cambridge: CUP.
[36] Klein, 1972, 'Social and Economic Factors in Muslim Revolutions in Senegambia'
*Journal of African History*, 13, 419–441.

but to fully understand the benefits to host farmers the nature of the Strange Farmer contract and working relationships need further elaboration and analysis, especially in smaller households. Strangers, young men usually in their 20s or 30s appeared in the villages before the rains, when they attempted to find host farmers who would give them food and lodging and a piece of land on which to grow ground-nuts. The host allocated land to strangers subject to the agreement and ultimate control of the *alkali*, which usually was easy as land was plentiful. In return, the migrant had to work on his host's farm for between two, and four days per week. After the harvest, the migrant moved on, or returned home. The essentially seasonal nature of this labour force is captured in the local Mandinka terminology, which refers to the system as *Sama manila*—rains abroad, while the stranger was referred to as *samalaa* (pl. *samalaalu*): the equivalent word in Wolof is *navet*, (pl. *navetanes*), which can be interpreted as either referring to the rains, or a shuttle, the latter suggesting the seasonal movement of workers.[37]

The number of days worked, and the length of the working day was negotiable, as well as other benefits such as the use of seeds and tools, and the payment of a proportion of the migrant's crop to the host after the harvest. Detailed accounts of the form of con-tract are very scarce in 19th century government reports, and rest on the observations of governors and administrators for 1849–50, who noted the exchange of money, a share of the crop and labour time for a piece of land. But central to the contract was the provi-sion of a farm for the migrant. More recent accounts, which include the views of elderly informants suggest that individual contracts between hosts and strangers changed according to their trust and familiarity as migrants might return to the same host year after year.[38] On the other hand, it appears that the contract itself changed over time. Such developmental changes are common to many forms of share contract, and have been classified by Robertson as *ontogenetic*, expressing the structure and dynamics of individual contracts, and *phylogenetic*, referring to wider long term structural change.[39] In effect there was a spectrum of contracts, which allowed for modifications

[37] Robertson, A.F., 1987, *The dynamics of productive Relationships*. Cambridge: CUP ch. 6. Also, K. Swindell, 1978, op. cit.
[38] Informants, 1977.
[39] Robertson, 1985, op. cit.

and adaptations, where contractual obligations reflected the shifts in
bargaining power between the two parties and the state of the groundnut trade.

By the end of the 19th century, the most widespread form of contract was that of shared time on the host's farm, together with local
tribute to chiefs, in return for a groundnut farm. The relationship
between the contracting parties has been described variously as that
of landlord- tenant, patron-client, father-son, farmer-labourer, or simply as collaborators. It mirrored working relationships within patri-
archal households, as well as showing similarities with the work
regime of slaves. Searing has suggested, serfdom among the Soninke
in particular served as a pattern for migrant work schedules, while
Weil's work on agrarian slavery in Wuli in The Gambia shows some
striking parallels too.[40] Junior freemen in households also worked
shared time schedules with elders, but when they became migrant
farmers they had sole rights to the disposal their groundnut crop,
which is probably why in the early 20th century as Gambia society
and economy changed more young Gambian men moved into villages in the prime groundnut zones to become Strange Farmers.

The system as it developed had a number of advantages for both
the Gambian farmer and the migrant. One way of looking at the
arrangement is that it was based on 'labour rents', whereby the
migrant gained access to land through giving the host an agreed
portion of his working time: moreover long distance migrants from
the interior were not only attracted by land, but land which was
proximate to the river and wharves, where prices were highest. In
the 19th century groundnut farming was concentrated around river-
side locations where traders set-up buying stations, and the extent
of the cultivated 'hinterland' around the stations depended on the
number of farmers, and the amount of time or money they were
prepared to spend on head-loading groundnuts, or carrying them by
donkey.

From the small farmers point of view, the system was one of giving land to workers in lieu of wages, in an area where land was in
surplus Here was a labour force which could be utilized without
recourse to cash, that could be effectively controlled and organized,
as the migrant was unlikely to leave the household until his own

---

[40] Weil, P., 1976, 'Agrarian Slavery to capitalist farming in a West African Society',
*75th Annual Meeting of the American Anthropological Association*, Washington, D.C.

crop had been harvested. This was an important given the need to perform jobs such as weeding as quickly as possible. While a wage labour market did exist in the 19th century, it was very shallow and uneven, being principally confined to Bathurst and the major trading posts and wharves. From the host's point of view, the success of the contract depended on how much labour he could extract from the migrant, which in turn depended on the number of days worked, and in turn what comprised a working day. A working day could be between sunrise and mid-day, or around 3.00 pm in the afternoon. It appears that the shorter working time could be accommodated by the migrant giving his host one-tenth of his crop, a practice known as *lajino*, which was common in the late 19th and early 20th centuries.[41]

But essentially this form of contract was about sharing of inputs, (that is labour and possibly seeds) not outputs. Labour was, and still is, central to *semboo*, a term in Mandinka, which encapsulates the notion of the resources or physical capacity that were essential for successful farming.[42] And, Strange Farmers became an increasingly important element in achieving this physical capacity as groundnut cultivation was integrated into local farming systems. However, physical capacity centred on labour required a sustained input of food, and food was an essential part of the host-migrant contract. But the provision of food throughout the farming season meant that migrants had to be fed during the pre-harvest 'hungry season', therefore sufficient grain had to be available from the *previous* season. Thus at an early stage in the development of the groundnut trade, any one groundnut season was inextricably linked to the previous wet season in terms of the amount of food which had been produced. An essential part of the migrant contract was that the migrant expected to know the amount of work required of him, and the amount of food he would be given; and it was this latter element which often created the most tension or argument. For the migrant and his household back home working away during the hungry season could be a distinct advantage, provided it did not seriously deplete the household's labour supply. And, for the migrant it was not a relationship without honour; he was not wholly subservient, he had bargaining power and self-esteem.

---

[41] Swindell, 1978, op. cit.
[42] Robertson, 1985, op. cit.

It appears that that not all households were able to take on extra
workers because of inadequate food stocks, and the ability of households to support more than one Strange Farmer was a measure of
their economic well-being, and an indication of social and economic
differentiation within a village. Calculations made by migrants of the
state of food farming during the current season they spent working
in The Gambia, was an important element in their decision to return
again next year. Furthermore, the information about the state of
food crops throughout Senegambia was disseminated on their return
home, and may have affected the number of new entrants into the
migrant system the following season. We shall discuss later the effect
of prices offered for groundnuts at the end of the migrants stay as
an incentive to return, and while this was no doubt extremely important, food availability was an essential part of the calculus for both
stranger and host. As subsequent chapters will show, the feeding of
migrants became not only a household issue but also a major strand
of colonial policy, as well as a source of disagreement among colonial officials and experts. It is true that an essential part of the
migrant contract was that they must work on the compound's communal food farms at the beginning of the season, something of the
order of two weeks. But the real issue was to what extent specialization meant more land and more time were allocated to groundnuts and less on food cultivation, so producers had to buy food to
support Strange Farmers and the compound in general.

There were other advantages for migrant farmers, beyond securing land for groundnut farming. Reports show that some migrant
groundnut farmers were combining their farming with dry season
employment in Bathurst, which as we noted earlier was a source of
casual employment prior to the groundnut trade. It was reported in
1868, that groundnut farmers went to work in Bathurst as day wage
labourers, and because of the manner in which they were paid they
were called 'wadjis'.[43] This is an early example of income diversification
by migrants, and what has been described as 'straddling', that is a
double participation in the waged and non-waged sectors. Also, the
combination of farming with trading was long established, and was
an important element in the migrant labour system whereby earnings were used as trading capital, albeit on a very modest scale. This

[43] Ibid.

form of income formation is associated with high levels of geographical mobility, and it became an integral part of West African
peoples' livelihoods and lifestyles as societies and economies changed
during the late 19th and early 20th centuries.[44] The combination of
on-farm and off-farm work, as well as farm and non-farm work has
been subjected to a variety of interpretations. It has been identified
as symptomatic of transitional economies in the process of development, or of an imperfect and blocked transformation to full capitalism. On the other hand, a plurality of jobs is commonplace among
the poor who are marginalized in even well developed capitalist
economies. The evidence from Senegambia, suggests that the seasonal integration of jobs embracing diverse relations of production
fulfilled several roles: for some it led to petty accumulation, for others
it was a means of survival, but it was certainly well established before
colonial rule, although it was subsequently accelerated by it.

### Local labour and groundnut production

The Annual Reports for The Gambia in 1848, 1851 and 1860,
together with Bocandé's account of Casamance emphasize the importance of migrant farmers, both as individuals and as groups, but they
also indicate that there were local sources of labour centred on
Gambian households. We have already alluded to the use of slaves
in the early years of the groundnut trade and they continued to be
a valuable labour source as the 19th century progressed. Slaves were
available as workers throughout the year, and in the dry season especially in Wolof households of the north Bank, they were weavers
making cloth for *pagns* used as the local currency. Although the trans-
Atlantic trade in slaves had almost disappeared by the 1850s, the
local and trans-Saharan trade continued, at times fuelled by local
wars and conflicts. Initially the use of slaves for groundnut cultivation
along the Gambia was not widespread, but in the late 1850s the
Soninke-Marabout wars increased the supply of captives and own-
ership spread. While these wars had negative effects on agriculture
because of the displacement of farmers and the disruption of the
groundnut crop, paradoxically there were also positive outcomes that

---

[44] Swindell, K. 1997, 'Labor Systems' in *The Encyclopedia of Sub-Saharan Africa*, ed.
J. Middleton. New York: Charles Scribner.

boosted the labour force through an increase in local slave trading.[45] Furthermore, as we noted in Chapter One, mercenaries also became migrant farmers.

As the Soninke-Marabout wars developed, an increased momentum was given to the internal slave trade, and a report of 1866 speaks of a demand from the liberated Africans and traders of the Colony for slaves taken as captives.[46] Slave traders followed the warring factions buying slaves, and much to the government's dismay, it appears that Europeans were also involved.[47] Slave raiding continued right up to the 1880s, and in Foni women were particularly valued as slaves and traded across the river to the Baddibus in exchange for cattle, grains and ammunition.[48] Women slaves were highly prized as they directly contributed labour to households and farming, as well as bearing children who became future producers. Thus the European philanthropists, who had hoped that the legitimate trade in oil seeds and tree crops would drive out the slave trade, were doomed to disappointment. Ironically the oil seed trade created new demands for labour, which in part were indirectly satisfied through local warfare.

By the 1870s groundnut farming was primarily centred on extended families, or joint-production and consumption units, who co-resided in compounds over which a headman exercised jurisdiction. In common with many areas of West Africa, the labour supply within social groups and village communities was shaped by status, age, gender, marriage, servitude, morbidity and mortality.[49] All compounds experienced expansion, maturity and decay as part of their demographic development cycles, and it was at periods of imbalance within households that Strange Farmers could be used to smooth the labour supply for one or more seasons. This was particularly important for smaller groups engaged in groundnut farming. But there were other differentials within villages: some groups were empowered by their social status (for example their relationship to the village head),

---

[45] CO 87/76, D'Arcy to Newcastle, 11th Sept. 1863.
[46] CO 87/87, D'Arcy to Blackall, 15th Nov. 1866.
[47] Ibid.
[48] CO 87/121, Gouldsbury to Governor in Chief, 3rd May 1883.
[49] Swindell, 1985, op. cit.

whether they held public office, or belonged to certain castes, as well as the number of slaves within their control. Access to land as well as labour could be important too, and possibly influenced by status. For example, permanent immigrants (*lutango*) who came into villages along the river attracted by the groundnut trade were allocated surplus land, but it might be less fertile, and on the periphery of the community's lands.[50]

Compound heads could also mobilize local labour outside their households, through *kafos*, which were village work groups arranged in male and female age-sets. Traditionally these groups were under the control of the *alkali*, and were summoned for communal works, such as road building. However, *kafo* labour could be called upon by individual households and paid in kind, and the use of such communal labour could be particularly important in easing labour bottlenecks when land had to be cleared, crops weeded and harvested.[51] While work groups could be used by individual households for a number of purposes, they were also being adapted to the needs of the expanding groundnut trade. In particular *kafos* were used at harvest time, and a report of 1871 described one village where the crop was so large that farmers feared the next season rains would have begun before the nuts were stored, so they called upon work groups to lift and store the harvest as rapidly as possible.[52]

The question is to what extent increased groundnut cultivation raised the demand for *kafo* labour beyond that for communal works and occasional household use? Did these workgroups redistribute labour towards those who could afford to mobilize them on a 'come one come all' basis, where marginal returns could be zero? Work groups were not paid as such, but were given food and drink, and it seems unlikely that all households had sufficient food stocks to be able to use the services of what might turn out to be large groups of workers. In addition to formal labour institutions such as *kafos*, occasional reciprocal labour exchanges might be made among neighbours and friends, while in Mandinka society women who had by custom

---

[50] Haswell, 1953, op. cit.

[51] Swindell, K., 1978, 'Family Farms and Migrant Labour: The Strange Farmers of The Gambia', *Canadian Journal of African Studies*, XII (1), 3–17.

[52] CO 87/99 extract from The Bathurst Times, encl. in no. 2, 1st May 1871.

moved to their husbands' compounds on marriage, might still return
to their fathers' households to give some help.[53] On the other hand
men in the process of contracting a marriage might give part of the
brideprice to their future father-in-laws through days worked on his
farms. But in addition to these inter-household transfers, many heads
were able to utilize domestic slaves.

### Strange Farmers in the late 19th century

As the 19th century progressed The Gambia continued to attract
migrants from a wide area, but probably the old reliance on pioneer itinerant trader farmers had diminished. Migrant flows were
now being shaped by the changing economies in the interior, and
there was greater 'push' factor behind movements of labour. The
year 1869 marked the opening of the Suez canal and while its arrival
posed problems for The Gambia, it was wholly detrimental to upper
Senegal where the groundnut trade was abandoned by French merchants.[54] The flourishing desert side economy we described in Chapter
One had sagged: by 1870s the gum trade of the Senegal valley had
begun to falter. The interior was now feeling the full impact of the
collapse of the Atlantic slave trade, followed by the decline in local
textile industries and inland groundnut cultivation, which occurred
between 1863 and the early 1880s. And, while Manchuelle is correct in arguing that neither local taxation nor poverty among the
Soninke were a sufficient reason for pushing men into labour migration in the mid-19th century, the changing economy of the interior,
and eventually the differentials in French and British taxation towards
the end of the century played a significant part.[55]

The 1860s were particularly troubled times in Senegal, and French
policies may have had an impact on the coastal groundnut producing area of Casamance, to the benefit of The Gambia. In 1861
Faidherbe introduced a head tax in all villages within the French
sphere of influence which was unpopular and arguably slowed the

---

[53] Pélissier, P., 1960, *Les paysannes au Sénégal*. St. Yriex: Imprimerie Fabrègue.
[54] Gallienni, L., 1883, 'Mission dans le Haut Niger à Ségou', *Bull. de la Soc. de
Géographie*, vol. 4, 345.
[55] Manchuelle, 1997, op. cit.

annual influx of navetanes into Casamance.[56] Also, a 3 franc per ton export levy was placed on groundnuts. Jaureguiberry who succeeded Faidherbe was more cautious, and allowed chiefs one-twentieth of tax collected to appease discontent and restricted taxes to St. Louis and Gorée, but the head tax was reintroduced in 1864.[57] And, as we observed in the previous chapter, the 1867–1868 season was hindered by hold-ups, as the Mandinka refused to sell unless the traders' buying-measure was reduced in size. In response the Mandinka and Soninke refused to pay their debts contracted in the previous wet season, and the Soninke from Bakel preferred to take their nuts into The Gambia and sell them for cash. The 1869 trade year was disastrous in French territories; trade goods increased in price, the measures was enlarged and the situation deteriorated into outbreaks of violence.[58] The disaffection with measures, taxes, prices of groundnuts and trade goods, pushed more migrant farmers into The Gambia. Governor D'Arcy surprisingly believed Britain could do worse than emulate the rigorous interventionist policies of the French, as this would suppress outbreaks of disorder and warfare, which were disruptive to the groundnut trade. However, he found no support from London who were intent on a laissez-faire approach, and on policies of minimal intervention consonant with their views on free trade.[59] As we noted earlier, one important influence exerted by migrants in The Gambia was their demand for payment in coin. This was reported as early as 1843 by the British Administrator, and the demands of migrants converged with those of the French merchants (discussed in the last chapter), who wished to trade in silver dollars, that is five franc pieces, valued at 3s 0d sterling. By 1880 it was estimated that 75% of the coinage in circulation along the river comprised five-franc pieces.[60]

During the period 1857–1888 the Gambian labour force underwent a huge transformation, as the rate of migration increased from the French enclaves and spheres of influence, where the relatively harsher political and economic policies of French imperialism were

[56] Roche, 1985, op. cit. pp. 120–124. For an alternative view, see Manchuelle, 1997, op. cit.
[57] Ibid.
[58] Ibid.
[59] CO 87/74, D'Arcy to Newcastle, 24th Nov. 1861.
[60] Hargreaves, J.D., 1963, *Prelude to the Partition of West Africa*. London: Papermac.

brought home to local populations, as well as the material advantages of groundnut farming abroad. As Bérenger Féraud observed in 1878, "in the fertile areas of The Gambia it is not rare to see Saracoulies coming in large numbers in the planting season to cultivate groundnuts. . . . Those who found a more prosperous soil. . . . stayed two, three, ten years at the same place, and some ended up with settling there indefinitely, when the advancement of their age and the extension of their families rendered them less mobile".[61]

*Summary*

The evidence from a number of sources indicates that pioneer migrant-trader farmers, both in groups, and as individuals were instrumental in the development of the early groundnut trade. Moreover, they were an integral part of the adaptation of coastal and interior economic networks to legitimate commerce after the decline of the Atlantic slave trade. As the groundnut trade gained momentum, more local farmers became involved in groundnut cultivation, using several types of labour. But the expansion of the trade became increasingly dependent on Strange Farmers, and by the late 19th century they were seasonally integrated into Gambian households, and were engaged under specific labour contracts, which reflected a land surplus, labour shortage economy.

A number of arguments can be adduced to explain the patterns and organization of migratory movements into The Gambia: some hinge on the motives of individuals or social groups, some on cultural history, while others embrace the shifting fortunes of both pre-colonial and colonial states, and the changing regional political economies of West Africa embedded in the global economy. Certainly, the gradual economic marginalization of the Upper Niger and Senegal basins, together with differential colonial policies contributed to the labour migration system, and shaped its volume and direction. The labour contracts between host and migrant changed as the century progressed, and the migratory system was being pushed into a different analytical category. Erstwhile pioneer trader-farmers were becoming incorporated into a pervasive labour-renting system, and by the latter

---

[61] Bérenger-Féraud, 1878, 'Étude sur les Sononkes', *Rev.d'Anthropologie*, 7, p. 604.

part of the 19th century the 'Serahullis' and 'Tillibunkas' comprised an important labour reserve for The Gambia, which allowed the agricultural labour force to be expanded and contracted to fit the vicissitudes of the world market. And, as we shall see later, migrants became an important means of breaking the bargaining power of local producers, when they attempted to raise prices through hold-ups (*tong*).

The migration of Strange Farmers in ever-increasing numbers continued well into the 20th century, when the migration system and the origins and destinations of migrants were altered and adapted, to meet the changing demands of the groundnut trade. However, one aspect of the increased use of migrant farmers was their impact on local food supply, which like groundnuts was subject to climatic variation. Local food supply and food farming systems in The Gambia, showed considerable resiliance to the expansion of groundnuts, but contrary to the vent for surplus thesis food importing relentlessly increased. It is necessary therefore, to understand the nature of Gambian food farming and its supplementation by food imports, as this became a central concern of the colonial administrations in the early 20th century, and beyond.

# CHAPTER THREE

# FOOD FARMING AND THE GROUNDNUT TRADE

One of the most remarkable features of the West African cash crop revolution was the manner in which myriad households integrated export crops into their farming systems. Unlike the 'Gentlemanly Capitalism' of the white settler economies of southern and east-central Africa, the production of export crops in West Africa was 'atomized'. Export surpluses were created and shaped through a nexus of household producers migrants and merchants, in addition to which there were the taxes and legislation imposed by colonial regimes.[1] As we have already observed, explanations of the emergence of a legitimate export economy in West Africa range from an emphasis on African agency and the success of African farmers in responding to the opportunities offered, to the invocation of the larger structural forces of merchant capital, which pushed African farmers into growing export crops, and an increasing dependency on world markets and the metropoles.

An integral part of these arguments has been the debate about the effects, or impact of the export trade on indigenous farming, especially the ability of small household farmers to maintain adequate levels of food production. In some cases it has been argued that the increased production of export crops undermined the ability of households to cope with natural disasters, such as droughts, floods and pestilence. Furthermore, where monoculture characterized production, it has been asserted that cash-cropping has resulted in environmental deterioration. For example, the 'peanut economy' in Senegambia and Niger, where an over dependency on groundnut farming allegedly damaged the soil, while the associated removal of vegetation adversely affected the hydrological and meteorological cycles.[2] Therefore the relationship between groundnut production,

---

[1] Cain, P. and A.G. Hopkins, 1994, *British Imperialism*. Longman: London.

[2] See for example, R.W. Franke and B.H. Chasin, 1980, *Seeds of Famine: Ecological Destruction and the Development Dilemma in the West African Sahel*. Monclair New Jersey: Allanheld, Osmun. For an alternative view see M. Mortimore, 1990, *Adapting to Drought*, Cambridge: CUP, pp. 211–213.

food production and environmental disturbance in The Gambia is an important theme, which at times was exacerbated by the effects of civil disturbance and warfare. Trying to establish the nature of Gambian farming and production systems in the 19th century is a necessary prelude to a discussion of colonial interventions, as well as providing a base-line from which to chart the relationship between groundnut and food farming during the 20th century. We begin by examining the physical environment of The Gambia and its peoples' farming systems, followed by an overview of production relations and land use systems. This is to recognize that the groundnut trade did not occur and develop within an ecological vacuum; it was integrated into particular kinds of farming systems and social settings. Ecology and farming systems are not especially conspicuous in vent for surplus theory and they are peripheral to many historical explanations of the cash crop revolution in West Africa, although during the 1980s there were several interpretations of the political history of the West African savannas and desert-side economy which have incorporated long term secular shifts in climate and environment.[3] Finally, we introduce an issue that began to dominate the groundnut trade: falling local food production and the necessity for imports.

However desirable an understanding of 19th century farming may be, it has to be admitted that the historical evidence is limited, and the analysis which follows is based on scattered qualitative archival accounts, together with interviews with elderly informants, and the backward projection of early 20th century agricultural reports. Evidence from the French reports for the Casamance is interesting too, while of especial importance are reports made in the early 20th century by Dudgeon, the first British Inspector for Agriculture and Forest Products in West Africa.[4] Much earlier, for example in the 1840s, as far as British officials were concerned, farming was primarily to do with the cultivation of groundnuts; the problem of an adequate supply of food had not yet arisen. The 1846 Blue Book includes the terse comment that . . . "with regard to agriculture, but little favourable can be said. No improvements have recently been effected in the

---

[3] See for example, G.E. Brooks, 1993, *Landlords and Strangers. Ecology, Society and Trade in Western Africa, 1000–1639.* Westview: Boulder.
[4] Dudgeon, G.C., 1910, *Fourth Report on Agriculture and Forest Products of The Gambia.* Gambia Gazette, Bathurst (Banjul).

farming operations of natives".[5] As for the environment and geography of the river, most early comments are concerned with its navigability and groundnut loading depots.

The 19th century reports may be slight in terms of details about Gambian farming practice, but they are unequivocal in their findings that insufficient food was being produced as the century progressed, which ultimately led to food importing. The suggestion is that crops were being neglected as more land and labour were being devoted to groundnuts, which as a wet season crop competed with millet and sorghum. Whether the actual yields of food crops declined, as opposed to the area cultivated, due to the diversion of labour towards groundnuts cannot be answered in the absence of any suitable data. The estimates of population from the 1890s show a population of some 90,000 for the colony and Protectorate, a total which was considerably boosted by Strange Farmers, who made additional demands on the local food supply.[6] The problem is we have no way of knowing exactly to what extent local food production for Gambians suffered as a result of increased groundnut production in the 19th century, or whether it was a case of topping-up local food supplies to meet the needs of Strange Farmers. However, the picture becomes clearer in the early 20th century, when both a neglect of food crops and an increased demand for food were apparent.

It is only in the opening years of the 20th century that we find any specific accounts of Gambian food crop farming, but we believe that these provide useful insights into the situation in the 19th century, as the farming practices and land use systems of 1910 were not significantly different from 1870. Also, the early 20th century reports are important as they demonstrate that while groundnut production had consistently risen, and despite producer dependence on groundnut incomes and rising imports of rice, The Gambia had still not become a monoculture: established crops and farming practices remained in place. On the contrary, the reports indicate the resilience of local agricultural practices to the pressures of the export trade, and the maintenance of a diversity of crop species and farming systems.

---

[5] Blue Book, 1846.
[6] Annual Report, 1891. The data excludes British Kombo, Ceded Mile, MacCarthy Island and the Fulladus.

Fig. 3.1: *Annual rainfall and rainfall decline for Bathurst, 1884–1934*

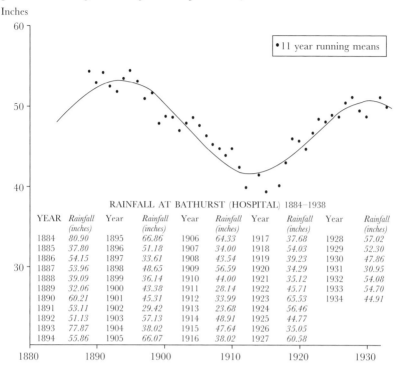

| YEAR | Rainfall (inches) | Year | Rainfall (inches) | Year | Rainfall (inches) | Year | Rainfall (inches) | Year | Rainfall (inches) |
|---|---|---|---|---|---|---|---|---|---|
| 1884 | 80.90 | 1895 | 66.86 | 1906 | 64.33 | 1917 | 37.68 | 1928 | 57.02 |
| 1885 | 37.80 | 1896 | 51.18 | 1907 | 34.00 | 1918 | 54.03 | 1929 | 52.30 |
| 1886 | 54.15 | 1897 | 33.61 | 1908 | 43.54 | 1919 | 39.23 | 1930 | 47.86 |
| 1887 | 53.96 | 1898 | 48.65 | 1909 | 56.59 | 1920 | 34.29 | 1931 | 30.95 |
| 1888 | 39.09 | 1899 | 36.14 | 1910 | 44.00 | 1921 | 35.12 | 1932 | 54.08 |
| 1889 | 32.06 | 1900 | 43.38 | 1911 | 28.14 | 1922 | 45.71 | 1933 | 54.70 |
| 1890 | 60.21 | 1901 | 45.31 | 1912 | 33.99 | 1923 | 65.53 | 1934 | 44.91 |
| 1891 | 53.11 | 1902 | 29.42 | 1913 | 23.68 | 1924 | 56.46 | | |
| 1892 | 51.13 | 1903 | 57.13 | 1914 | 48.91 | 1925 | 44.77 | | |
| 1893 | 77.87 | 1904 | 38.02 | 1915 | 47.64 | 1926 | 35.05 | | |
| 1894 | 55.86 | 1905 | 66.07 | 1916 | 38.02 | 1927 | 60.58 | | |

RAINFALL AT BATHURST (HOSPITAL) 1884–1938

*Source*: L.S. Matthews, 1939.

## The farming environment

The physical environment within which Gambian farmers operated both as food farmers and groundnut producers was (and is) fundamentally influenced by two sets of conditions. First, the alternating of wet and dry seasons related to the general monsoonal regime of West Africa, and second the morphology and hydrology of the river Gambia. The climate of The Gambia and of West Africa as a whole is conditioned by the north-south movement of a frontal system (the Inter-Continental Discontinuity) that separates dry tropical Saharan air from the humid maritime air over the Gulf of Guinea. The northward advance of the front brings the summer monsoon rains, which can vary according to the extent of the frontal movement northwards and its speed of advance and retreat, something that affects both rainfall totals and seasonal incidence. The rainy season in The Gambia lasts approximately from April to October, and rainfall totals

recorded at Bathurst from 1884 onwards have shown annual variations of between 30 and 66 inches (750 mm–1650 mm). (Fig. 3.1)
Also, there are regional and local variations between the lower and
upper river; for example 52 inches (1300 mm) near the coast to 24
inches (600 m) at the eastern extremity of the country, while there
are small scale differences of an inch or two from one bank to the
other. The latitudinal position of the Gambia together with its east-
west extension, place it within a transitional zone. The lower river
is Guinea-Savanna with oil palms, while further up stream it has the
characteristics of grassland savanna.

The reconstruction of past climatic conditions relies on qualitative
written and oral data, while there are also series of records of rainfall and temperature from meteorological stations. The data given
in Fig. 3.1 comprise rainfall totals for Bathurst 1884–1938, together
with a smoothed curve based on running 11-year means. The rainfall data, in common with many locations in West Africa pose problems of accuracy, consistency and comparability. For example, a
report of 1939 indicated that the total for 1884 and 1885 at Bathurst
were considered unreliable, while the position of the gauge was lowered in 1892. At Georgetown the disposition of the gauge was not
known and was moved in 1933, and the data for 1928 onwards
appeared to be 20% too low.[7] Such technological shortcomings affect
the quality of the data and require cautious interpretation. The rainfall data show that annually the amounts varied quite significantly;
there were clusters of good and bad years in common with much
of the West African savannas and Sahel. The running 11 year means
calculated by meteorologists in the 1930s, show good rainfall years
until the mid-1890s, after which there was a downward trend until
1919, followed by an improvement, the causes of which and their
impact we discuss in subsequent chapters.[8]

Agriculturally, low annual rainfall totals can affect the weight of
groundnuts in shell and the maturation of rice, but there are other
important factors: annual rainfall figures can hide as much as they
show, because of the absence of any indication of the length of the
wet season, as well as the daily and monthly incidence of rainfall.
If the bulk the rain comes at the beginning of the season much is
lost through rapid run-off when the ground has minimal vegetation

---

[7] GNA 2/238, L.S. Matthews, *Variation in Rainfall in The Gambia*, 30th June 1939.
[8] Ibid.

cover; therefore a relatively small rainfall well distributed throughout the farming season is much better than a heavier unevenly distributed rainfall. On the other hand, sporadic rainfall at the beginning
of the wet season can be particularly harmful for early millets, while
erratic rainfall at the end of the season can adversely affect the maturation of rice. From the point of view of groundnut producers, a
wet season which ends slowly is preferable to one which ends suddenly, as the latter causes rapid soil hardening which makes it difficult
to lift groundnuts. Therefore, there are a number of variables to
consider when judging the 'effectiveness' of rainfall, while any particular rainfall year can be good for some crops, and less good for
others. In the light of this kind of rainfall variability, Gambian farmers over centuries have developed farming practices such as multi-
cropping and crop relays, which take account of general, as well as
quite local variations.

The historical record shows that over long periods there occur
clusters of wetter and drier years, as well as longer climatic shifts.
Across the whole of the West African Sahel and Sudan there is a
long history of droughts, floods and famines that appear in local
chronicles, oral histories, travellers' accounts and colonial records, as
well as being encapsulated in poetry, song and dance. However,
reconstructions of past climates differ over the occurrence of wet and
dry periods, and Webb has drawn attention to the lack of agreement between two of the better-known accounts, those of Brooks a
historian, and Nicholson a meteorologist.[9] According to Nicholson,
the beginning of the 19th century was marked by a drought from
1828–1829, but then rainfall improved until 1895, which was propitious for the beginning of the groundnut trade. Afterwards Nicholson
believes the climate became drier, while Brooks subdivides the 20th
century, recognizing clusters of poor and better years.[10] (Fig. 3.2)
Webb prefers to concentrate on a gradual decrease in rainfall from
the 18th century onwards, rather than specific periods of wet and
dry climate which are contentious.[11]

---

[9] Webb, J.L.A., 1995, *Desert frontier: Ecological and Economic Change along the Western Sahel, 1600–1850*. University of Wisconsin. Also, 1992, 'Ecological and economic change along the middle reaches of the Gambia river', *African Affairs* 91 (360), 543–565.
[10] Nicholson, S.E., 1978, 'Climatic Variations in the Sahel and other African regions, during the past five centuries', *Journal of Arid Environments* 1, 3–24. Also Brooks, G.E., 1993, op. cit.
[11] Webb, 1995, op. cit.

Fig. 3.2: *A Comparison of climatic periodization for West Africa, c. 800–1990s*

|                | *Nicholson*                                 | *Brooks*             |
|----------------|---------------------------------------------|----------------------|
| Wet            | c. 800 to 1300s                             |                      |
| Dry            | c. 1300s to c. 1450                         | c. 1100 to c. 1500   |
| Wet            | late fifteenth to late eighteenth century   | c. 1500 to c. 1630   |
| Dry            | late eighteenth to late nineteenth century  | c. 1630 to c. 1860   |
| Wet            | late nineteenth century                     | c. 1860 to c. 1900   |
| Dry Moderate   | late nineteenth century to the present      | early 1900s          |
| Sporadic       |                                             | 1930–1960            |
| Drought        |                                             | 1960 to the present  |

*Sources*: Nicholson, "A Climatic Chronology for Africa", 75–81, 251–254, and "Climatic Variations in the Sahel," 3–24; Brooks, *Landlords and Strangers*.

The implications of these records is that the climate of the Sudan-Sahel experiences secular change as well as clusters of low rainfall years, which can also be discerned in The Gambia although it lies at the southern and western margins of this region. As far as the groundnut trade was concerned, it was the clustering of good and bad years within any larger climatic shifts that was important for producers and traders. However, while these periodic low rainfall years affected groundnut and food supplies, it is important to appreciate that seasonal hunger within any one year was a condition that affected many households. Seasonal hunger occurs around the beginning or middle of the rains, when people are working hard before the harvest of the first millets and rice. At this time households were (and are) dependent on the *previous* season's harvest, which may be almost, or totally exhausted. Therefore, there is a time-lag in food supplies: although the current season's rainfall may be good, household food supplies initially reflect the previous year's rainfall.

The Gambian groundnut trade, as well as food farming has also been shaped by the hydrology of the river's catchment and its longitudinal and cross-sectional morphology. The Gambia River rises in the Futa Jallon uplands, and the 300 miles (480 km) of its lower course comprises both the present country and the riverine tract along which the groundnut trade developed. The 300 mile limit was effectively imposed by the Barrakunda falls just to the east of the

Fig. 3.3: *Land use cross-section, Bintang Creek, near Kerewan*

*Source*: G.M. Roddan, in K.W. Blackburne, 1943.

present boundary, which limited the movement of cutters and sailing barges which were the primary means of shifting groundnuts
downstream to the point of shipment to Europe. After the 1850s
ocean steamers penetrated 150 miles (240 km) up-river, to the port
of Kuntaur, while Bathurst offered a deepwater anchorage as well
as controlling the narrows between St. Mary's Island and Barra Point
(Fig. 1.1).

Along the river one can discern differences between the lower and
upper river; for example, the contrast between saline and fresh-
water swamps, and the amount of flooding in the lower and upper
reaches. The river is 5 miles (8 km) wide east of Banjul (Bathurst),
but it narrows to a mere 200 meters at Basse, where it is incised
into a low plateau of some 15 meters. In the upper section (beyond
MacCarthy island) the floodplain narrows, and the water is fresh-
water, while below this point the floodplain widens into marshy tidal
mangrove swamps and grassland, the inner portions of which provided tracts of alluvial rice land generally known as *banto faros*. (Fig.
3.3)[12] Importantly the extent of the salinity and flooding of the inner
swamps varies seasonally as well as annually, according to a combination of the amount of local rainfall, and the rainfall of the upper
basin on the flanks of the Futa Jallon plateau. Therefore flood levels vary from year to year and can be disastrous in the upper river
where the floodplain in limited, but at the same time beneficial to
the lower river where more swampland is flooded.

There are also important cross-sectional differences stretching across
the low plateau and river plains which show a marked soil variation: the upland comprises light sandy loams, while the river margins

---

[12] Since the late 1940s rice land has been extended by clearing mangrove swamps,
therefore the rice area was smaller during in the period under discussion.

Fig. 3.4: *Land use zones for upland and lowland villages in The Gambia*

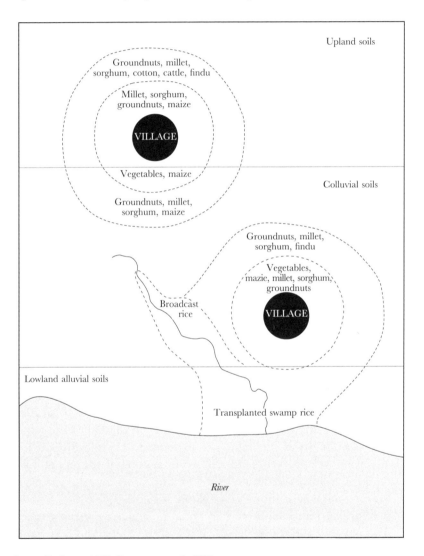

*Sources*: Dudgeon, 1910. Dunsmore *et al.*, 1976.

with have alluvial soils and variable degrees of salinity.[13] However the river bluffs and slopes that separate the upland and the swamps have mixed colluvial soils, which are produced by downwash during the rains. The tributaries of the mainstream also reproduce the contrast in soils and slope types on a smaller scale. Thus the location of villages along the cross-section of the Gambia valley endows them with different physical resources, and it is possible to identify them as either upland or lowland villages. (Fig. 3.4) What is of some importance is how local farmers manage these different physical and ecological zones, and how in some instances they integrate them into a diversified farming systems: some farmers in upland villages may have access to swampland, and vice versa. In this way an array of crops can be grown which reduce risks of a variable climate, because it does not affect all crops in the same way.

In effect, farmers past and present face multiple choices ranging over a wide spectrum of ecological niches with a variety of uses. Such local environmental and farm management systems were a particular focus of attention during the 1970s and 1980s, when social scientists and some of those interested in development and agrarian change began to examine the role of ethno-science, or indigenous technical knowledge, as it affected farming practice and land use management.[14] The 'populist' approach of the 1980s was a rejection of modernizing 'top-down' technical interventions that emanated from Europe and North America, as well as those promoting the radical reconstructions of society. Rather than the eradication of past practice, the emphasis was on long established, tried-and-trusted farming methods that were the result of centuries of innovation and experiment which have produced not only techniques, but an abundance of locally generated 'races' and types of cereals and tubers suited to local conditions. And, it has been argued that in the Sudan-Sahel environment both farmers and pastoralists have an acute perception of environmental variations and climatic variability, and accordingly use appropriate farming methods and land use systems. We would argue such contemporary studies are useful in re-interpreting some of the observations made by Europeans about African

---

[13] Brunt, M.A., 1959, 'The Gambia Land Use and Vegetation Survey' Paper Third International African Soils Conference, Dalaba, Guinea.
[14] Richards, P., 1985, *Indigenous Agricultural Revolution*. Heineman: London.

farmers and farming during the colonial period, and especially what was regarded as their resistance to new farming methods. An understanding of Gambian farming practice is of importance not only as a means to re-evaluate the sentiments of 19th century Europeans, but also the British Administration's attempts in the 20th century to introduce a number of innovations connected with growing and harvesting groundnuts and food crops.

### Gambian farming systems

It is clear from 19th century and early 20th century accounts that there was an important distinction between upland rain-fed farming systems, requiring fallowing and rotation, and lowland cultivation of swamps and flood plains with semi-permanent intensively cultivated plots. As we have already noted, the latter was physically restricted in the upper portions of the river where the floodplain is narrow and flood land cultivation was limited to tributary streams. However, it is important to appreciate that many farmers combined both upland and lowland farming systems, albeit in different proportions according to the locations of their villages and lands. The food crops on upland farms, that is those on the low sandy plateaus were millet, sorghum and 'hungry rice' combined with groundnuts, while patches of broadcast swamp rice could be accommodated in moister hollows and along the edges of streams. Thus there was a particular patterning of crops and landuse around villages, and spatially groundnuts competed with food crops and for the better soils. (Fig. 3.4) The first useful accounts of upland farming occur in the early 20th century when Dudgeon recorded the various crops and methods of cultivation in the Agricultural and Forestry Reports.[15]

The principal food crop in the Gambia in the late 19th century was millet (*penisetum typhoidium*) and Dudgeon's reports on the North Bank Province (the most specialized groundnut area) were sufficiently detailed and observant as to describe several local variants of millet. These included 'suna' a three month crop, and 'sanior' (sometimes called 'sanyo') a four or five month crop that had the advantage

---

[15] Dudgeon, 1910, op. cit.

of the grains being protected from predators by a spike. Another later maturing variety called 'madjo' was grown in the Kombos. Dudgeon was particularly interested in those areas where he found suna being grown annually on the same patch of ground, the fertility of the soil being maintained by cattle grazing on the corn stubble after the harvest. In one instance he found that land had been under suna for three generations. However, the importance of cattle being grazed across farmland, usually by the Fula, had been understood for some time as shown by a report of 1869 written by Patey the Administrator, sent to the Secretary of State. Patey regretted the frightful cattle plagues of 1863–64 and 1868, which also attacked sheep and goats "whereby the land lost its usual supply of manure".[16] Dudgeon's report indicates that it was the small straight-back cattle, the variety that is now known and 'Ndama', which were kept around these villages. This is a hump-less variety which originate in the uplands of the Futa Jallon, and which as Dudgeon realized had a good level of resistance to tsetste infestation. This use of animal grazing for dunging during the dry season either by locally kept herds or by nomadic Fula is widespread across the whole of the Sudanic belt of West Africa, and commonplace in northern Nigeria.

Guinea corn (*sp. sorghum*) of which there are two local varieties known as 'bassi' (or 'basso') and 'kinto' was another grain which gave good yields, but unfortunately seems to have been cyclically affected by sorghum aphids. Another important support crop was 'hungry rice', known generally as 'findu' or 'finde' (*digitaria exilis*), which was regularly planted on the outermost fields around the villages. (Fig. 3.4) This was the crop which required little weeding, minimal ground preparation and had the supreme advantage of maturing very quickly and thus became the means of breaking the hungry season prior to the main harvest. Dudgeon's North Bank report recorded three varieties which were separated according to their length of maturation: 'findu wolomo' harvested after 60 days, 'findu momo sato' harvested after 75 days and 'findu ba' harvested after 95 days. Dudgeon's reports together with incidental colonial notes and letters, although patchy and limited are sufficient to demonstrate that in the 19th century Gambian farmers had systems of

---

[16] CO 87/93, Patey to SS, 4th April 1869.

cultivation, which were consonant with the vagaries of the climate and the different physical conditions of their farms. The several varieties of crops and their different maturation periods indicate that risks of poor harvests could be spread and offset, together with a spreading of that most crucial input, labour.

The methods, or systems of upland farming adopted by Gambian farmers comprised a combination of rotational bush fallowing and permanent fields with crop rotations, the fertility of the latter being maintained by the use of animal manure. Rotational bush fallowing was widespread in both forest and grasslands in West Africa, where this extensive form of land use could support medium population densities. Cutting bush and then burning cleared the ground as well as cleaning the ground of pests and weeds, while burnt vegetable matter was a source of potash. Slash and burn clearing and hand hoe cultivation did not impress colonial officials, and Patey's letters we referred to above stated, "the land is merely turned over some 6 inches before the rains, the seeds dropped and crops gathered when ripe. The land then lies fallow without the slightest attempt to manure except by burning rubbish before the dry season terminates. . . . The soil would easily admit to the use of ploughs, but I am afraid it would cost a European his life to endeavour to teach them the use of it".[17] The use of ploughs recommended by Patey was primarily aimed at the improvement and extension of groundnut production, but as we shall see later there were also concerns in the 1860s about food production. The subject of plough cultivation and its non-adoption was a recurrent theme (along with the adoption of European strains of cotton) and in the Administrator's report for 1889 he bewails the lack of ploughs despite the gift of several implements several years earlier by the Philanthropic Society to the MacCarthy Island Mission, where the ploughs were "now rusting away".[18] Deep ploughing is a questionable technique under tropical soil conditions, and ox-plough cultivation was not effectively adopted in The Gambia until 1949, after which its use spread rapidly as farmers bought or hired ploughs.[19]

---

[17] Ibid.
[18] Report on The Gambia, 1890, c. 5897 XLVIII 1890, University of London Library.
[19] Weil, P.M., 1970, 'Introduction of the Oxplow in Central Gambia' in P.F.M. McLoughlin, *African Food Production Systems: Cases and Theory*, Johns Hopkins Press, pp. 229–243.

Farms were cultivated for two or three years, then in areas of heavy bush long fallows of up to 25 years restored fertility, although in grasslands regeneration was possible over shorter periods. Informants have suggested that farming households cleared and planted larger areas than could be worked thoroughly. This was a device which allowed for flexibility, as land could be planted and tilled in varying degrees, some of it in a perfunctory fashion if labour was insufficient, but if enough workers were available then advantage could be taken of a larger cleared area. Bush farms were rarely consolidated, and scattered clearings on different sites with different ecological capacities were part of risk spreading and equity within village communities. However, it appears from the evidence of informants and Dudgeon's account for the early 20th century, that on land in the immediate vicinity of villages there was continuous cultivation using rotations. Therefore a distinction could be made between bush farms, and village farms.

Whether the intensification of the more accessible land around villages was a result of integrating groundnuts into the cropping system is a question that cannot be answered, although it appears groundnuts were integrated into both remoter bush farms and the village farms. Dudgeon reported that in North Bank there were common crop rotations, where bush farms generally grew groundnuts in the first year, followed by millet (suna) or hungry rice (findu) and then in the third year groundnuts again. In some instances sorghum (bassi) was introduced into the rotation.[20] On village farms, as mentioned above, millets might be grown continuously if there were sufficient cattle to manure the farms, otherwise they were grown until the ground showed signs of depletion, then groundnuts were introduced for one year followed again by millet. According to Dudgeon, in North Bank groundnuts were never grown consecutively although this had been the practice in the past. The abandonment of successive groundnut cultivation stemmed from the disease that affected groundnuts (presumably rosette disease), which can be attributed to over cultivation. The intensive cultivation of village farms, together with bush farms being left fallow for as little as four years in North Bank, looks very much a product of the early development of this core area of groundnut farming, combined with above

---

[20] Dudgeon, 1910, op. cit.

average population densities. It cannot be assumed that such intensive cultivation of groundnuts obtained everywhere in either the 19th or 20th centuries, and there were particular regional variations in the production of both food and groundnuts.

Millets, 'hungry rice' and sorghum, integrated with groundnuts were the principal components of the upland farm, but there were other upland food production niches that were utilized by farmers. Small areas around compounds manured by domestic animals provided vegetable and fruit gardens, and the Administrator in 1884 remarked on the large amounts of tomatoes consumed by the Wolof, who also preserved the fruit in large clay pots.[21] Cassava, yams, sweet potatoes, okra, beans, tobacco, peppers, oranges and pawpaws were commonly grown around huts and compounds, while various curcubits climbed up and over the huts. Dudgeon, noted that shallots were planted in shallow beds near to the village wells and watered through the dry season: such comments pre-figure the government and Non-Governmental Agencies attempts in the 1970s and 1980s to introduce vegetable gardens in the Banjul hinterland, which were launched as an innovation![22]

Another diverse and rich source of foods, fibres, and medicines was the forest and bush, which surrounded and separated settlements. The collection of bush products was widespread, being especially well developed among the Jola in the moister forest on the South Bank and Casamance.[23] British interest in the forest and bush was chiefly as a source of palm produce and exportable timber, therefore there is only passing mention of the local use of bush products, although officials were aware that the collection of fruits, leaves and roots was an important means of coping with food shortages before harvest, or after crop failures. The best insight we have at this time into forest products and their uses was provided by Bocandé the French Resident at Carabane in the Casamance.

Bocandé's listing and comments on collected products form the single largest section of his report of 1856.[24] And, while he admits

---

[21] Report on the Gambia, 1886, c. 4904, XLV, University of London Library,
[22] Dudgeon, 1910, op. cit.
[23] Madge, C.E., 1993, *Medicine, Money and Masquerades: Gender, Collecting and Development in The Gambia.* Unpublished Ph.D., University of Birmingham.
[24] Bertrand-Bocandé, E., 1856, *Les résources qui présentent dans leur état actuelles comptoirs français établis sur les bords de Casamance, à Carabane et Sédhiou.* Extrait de la revue coloniale, encl. CO 87/3, 12th July 1861.

to his interest being motivated by the possibilities for French commerce, nonetheless, his reporting suggests his acute observation and
awareness of the importance and wide ranging usefulness of bush
products. Bocandé's account covers the collecting of garnishes which
were used in food preparation, as well as wild fruits and medicines.
Wild fruits (the *nymphaceas* were an important class) were used to supplement the diets of those households unable to produce enough
grain because of shortages of labour. Other fruits such as locust
beans (from *parkia* Clappertonia) were eaten in times of famine, or
before the harvest when the granaries were exhausted. In addition
to identifying fruits and their uses Bocandé remarked upon the manner in which flowering and fruiting of various species were used by
local people to divide up the year and seasons, and signal the various stages in the cultivation cycle. On the subject of medicine he
noted that local people were not just reliant on fetishes and Maraboutic
practices, but were also actively engaged in using the resources of
the bush. People around Carabane were using leaves, gums, barks,
roots, minerals and vegetable oils in a variety of forms such as pow-
ders, infusions, poultices, astringents and tinctures, which provided
emollients, purgatives and plasters for the treatment of skin complaints, fevers, gastro-intestinal disorders, tumours, haemorrhages and
eye complaints. While the listing is in itself useful, Bocandé also hits
upon something that has recently been recognized, that in many
instances food was medicine, and medicine was food; the distinction
between the two often being superfluous.[25]

## Land

All of the 19th and early 20th century accounts suggest that Gambia
was an area of land surplus, and there is little evidence of the emergence of land sales and the commoditization of land as groundnut
farming took hold along the river. Villages were surrounded by
acknowledged 'territory' which was not necessarily continuous, and
which comprised bush and farmland under the jurisdiction of the
village head (*alkali*). Each compound and its constituent farming

---

[25] Etkin, N.L. and P.G. Ross, 1982, 'Food as Medicines, Medicines as Food. An
adaptive framework for the interpretation of plant utilization among the Hausa'
*Social Science and Medicine*, 16, 1559–1573.

households had access to land generally according to their need or
ability to cultivate it. And while at the end of the farming year land
was symbolically returned to the *alkali*, usufruct rights were rarely
abrogated. Within a compound farmland was divided into those
farms which were cultivated communally under the head of the compound, and were primarily devoted to securing a supply of basic
foodstuffs; and those individual plots of land allocated to household
members and to Strange Farmers. Among the Mandinka these different
plots were referred to as *maruo* (collective) and *kamanyango* (individual), and the importance of the latter was heightened, as commercial groundnut farming increased, especially in response to the needs
of Strange Farmers.

Land could be held for absent members upon their return, while
additional land could be acquired through loans among neighbours.
There also existed possibilities of acquiring rights to extra land by
clearing unclaimed tracts: moreover the rights of clearance precluded
subsequent forfeiture to either any other individual or authority. In
essence this was a flexible system of access to land based on the
ability to cultivate it. However, as we suggested in the last chapter,
differentiation among households lay not only in their size and demographic composition, but also because the households of certain individuals such as chiefs and Imams could create larger farms because
they were able to summon additional labour from their slaves, clients
and Strange Farmers, as well as through obligations from other members of the community. Thus the control of manpower and to some
extent status, were means of land 'accumulation' in a land surplus
economy where there was little commoditization of land.

The inheritance of farms and possessions was patrilineal. Inheritance
rules allowed wealth (money and goods) to be shared among sons
and daughters, but land rights were not shared. Among the Mandinka
and Wolof land rights were inherited without fragmentation by male
successors of the deceased, and, despite Islamicization after the
Soninke-Marabout wars, local customs of land inheritance were not
materially transformed, and it is arguable that the inherent stability
of land succession among the Mandinka and Wolof was an integral
part in the development of the groundnut trade. Women who were
principally rice farmers were often given surplus rice farms as part
of their dowry, and marriage was another route to land accumulation. However, this might only be a temporary transfer of rice land,
as there was an understanding that such land would be returned to

a wife's family if it were urgently needed. On the other hand, rice land could be kept within a man's compound when husbands gave the rice farms of their mothers to their wives.

### Rice Farming

The cultivation of wetland rice (*oryza sativa*), including the transplanted method was described by Jobson in 1623.[26] Alternatively some rain fed upland rice (*oryza glaberrima*) was grown in moist hollows and depressions. By the 19th century, swamp rice could be found along the length of the river, but as we observed above the nature of the floodplain meant that its cultivation was particularly important along the middle and lower river on the *banto faros*. The careful use of flood land was important as The Gambia is somewhat marginal for rice cultivation, as the rainfall is well below the 80 inches (2000 mm) needed for guaranteed high yields. Localized flooding related to rainfall in the upper catchment of the basin, together with local run-off was crucial for successful crops, especially the adequacy of moisture at the end of the growing season, which ensures the ears of grain fill satisfactorily.

Dudgeon's account of farming in Niumi in North Bank Province in 1909 is particularly illuminating about lowland rice farming, and it begins by noting that it was the Mandinka who were the principal rice farmers, with women doing the cultivation, harvesting and food preparation, but with boys and men transporting the rice from the fields to the compounds.[27] Dudgeon also described the methods of harvesting of rice by women, as a highly labour-intensive process of cutting the ears with a curved knife and then tying them into small bundles. As for preparation, very little rice appears to have been steamed except by the Jola, who also produced cracked rice (*dempatong*) by pounding ripe grains. Dudgeon described how rice was planted broadcast in small patches of ground along the river margins, which had been prepared by deep hoeing to turn-in the previous season's crop residues. Water was then applied until the crop was 12–18 inches (300–450 mm) high and then transplanted after

---

[26] Jobson, R., 1968, *The Golden Trade*, The Colonial History Series. London: Dawson. First published, 1623.
[27] Dudgeon, 1910, op. cit.

two weeks into the submerged river flats, small bundles being planted about 8 inches (200 mm) apart. This method was and still is widespread along the coastal littorals and riverine swamps.

Of particularly importance in rice cultivation systems was the way in which farmers had a repertoire of varieties or local 'races', which were used to satisfy local rainfall and moisture conditions, as well as culinary preferences. In 1856 that indefatigable observer Bocandé, noted differences in rice types and rice cultivation in lower Casamance.[28] According to Bocandé, two types of rice were grown, white and red, and he carefully distinguished between the two as the former—of which there were three varieties—was rain fed upland rice, whereas the latter was grown in flooded swamps during the wet season. Red rice also had the advantage of early and late varieties; the one being harvested at the end of October, and the other at the end of December. One other rice variety is mentioned but not named, that which had a barbed ear, which reduced predation from birds.

A more sophisticated appraisal appears in Dudgeon's 1910 report when he comments on different local varieties of rice, with their several qualities, maturation dates, and their sequential planting.[29] Dudgeon's descriptions almost pre-figure recent accounts of the use of local varieties and planting techniques, which have caught the attention of those interested in indigenous science and African cultivation systems. And it is of some interest to consider why these perceptions of indigenous agriculture were subsequently lost or ignored, only to be revived in the 1980s. In general it was the post-Second World War conviction that the transfer of western technologies were likely to transform agriculture, although as we discuss in Chapter 6 the foundations for this approach had been laid in the 1920s and 1930s. In his report of 1910 Dudgeon recorded eleven different types of rice and noted their Mandinka names. The first to be sown was 'Tung-kung-o' in mid-June, which matured in three months and could be harvested in late August. The latest maturing kinds were 'Yacca' and 'Morototo' which were gathered at the end of December. Different maturation rates allows the spreading of work load and the

---

[28] Bocandé, 1856, op. cit.
[29] Dudgeon, 1910, op. cit.

most effective use of labour, but, in addition, different races or varieties are suited to particular ecological niches; some strains growing near the mainstream in deeper water and others on the elevated river margins. Variations of this kind also spread risks and are extremely important given the year to year variations in flood level; early rice might be flooded by excessive water levels, but later rice could flourish, and vice versa. Dudgeon's account of 1910 indicates that at least in some parts of The Gambia rice cultivation and its techniques had been maintained in the face of the increased efforts spent on groundnuts and increased quantities of imported rice, while it also emphasizes the importance of women as food producers.

### Groundnut cultivation and food supply

The evidence from these early 20th century reports reinforces the suggestion that The Gambia did not become a groundnut monoculture, in the fullest sense of the word, but there is evidence that during the second half of the 19th century the significant shift towards groundnut production had important implications for the supply of local foodstuffs and the feeding of migrant farmers. In those areas where groundnut specialization had proceeded quickly, rural households were increasingly dependent on purchases of rice, as local production of rice, millets and sorghum proved insufficient. It appears that 1857, the year of the Anglo-French (trade) Convention was a threshold: before this date producers maintained some kind of balance between food and groundnuts, while afterwards foodstuffs were not only purchased, but also there were periods of conspicuous food shortage.

One of the earliest reports giving details of food production and food trading was that made by Governor O'Connor when he toured the river during November and December of 1853, travelling between Bathurst to MacCarthy Island. The purpose of the Governor's tour was to try and put the groundnut trade on a firmer basis, and to hold 'palavers' with all the kings and chiefs, but his incidental observations on food farming suggest that farmers were coping with the integration of the groundnut without detrimental effects on the production of rice, millets and sorghums. In Lower and Upper Kombo he reported "they grow more food than it is possible to eat, and there is a great transaction of exchanging articles among themselves at their market place".[30] Again, in the extensive Wolof kingdom of Saloum, O'Connor reported "they also produce fine crops of abundance (sic) grains, doing much buying and selling among themselves. These natives still have plenty of uncultivated land."[31] His observations on Nianimaru in Niani are particularly interesting as he reported not only abundant grain crops and the exchange of produce among the surrounding villages, but also that, "Their fields being crowded to the extent that only the most trained mind in native diet can distinguish one crop from another".[32] Such an account suggests diverse and flourishing crops, but it also may imply some form of intercropping, which is common in the intensively settled and cultivated parts of West Africa, and which can be seen in some parts of contemporary Gambia where groundnut, millets and sorghums are intercropped. The general conclusion to be drawn from these reports is that despite the rapid expansion of the groundnut trade, local farmers were achieving a reasonable balance between groundnuts and food crops.

In 1857 the first indications of food shortages were reported, together with indications that local food production was being neglected in favour of export crop production. A general shortage of food was recorded in many villages, especially in the highly productive groundnut area of North Bank in a year when the export of groundnuts reached an all-time high of 13,544 tons. In 1857 O'Connor wrote, "The natives until the present year cultivated enough grain crops for their own sustenance—as indeed witness my reports on the many villages and districts that I visited in 1854. But an alarming scarcity of foodstuffs have (sic) this year (1857) struck considerable parts of the river, including alas, the very extensive places I visited three years ago".[33]

If food was short in some areas, then two questions arise: were the defecits made good locally, or if not where did the food come from? The accounts of the 19th century indicate that the important rice producing areas in The Gambia were in the Kombos, the South Bank and in lower Casamance, and that all these areas were

---

[30] BA, class 54, File no. NN1/1 Governor's Tour of the River, 1853.
[31] Ibid.
[32] Ibid.
[33] CO 87/64, O'Connor to Labouchere, 31st May 1857.

capable of producing tradable surpluses. Here the climate is wetter, there are more extensive areas of swampland compared with the upper river, they are occupied by the Jola and Mandinka, the former being particularly associated with rice cultivation. Both the British and French accounts indicate the importance of these rice growing areas and the surpluses they produced. Vallon's description of Casamance in 1862 indicates there were two distinct kinds of trade: in the middle region groundnuts were grown and traded, while in the lower region rice was predominant.[34] The Jola exchanged rice for cotton supplied by the local Mandinka, although a better variety of cotton was traded from the Gambia, and together with the Bangnons, the Jola also traded palm-nuts, hides and beeswax. Vallon's report indicates that rice in addition to being sold to the local European factories and seafarers in Casamance, was also exported in considerable quantities along the coast to the French forts and factories in Senegal, and significantly along the Gambia river. Vallon was concerned that the Portuguese dominated this coastal trade, while Bocandé's earlier report of 1856 shows that St. Louis and Gorée were dependent on Casamance rice.[35] The trade into The Gambia was such that Vallon reported the movement of porters carrying rice northwards had led to the error of believing that the river Songrougrou flowed into The Gambia and not the Casamance.

Rice was also coming into the Gambia from the English trading station at Lincoln, sited at the mouth of the Casamance river, and Governor D'Arcy, reporting to the Colonial Office in 1861 noted that there were" people annually producing great quantities of groundnuts and rice, together with an abundance of corn and millet and vegetables.[36] The Governor refers to this area as, "this African Egypt", which was supplying Bathurst with rice, and he entertained the idea that this situation might be replicated in North Bank where food was being neglected. In fact the two Bathurst firms that had groundnut agents at Lincoln were already purchasing rice from farmers there, and selling it along the Gambia where producers were concentrating on groundnuts. But it is also clear from Gambian reports that the South Bank and the Kombos were important for their food

---

[34] Vallon, M., 1862, 'La Casamance, Dépendance du Sénégal'. *Revue Maritimes et Coloniale*, tome 6, pp. 456–474.
[35] Bocandé, 1856, op. cit.
[36] CO 87/71, D'Arcy to Newcastle, 24th July 1861.

surpluses too, and in effect they were an extension of the Casamance rice area that collectively comprised the ethnic and cultural core of the Jola. When Governor D'Arcy visited Yundum, the capital of the Kombo king in 1860 he observed that, "natives came from various districts, even from the other side of the river, to buy food".[37] All of these reports indicate that the trade in grains, which was such a feature of the lower Gambia and Senegal rivers during the Atlantic slave trade continued, but in addition to supplying European trading posts the emphasis had now shifted towards supplying and supporting legitimate trade, especially the North Bank of the Gambia which by the mid-19th century was the important area of groundnut production. It appears that new markets for the commercial grain farming was also part of the process of adaptation and transition after the ending of the Atlantic slave trade, and farmers and traders were exploiting new markets associated with the groundnut trade. Such developments in food farming and trading would seem to support one of Myint's tenets about the effects of the development of legitimate trade.

After 1857 a dichotomy seems to have developed between the North Bank and South Bank, which was reflected in the greater emphasis on groundnuts on the former, and the continued cultivation of surplus foodstuffs on the latter in response to the rising demand for rice in the groundnut exporting zones. To this extent supplies from the South Bank and the rest of Casamance were limiting the necessity for internationally imported rice to maintain the groundnut trade. However, this division should not obscure the fact that groundnuts were also being produced in the South Bank, especially at Kombo, Kiang and Jarra. In 1860 Governor D'Arcy was pleased to note during his visit to Gunjur that, "the people have not forgotten their food crops of cereals and vegetables. The groundnut advances but the natives of Gunjur attend to their foodstuffs bringing also great amounts of groundnuts to the two European firm established there".[38] And, at Sabiji the Governor was gratified to observe that the people were resisting the growing habit of neglecting food crops.[39] These sentiments of D'Arcy suggest an emerging awareness on the part of the Administration of the consequences of

---

[37] CO 87/69, D'Arcy to Newcastle, 14th June 1860.
[38] CO 87/69, D'Arcy to Newcastle, 24th May 1860.
[39] CO 87/71, D'Arcy to Edwards, 8th January 1861.

the spread of groundnut cultivation, and also they were the first expressions of a hope (much repeated in the colonial period), that sufficient food production could be maintained along with increased groundnut cultivation.

On the North Bank by the late 1850s groundnuts had taken a much stronger hold. Agriculture was becoming more intensive in this well populated zone, which was situated in open grasslands with sandy soils suited to groundnut cultivation and which economically always had been more important than the South Bank as it contained the five powerful 'petty kingdoms' of Niumi, Baddibu, Saloum, Niani and Wuli. By 1860–61 Baddibu (along with Niumi) had successfully converted from a slave trade economy and consolidated its position as a 'cradle' of commercial groundnut production. Governor D'Arcy's visit of 1861 alludes to the dependency of the Baddibu on external food supplies, when he went there to try and obtain redress for merchants whose goods were alleged to have been pillaged. D'Arcy was moved to comment on the lawlessness and power of the King of Baddibu and his ability to withstand attack, but he also noted the King's vulnerability from the river and that it was possible "to blockade his country, which would force him to submit. For his people need food, considerable quantities of which come from the south bank of the river—the Baddibu people themselves growing ever increasing quantities of groundnuts, but rarely do they now grow sufficient food to feed themselves."[40] And D'Arcy also noted that the situation was the same in neighbouring Niumi.

In the same report of 1861 there is also the suggestion that a gendered division of labour was emerging based on food crops and groundnuts. D'Arcy noted "the men are no longer devoting effort to food cultivation. They leave the task entirely to women, while they pursue the groundnut in earnest. . . . It is my opinion that this situation is a great ill, which the extension of commerce has brought to the river. . . as long as groundnuts pay to cultivate, the people will continue to devote their time to the cash crop, using the rewards of commerce to purchase imported rice, and local foodstuffs where available".[41] A rather more censorious comment came from the trader Whitford in the 1870s who opined that "the women till the soil and

---

[40] CO 87/71, D'Arcy (aboard HMS "Torch", Baddibu Creek) to Newcastle, 26th Feb. 1861.
[41] Ibid.

cook the yam . . . a few of the men only work to buy rum and other luxuries.[42] Therefore, by the early 1860s, it would appear that on the North Bank in Saloum, Baddibu, Niumi, Niani and Wuli the male labour force concentrated on groundnuts, while along the South bank men as well as women were committed to food production, although as we have observed, groundnuts were also part of South Bank farming systems.

The issue of the gendered division of labour expressed as men cultivating groundnuts and women rice, does however need some further discussion. Certainly Mandinka women did not have individual (*kamanyango*) upland plots on which they could cultivate groundnuts, and they were predominantly rice cultivators. Wolof women had small groundnut farms, while among the Serahuli in the upper river, women were growing groundnuts for export because there were limited areas of flood land suited to rice cultivation. But in both Mandinka and Wolof communities men prepared rice farms for women before planting, although this was a task which men were gradually to discard, as they expanded groundnut production after 1857.

However, the idea women started to cultivate rice in the mid-19th century because men cultivated groundnuts is wide of the mark: women had been cultivating rice for centuries. In the early 17th century Jobson wrote "I am sure there is no place where women can be under more servitude for they beate and cleanse the rice . . . which is only women's work, and very painfull".[43] Also, women assisted in the harvesting of millet although it was grown by men, while cotton was planted by men, but the intermediate processes of picking, cleaning and spinning were done by women, after which men did the weaving. The growing of maize involved both men and women while women chiefly grew vegetables that they harvested and sold in the market place. As in many West African societies it was less a case of a single crop being grown by men or women, and more a case of complementary tasks, or a combination of jobs involving sowing, harvesting and processing, which varied with specific crops. However, the proportion of male and female labour varied according to circumstances and the crops grown, but in the longer term

[42] Whitford, J., 1967, *Trading Life in Western and Central Africa*, London: Frank Cass, 2nd Ed.
[43] Jobson, R., 1904, *The Golden Trade, or a Discovery of the River Gambia and the Golden Trade of the Aethiopians, 1620–21*. Teignmouth.

the development of the groundnut trade importantly shifted the control of cash crop farming towards men. In addition to cultivation, men also spent time transporting groundnuts to the wharves during the trading season, which could begin as early as late November, and continue until May, although December and January were the important times for sales.

### Changing patterns of food production and rice importing

By 1857 it may have been the case that as the specialization in groundnuts increased, so women became more involved in rice farming, but it is also clear that local supplies of millet and rice were not sufficient and imports of rice began to climb. More land was put down to groundnuts, while the needs of Strange Farmers, together with the disturbances caused by the Soninke-Marabout wars began to raise the demand for imported food, which meant rice. Therefore, an important change in diet was taking place at this time for those who hitherto had relied principally on millet as their food staple. The production of groundnuts had increased by 400% between 1843 and 1857; and in 1858 £19,351 of rice was imported which by the next year (1859) had risen to £28,208.[44] The neglect of local food crops and the preference for a cash crop not only fuelled the demand for imported rice, but also a range of other imported goods which could be bought from the proceeds of the groundnut harvest. As we mentioned earlier, between 1842 and 1847 imports of cotton piece goods increased by 300%, chiefly from Manchester and Glasgow.[45] By 1852, 24% of all imports by value were cotton piece goods, while unprecedented increases were recorded for guns (largely British army rejects), gunpowder, rum, spirits and tobacco.[46]

There were also some changes in the crops grown. For example, maize had been an important crop until the 19th century, as it was highly prized for its' relatively good calorific rating, and moreover it was the first of the cereals to be harvested in August and September, which helped to break the hungry season when food supplies were scarce. Maize was probably the first New World plant to cross the

---

[44] CO 90/31–33, Blue Books, 1857, 1858, 1859.
[45] CO 87/41, Annual Report, 1847.
[46] CO 90/30, Blue Book, 1856.

Atlantic, but when it first reached West Africa has been much dis-
puted.[47] The Portuguese reported *mihlo zabura* in the Senegambian
littoral in 1502, but whether this referred to maize or sorghum is
unclear, while there is some speculation whether maize came from
across the Sahara from Spain.[48] The first unambiguous account of
maize was given by the English in 1555 when expeditions to the
Gold Coast revealed its presence, while a Dutch expedition of 1601
described how it came from the West Indies to Sao Tomé.[49] Maize
appears to have been well established along the coast at the slave
trading depots, and reports of its cultivation in the interior are sprin-
kled through the accounts of the travels of Mungo Park, but never
referred to as a dominant staple.[50]

Webb has suggested that the decline in maize in favour of millet
is a reflection on the steadily deteriorating climate, from the 18th
century onwards.[51] But like the disappearance of forests as indica-
tors of dessication, the decline in maize farming is capable of alternative, or complementary explanations. The popularity of maize
along the coast stemmed from its usefulness as a basic foodstuff for
slaves in transit, which created a considerable demand (10,000 tons
per annum). Maize was particularly suited to supplying the Atlantic
slave trade as it stored better than millet, and could be more easily
transported over long distances. But with the decline of the slave
trade it seems likely there could have been a corresponding decline
in the demand for maize. It is true that maize is susceptible to poor
rainfall, but its replacement by millet and more importantly 'hungry rice' is most likely to be due to the fact they require less labour.
The cultivation of hungry rice (*findu*) is widespread in contemporary
Gambia and is used to break the hungry season in much the same
way maize can be used, but unlike maize it is sown broadcast and
rarely weeded. Maize requires careful weeding, especially in its early
stages after it has germinated; it grows slowly at first, and if it is to
succeed then correctly timed weeding is of the essence. In situations
where increased labour inputs for groundnuts were required, especially

---

[47] Alpern, S.B., 1998, 'European crops in pre-Colonial Africa', *History in Africa*.
[48] Ibid.
[49] Ibid.
[50] Park, M., 1878 edition, *Travels in the Interior of Africa in the years 1795, 1796 and 1797*, London.
[51] Webb, 1995, op. cit.

for weeding, then maize is far more expensive in terms of labour costs than hungry rice or early millet, which probably led to its reduction as the groundnut trade developed, rather than being a response to the worsening of the climate. Therefore, an alternative explanation for the reduction of maize because of climatic deterioration is the possibility that it represented another adaptation to the ending of the slave trade and the development of the groundnut trade.

However, the climate was certainly not unproblematic, *vide* the rainfall figures shown in Fig. 3.1, but from the point of view of the Gambian producer (and the government), it was short-term climatic perturbations that attracted their concern. Poor rainfall and badly distributed rainfall, together with outbreaks of crop pestilence and human and animal disease directly and indirectly exacted their toll on groundnuts and food crops, which as we have stressed are interconnected. In some years both groundnut and food crop outputs were affected, in others one or the other. But as specialization of the groundnut industry took hold and food imports rose, then a bad groundnut crop could have significant consequences for producers relying on rice, either purchased or on credit. There were other circumstances too converging with climate and changing farming systems, which caused disruptions in supply and necessitated food imports. These were epidemics, and the effects of warfare and civil disturbance (to which we have referred earlier). In 1859 and 1866 there were yellow fever epidemics, while cattle plague was recorded in 1863, 1864 and 1868, and in 1869 there was a severe cholera outbreak that spread from Senegal. Yellow fever in August 1859 brought all trade to a halt as "European merchants, who on the outbreak of the sickness, promptly left for the island and England. The year consequently saw a falling off of the revenue and exports of the groundnut".[52]

The cattle plagues also indirectly reduced the productivity of groundnut land as manure was lost, and while the 1863–64 outbreak only affected cattle, that of 1868 was worse as sheep and goats were affected too. As Patey explained to London, "the whole of the groundnut land up the river has suffered considerably",[53] and exports

---

[52] Archer, F.B., 1967. *The Gambia Colony and Protectorate: An Official Handbook.* London: Frank Cass.
[53] CO 87/93, Patey to SS, 4th Aug. 1869.

fell accordingly. (Fig. 1.6) Among the human population, the cholera
epidemic of 1869 accounted for 1,162 deaths out of a population of
4,000 in Bathurst and district,[54] while Gray believed that the effects
up-river were just as disastrous, where villages were overcrowded
and stockaded because of the Soninke-Marabout wars.[55] Estimates
suggest that within a three month period one quarter of those in
the river bank settlements fell victim to cholera. Epidemics can have
serious effects on labour intensive systems of agricultural production,
while they also contribute to the dislocation of food distribution and
trade. However, although many observers may have believed epidemics, food shortages and warfare were discrete events, it is now
accepted that they are frequently linked and mutually reinforcing,
which causes widespread and persistent dislocation.

As we have observed in Chapter One, the Islamic wars that intermittently erupted across Senegambia spanned some 30 years, from
1862–94. The wars affected the production of groundnuts, but they
also disrupted local food farming. In February 1863 a minor refugee
crisis emerged, as some 2,000 Wolofs and Serer from Saloum arrived
at Barra Point seeking the protection of the British. Five months
later 700 more refugees arrived at Barra, reporting that many of
their fellow villagers had died on the way.[56] The Annual Report for
1863 notes the "the corn growing districts desolated in default of
corn and millet; these starving immigrants have adopted as food,
bread and imported rice, exchanging a few crude articles of native
ornaments and dresses saved by them in the sacking of their towns
for more essential articles of life".[57] Two years after this report Colonel
Ord, the Commissioner appointed to inquire into the conditions of
British settlements on the West Coast, observed that in The Gambia
the recent wars had disturbed trade and that since 1854 the principal imports were cotton goods, rice and tobacco. He went on to
say that rice had become a large article of commerce due to famine
caused by recent native wars and that as it could be procured at a
reasonable cost it was likely to "continue to form a considerable

---

[54] CO 1869 Paper relating to an outbreak of cholera in the settlement of The
Gambia, 1869.
[55] Gray, J.M., 1966, *A History of The Gambia*. London: Frank Cass.
[56] CO 87/76, D'Arcy to Newcastle, 11th Sept. 1863.
[57] Annual Report, 1863.

portion of the food of the people, who will devote more time to the cultivation of produce and less of corn".[58]

As Ord's report makes clear, Gambian households, at least in the areas of specialist groundnut production, were buying-in food both as a response to periodic drought and civil disturbance, and as part of their increased commitment to groundnuts. This was a particularly attractive option when the prices of groundnuts were good and the terms of trade in favour of Gambian producers. Until about 1870, the terms of trade were favourable towards Gambian producers and they were able to conveniently purchase both imported trade goods and foodstuffs. The merchants not only exported groundnuts and imported manufactured goods they also imported and distributed food. As food and trade goods were advanced on credit Gambian producers after 1857 became increasingly susceptible to being drawn into webs of indebtedness. The growing dependency on imported rice combined with groundnut exports, rendered Gambian producers much more vulnerable to the fluctuation in world prices for both these commodities. Myint's scenario of commercial export crops stimulating local food production had now changed; exports had stimulated food imports. By the late 19th century a picture was emerging of a nexus of interacting physical and social circumstances, wherein food production, labour supply, a variable and changing climate, epidemics and civil disturbance were embedded in the rapid expansion of groundnut production for export.

Ord's report contained selected import and export figures for 1855 and 1863, some 20 and 30 years respectively after the inception of the groundnut trade. The list of imported goods demonstrates the importance of cotton goods, tobacco and wines for each year, but also it highlights the significant increase in rice between 1855 and 1863 when collectively imports underwent an exponential increase. By 1878 Skipton Gouldsby, the Administrator of The Gambia was reporting once again that cotton goods, kola and rice had shown a bigger value increase than any other, largely as a result of exceptionally good groundnut exports in that year.[59] Certainly good groundnut harvests stimulated imports when prices were reasonably good,

---

[58] Report of Colonel Ord, Commissioner appointed to inquire into the conditions of British Settlements on the west coast of Africa British Parliamentary Report, 1865, XXXVI (412), University of London Library.

[59] Report on The Gambia, 1878, c. 2598, XVI, University of London Library.

but if farmers became indebted to traders when prices fell they tended to respond by planting more groundnuts, which meant less food crops and so the vicious circle was intensified. Also, by 1879 the local supply of food from South Bank showed signs of deterioration: the Jola were so embattled in local wars they were no longer making an effective contribution to the food market as they had done in the 1860s.[60] By 1884, Moloney, the Administrator, was emphasizing that there "was not enough cereals for home consumption as rice has been imported", and this is a clear indication that an important shift in food production had taken place, and producers now looked to imported rice as their food staple.[61]

But where did the rice come from in the late 19th century to supply the growing demand from groundnut producers along the river? An example from the Blue Book of 1876 shows the new directions of the rice trade, and how rough and clean rice were being brought into The Gambia from distant sources, which in effect meant Britain or British possessions.[62] Of the rice imported in 1876, 60% came indirectly from Britain itself, although a significant amount, some 20% came from the Windward Coast including Senegal, Gorée and Cape Verde. Small amounts by value came from Sierra Leone and the Leeward Coast, together with slightly more from the British West Indies. Interestingly while the overwhelming proportion of the groundnuts exported from The Gambia went to France (82%), only a minute proportion (£436) of rice came from this country. Thus food trading in The Gambia by the 1860s had developed beyond the local and regional redistribution of grains from areas of surplus towards the burgeoning groundnut areas, and had been replaced by a situation where producers were increasingly dependent on the international trading of rice and international food prices. Another threshold had been reached in the development of the groundnut trade.

*Summary*

The Gambian farming environment as reported during the 19th century was influenced by the regional climate of the western Sudan,

[60] CO 87/110, Cooper to Gov. in Chief, 2nd Jan. 1879.
[61] Report on The Gambia, 1886, c. 4904, XLV, University of London Library.
[62] Blue Book, 1876.

together with the physical nature of the Gambia valley. There were problems of clusters of poor and good rainfall years which affected groundnut production, as well as corn and rice. Nonetheless Gambian farmers by careful niche management, and the deployment of a suite of corn and rice varieties were able to offset climatic vagaries and outbreaks of pestilence. However, it appears that 1857 was an important turning point in the Gambian groundnut trade, because it marked the beginning of food deficits in the major producing areas. By the 1870s the initial stimulus to local food production had proved insufficient: food imports from overseas were required, a process which accelerated and became an integral part of expanding production.

Yet if there was a discernible shift towards prioritizing groundnut cultivation, and an increasing dependency on groundnuts and imported rice, it cannot be said that The Gambia became a monoculture. One of the important insights from the early 20th century reports of the Agricultural experts, such as Dudgeon and Blackburn, was that farmers had maintained their local food producing and marketing systems in the face of an expanded groundnut export economy. But imported foodstuffs were vital for two reasons: first, as the means of feeding the ever growing number of Strange Farmers who poured into The Gambia as the 19th century progressed, and second, as the means of overcoming years of poor rainfall. If groundnut prices were good in times of environmental difficulty, Gambian producers had sufficient exchange entitlement to foodstuffs: the real problem arose when environmental disasters (as well as civil disturbance) occurred *simultaneously* with poor producer prices. Lower prices were encountered more frequently after the 1870s, exacerbated by the Great Depression in Europe, when the terms of trade moved against Gambian producers. The nexus of groundnuts, local food, imported food, environment and migrants became a much more sharply focused issue under the political economy of colonialism, because it affected government revenues and expenditure. The next chapter begins to investigate how the creation of a Protectorate, and the British Administration of The Gambia, affected the groundnut trade and the lives of Gambian producers.

CHAPTER FOUR

# THE BEGINNINGS OF COLONIAL RULE, 1893–1913

In 1893 British rule was extended beyond the colonial enclaves of
Bathurst and MacCarthy Island, through the creation of a Protectorate
stretching 300 miles inland along the north and south banks of the
river. From the outset there were doubts about The Gambia's viability, and there was an extended debate on the merits of cession.
However, once established it was inevitable that groundnuts became
the economic mainstay of the Protectorate, but almost immediately
production was hindered by weak groundnut prices and erratic rainfall: output fell from 25,218 tons in 1893 to a low of 10,006 tons
in 1895.[1] (Fig. 4.1, 4.2.) Thereafter production recovered for a few
years, and continued to increase despite serious price fluctuations,
and by 1913, 67,404 tons were exported. (Fig. 4.2) The cultivated
area was extended, migrant farmers flooded in, and the merchants
continued to advance credit to producers, but relations between the
two deteriorated as the bargaining position of the farmers was substantially eroded. A critical point was reached in 1900 when high
levels of credit and indebtedness were followed by very low prices,
which initiated a series of 'hold-ups' accompanied by outbreaks of
violence. The merchants re-acted by collectively fixing prices and
abandoning credit. Unfortunately these events coincided with another
run of poor rainfall years, and producers bore the full brunt of a
climatic downturn and changed economic conditions. Yet despite the
economic and environmental turbulence during the early years of
the 20th century, production was sustained and at times increased,
for reasons we shall discuss later.

---

[1] To what extent liberal free trade was curtailed by the Great Depression after
1870 is a matter of debate, but there were clear signs of a downward trend in
groundnut prices in The Gambia, with the terms of trade moving against the
producers.

Fig 4.1: *Gambian groundnut exports and public finance, 1893–1913*

| Year | Groundnut Tonnage | Value of Groundnut Exports (F O B) | Government Revenue | Government Expenditure |
|------|------|------|------|------|
| 1893 | 25,218 | 172,765 | | |
| 1894 | 20,010 | | | |
| 1895 | 10,006 | | 35,403 | 29,875 |
| 1896 | 12,107 | | | |
| 1897 | 20,279 | 126,605 | | |
| 1898 | 33,078 | 200,308 | 39,908 | 27,499 |
| 1899 | 34,353 | 210,005 | 46,840 | 30,405 |
| 1900 | 35,805 | 221,841 | 49,161 | 25,813 |
| 1901 | 25,750 | 172,405 | 43,726 | 29,886 |
| 1902 | 31,612 | 193,485 | 51,016 | 38,775 |
| 1903 | 45,477 | 275,394 | 55,564 | 44,792 |
| 1904 | 43,436 | 229,287 | 54,180 | 45,078 |
| 1905 | 29,499 | 169,426 | 51,868 | 48,568 |
| 1906 | 36,050 | 278,055 | 65,430 | 45,971 |
| 1907 | 40,858 | 256,685 | 65,892 | 52,659 |
| 1908 | 31,964 | 245,084 | 57,898 | 52,823 |
| 1909 | 53,644 | 323,231 | 72,676 | 50,728 |
| 1910 | 58,456 | 387,934 | 82,880 | 55,476 |
| 1911 | 47,931 | 437,472 | 86,454 | 58,678 |
| 1912 | 64,169 | 503,069 | 96,222 | 58,466 |
| 1913 | 67,404 | 622,098 | 124,995 | 67,405 |

*Sources*: Blue Books, 1893–1913 and K.W. Blackburne, 1943.

The groundnut trade had been established for some 60 years when partition occurred, and although colonial rule was of considerable significance in the long run the Administration had a limited capacity to effect a profound structural transformation of the groundnut economy. However, there were initial transformations through the introduction of trading licenses, taxation, the abolition of domestic slavery and a new legal system. After these early interventions the Administration generally tried to mediate the several interests involved in the groundnut trade. Over all The Gambia remained an, 'open economy', and government interventions were often the means of 'holding the ring' among several conflicting interest groups, or of alleviating the effects of environmental and economic turbulence. However, as the 20th century progressed the economic hold of the firms over producers tightened, and the benefits enjoyed from their engagement in the overseas exchange economy appear to have been limited. Certainly households had to further internalize the externalities of groundnut production for the world markets, which led to changes in household relations of production and distribution. In

Fig. 4.2: *Gambian groundnut exports (tons), 1893–1913*

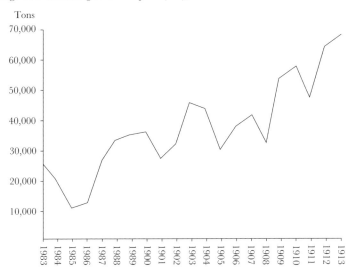

*Source*: Blue Books.

the period under discussion (as well as afterwards), the amount of government investment was minimal, and as elsewhere it was 'colonialism on the cheap': indeed one of the inner dramas of colonial rule was finding the means to pay for itself. It has been argued that far from exploiting Africans, colonial regimes did not 'exploit' them enough; in other words there was no real attempt to transform them into modern capitalist societies.[2] In The Gambia the Administration's concern was primarily the successful production and evacuation of groundnuts, of keeping income above expenditure, and in the long run it was not a case of what the government did do, but what it failed to do.

One important result of the extension of formal British rule along the river was the production of better records and observations, as a growing band of colonial officers travelled and worked throughout the new Protectorate. More information had to be collected and censuses carried out because the British administration had to introduce new systems of taxation, as well as addressing the issue of domestic slavery and the local slave trade. Also, the increased amount

---

[2] Kay, G. 1975, *Development and Underdevelopment*. London: Macmillan.

of information (despite its deficiencies), is particularly important in improving our insights into the nature of the relationships among the size of the groundnut crop, the environment, producer prices, the number of migrant farmers, and the amount of food imported.

## Partition and the proposed cession of The Gambia

There has been an extended, and indeed continuing debate about reasons for British imperialism and expansion overseas, including the partition of Africa. Both liberal and Marxist analyses have placed great emphasis on imperialism being shaped by the Industrial Revolution and its need for raw materials and markets, while the decline of empire was part of industry's fading strength. And, a distinction has been made between informal empire rooted in free trade in the early 19th century, and formal empire underwritten by political control in the latter half. Analyses by Cain and Hopkins have sought to re-interpret British imperialism, drawing attention not just to relations between the metroples and overseas interests, but of the interaction between economic development and political authority within the metropoles.[3] They have drawn attention to the several strands of modern British history, which include agriculture, commerce and finance, and the importance of capitalistic enterprises beyond the industrial sector. What they propose are two periods of 'Gentlemanly Capitalism'; the first the old colonial system from 1688 to 1850, the second from 1850 to 1945. Cain and Hopkins point to the landed classes and rentier capital of the 17th century gradually becoming merged with commercial capitalist agriculture in the 18th century. In the period 1688 to 1850 British administrators and civil servants were drawn from the ranks of landed, rentier or service sector wealth, not from industry. After 1850 Gentlemanly Capitalism in its landed form was replaced by service sector capitalism, when financial and city magnates assumed control of the British economy. Yet they were still part of an agreed culture shaped by the values of landed aristocracy and the Public School.

In the period up to 1850 important landmarks were the creation of the Stock Exchange, the emergence of the National Debt and the

---

[3] Cain, P.J. and A.G. Hopkins, 1994, *British Imperialism*. London: Longman.

confirmation of the Gold Standard. The National Debt was the price
of foreign wars and an imported monarchy, which demanded management by the moneyed interest. Free trade was a result of pla-
cating taxpayers and containment of the National Debt through
customs dues, rather than being initiated by industrialization. The
City, like industry had to look abroad for new areas of expansion
if they were to launch sterling on its international career. Moreover,
exporter and industrialist alike were dependent on the City for credit.
Overseas possessions were a response to the growing political and
commercial power of Europe, and then America. Overseas interests
also were solutions to domestic problems, such as social discontent
(for example Chartism). But after 1850 the old colonial system was
destroyed by the success of free trade: one phase of Gentlemanly
Capitalism was succeeded by another as the City and service sector
of southeastern England required the rapid expansion of world trade
and colonial development. After 1850 there was a relative decline
of manufacturing, but from 1870 to 1945 the service sector flourished,
and the City advanced as the banker and carrier of the world's
trade. The groundnut trade was a good example of an industry heavily dependent on the shipping lines, and the provision of mercantile
credit through the banks.

The partition of Africa, and more to the point in our case West
Africa has received extended discussion and has produced a variety
of interpretations. Some authors have cited the Egyptian crisis of
1882 as the key, or the Berlin Conference of 1884–85, while specific
military and political figures have also been held to be crucial factors.[4] But the circumstances which led these individuals to act as
they did are important too. The economic expansion of Europe in
the 19th century had a destabilizing effect on West Africa, as the
old Afro-European understandings which made the Atlantic slave
trade possible were dislocated as export production involved the
region in the trade cycle and European markets. Indeed much what
follows in this book is concerned with the impact on Gambian producers of booms and slumps in the groundnut trade. And, as we
have suggested earlier, the emergence of myriad small producers
posed new challenges to established authority, and contributed to

---

[4] See Robinson and Gallagher, 1981, *Africa and the Victorians; the Official Mind of Imperialism* (second edition).

the Soninke-Marabout wars.[5] The balance between Africans and
European traders was tipped towards Europeans in the late 19th
century, as the terms of trade deteriorated for producers, while the
shifting balance of power in Europe among Britain, France and
Germany created rivalries exacerbated by the Great Depression
(1873–1896). Thus there was a struggle to control African markets
and enlarge merchant influence.[6] In The Gambia, declining profits
had to be countered, and a number of practices emerged on the
part of the merchants such as dilution of measures and price fixing.
On the other hand producers resorted to hold-ups. Throughout West
Africa merchants began to press for a more active policy on the part
of their governments, and in putting their case they were well aware
of lowered costs of coercion and intervention through the mecha-
nization of warfare and the development of the Maxim and Gattling
guns.

The establishment of The Gambia Protectorate as a British sphere
of interest was troubled by doubts because of its size and shape, and
it was preceded by an extended debate about cession to France,
which in part was fuelled by falling groundnut prices and fluctuating
production. Rather than supporting the merchant interest, the British
government and Gambian Administration expressed doubts about
the continued viability of The Gambia, especially given the strength
of French merchants. Cession of The Gambia to France had been
discussed as early as 1866, when France proposed an exchange of
The Gambia for stations in the Ivory Coast, but the momentum for
cession increased during the latter part of the 19th century as the
groundnut trade faltered.[7] Arguments about cession developed between
the Administration and the merchants: the former setting-up official
visitations and inquiries, while the latter used the well-tested practices of political lobbying, and the submission of memoranda together
with appeals to their Chambers of Commerce.

Sir Arthur Kennedy, the Governor of the British West African
Settlements visited Bathurst in 1869 and reported that the £20,000
spent on troops exceeded the mercantile profit; furthermore, he

---

[5] Klein, M.A., 1972, 'Social and Economic factors in Muslim revolution in
Senegambia', *Journal of African History*, 13 (3) pp. 419–441.
[6] Hopkins, A.G. 1974, *An Economic History of West Africa*, London: Longman,
ch. 4.
[7] Gray, J.M. *A History of The Gambia*. London: Frank Cass. p. 435 and ch. 29.

stressed that the trade was in the hands of the French.[8] This view
was supported by Patey, the Administrator of The Gambia, who
pointed out that the French firms were expanding and had close ties
with the oil-milling interests in Bordeaux and Marseille.[9] Patey in
turn was supported by Fowler, the Acting Collector of Customs who
in 1870 thought that British mercantile capital in The Gambia was
insubstantial and declining, whereas French investment was expanding.[10] British interest comprised individual firms or traders, whereas
the French firms were branches of larger metropolitan businesses.

Not surprisingly the British merchants were vociferous in their
opposition to the government view, and joined forces with the
Liberated Africans who also had a stake in the groundnut trade. Led
by two prominent Bathurst merchants, Brown and Quinn, they lob-
bied the Colonial Office and Manchester Chamber of Commerce,
and by May 1870 two petitions had been delivered to the Colonial
Office.[11] In July of 1870 the merchants further pointed out that government reports had concentrated on Bathurst, and overlooked the
investments in vessels and up-river factories and the supplies kept
there.[12] Details of merchant trading emerged in the correspondence
as never before, and Brown alone stated he had £28,500 invested
in houses, boats and factories. as well as £35,000 tied up in credit
along the river, which approximated to annual government expenditure.[13] The merchants also reminded the government that although
the French might dominate the groundnut trade, it was the British
who provided imported trade goods, luxury items and food.[14] However,
the Gambian Administration and the British Government remained
unimpressed, and furthermore they turned the issue of barter trade
against the merchants arguing it exemplified their anachronistic and
exploitive attitudes.[15] The merchants stoutly defended their use of
barter, although as Kennedy noted, it was advantageous to merchants but not to the farmers, with whom it was becoming increasingly unpopular.

---

[8] CO 93, Kennedy to Elliot, minute no. 10698, 23rd Sept. 1869.
[9] CO 87/95, Patey to Mansell, minute no. 11416 1st Oct. 1869.
[10] CO 87/98A, Fowler to Kennedy, 12th Mar. 1870.
[11] CO 87/96, Kennedy to Granville, April 1870 and 10th May 1870.
[12] CO 87/97, T. Brown and T. Quinn to Kennedy, 12th July 1870.
[13] CO 87/97, Brown to Kimberley, 21st July 1870.
[14] CO 87/97, Chown and Chown to Kimberly, 30th July 1870.
[15] CO 87/97, Kennedy to Kimberley, 20th Sept. 1870.

While the several parties argued about cession, the French continued to move southwards and eastwards, from their bases in Senegal. After 1879 there was a distinct change in French attitudes about the role and costs of the military presence in the colonies, and under Freycinet and Jaureguiberry, the tradition of limited intervention was broken. Alarmed by foreign competition, convinced of the wealth of the interior and a supposed population of 80 million, together with pressure from the Bordeaux merchants, French policy changed. The firm of Maurel et Prom were especially supportive of the extension of French influence, and backed a proposed railway to link Sudan with North Africa, and the establishment of river steamers on the Senegal from St. Louis to Kayes.[16] In 1880 an Anglo-French treaty had halted French territorial advances, but the Gambia was already encircled, while the hinterland of Sierra Leone was also curtailed effectively limiting its economic potential. Prior to the Berlin Conference in 1884–5, the Liverpool and London merchants pressed the government to save the Gambian and Sierra Leonean hinterlands, expressing bitter disappointment over the splitting of the two territories by French advances.[17] But their influence was nowhere near as strong as the powerful lobbies of the Indian and Eastern commercial interests, and it has been argued that during the 'scramble for Africa' the British in West Africa held back and were primarily interested in a holding operation against the French and Germans.[18]

West Africa was an area where there were no big financiers or groups of settlers wishing to stake out claims, although as noted above there was a vociferous defence of British interest from some merchant quarters. But it has also been suggested that the British were keen to accommodate the French in West Africa, in order to further British policy in Egypt vis a vis France.[19] In the case of Senegambia this argument seems difficult to sustain, as the French had well established coastal enclaves by 1860 (for example Carabane), as well as already having spread inland along the Senegal and Niger[20] Thus the French were in place, and it was more a case of sorting

[16] Newbury, C.W. and A.S. Kanya-Forstner, 1969, 'French Policy and the Origins of the Scramble for Africa', *Journal of African History*, 10, 253–76.
[17] See Robinson and Gallagher 1981, op. cit.
[18] Ibid.
[19] Ibid.
[20] Newbury and A.S. Kanya-Forstner, 1969, op. cit.

out respective spheres of established interest. In the end The Gambia remained British, because the French failed to keep their side of the bargain proposed under a settlement of 1888 whereby the British would receive Dahomey, adjacent to the Niger delta where British influence was assured.[21] By 1891 the Senegal-Gambia frontier had been provisionally drawn, and the boundary finally agreed in 1894. However, the boundary was a formal arrangement between Europeans, and as the continued flow of Strange Farmers demonstrated it rarely constrained the movement of people or goods. Thus the social and economic hinterlands of The Gambia from its' inception stretched well beyond its' political boundary, as it still does today.

*The establishment of the Protectorate and the introduction of taxation*

In 1893 the Bathurst government appointed two Travelling Commissioners, Ozanne and Sitwell, who were to work on the north and south banks of the middle and lower river. By 1906 three more administrative areas (known as Provinces) had been added; Kombo and Foni, MacCarthy Island and Upper River. (Fig. 4.3) The role of the Commissioners was to facilitate trade by spending the months between January and June travelling through their districts to keep the peace between producers and traders, and to prevent theft and fraud associated with groundnut trading.[22] The initial legislation was provided by the Protectorate Ordinance of 1894, which provided administrative and judicial services in the protected territories, established native courts and a police force under the supervision of the Commissioners with ultimate power vested in the Governor.[23] The Ordinance opened the way for further Ordinances implementing direct taxation and the suppression of the slave trade, both of which were associated with the establishment of British control throughout the Protectorate.

While Sitwell's first tour of 1893 recommended a Hut Tax, the government initially preferred to address the groundnut trade through the implementation of traders' licenses and Strange Farmer rents,

[21] Ibid.
[22] CO 87/141, Llewelyn to Chamberlain, 20th May 1892.
[23] CO 87/147, Maxwell to Llewelyn, 28th Dec. 1894.

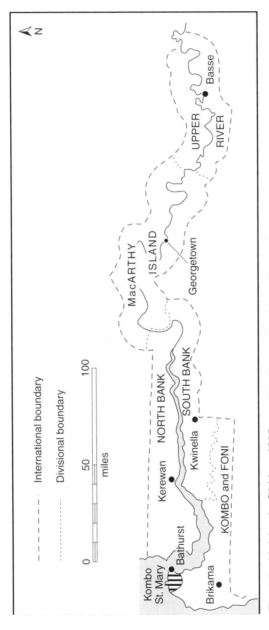

Fig. 4.3: *Administrative Divisions, 1906*

which in effect was a re-shaping of the existing practices of paying tribute to local chiefs.[24] These two issues were gradually dealt with by government as political control was established and consolidated, but both led to a conflict of interest among the government, chiefs and merchants, something which became a persistent feature of the governance of The Gambia, as elsewhere in West Africa. It was not just the level of taxation that concerned chiefs, but the division of the revenue collected from the traders and Strange Farmers. The Traders' Licenses Ordinance was passed in October 1893, abolishing the long established practice of traders paying 'custom' to chiefs for permission to trade in the interior.[25] The new legislation, much resented by the merchants now required traders to pay for a license in Bathurst, which they then presented to chiefs in whose areas they were trading. The government believed this new system would deter fraudulent traders, and so end the interminable arguments with chiefs about the payment of 'custom'. Hitherto 'custom' had amounted to goods to the value of £6 2s 0d paid to the chiefs, whereas Governor Llewelyn suggested a fee of £4 0s 0d per trader payable in Bathurst to the government. Under the new system traders had to pay cash, rather than their preferred method of advantageously using goods in lieu of payment in coin. Once issued the traders handed the licenses to the chiefs in whose districts they traded, who received £1 0s 0d for every license presented to the Treasury at the end of June. The *alkalos* of the villages were to be given a fee, after consideration by the Governor of any complaints made against them.[26]

At first returns from the tax were pitiful: in 1895 a mere £325 from the North Bank, and £100 from the South Bank, and £50 for the Kombos.[27] These low figures suggest evasion: it was one thing to legislate for taxation but another to collect it and supervise its implementation given the limited manpower. The license fee in the end was scaled according to different 'classes' of trader and the evidence relating to Traders' Licenses reveals a good deal about the types of traders who were operating along the Gambia river. (Fig. 4.4) No less than nine 'classes' of trader were identified for the purposes

[24] CO 87/146, Mr Sitwell 27th Dec. 1893.
[25] CO 87/144, AWLH to Bramston, minute no 19852, 25th Nov. 1893.
[26] CO 87/141, Llewelyn to Chamberlain, 20th May 1892.
[27] CO 87/149, Llewelyn to Chamberlain, 27th July 1895.

Fig 4.4: *Traders' Licences by category of trader*

| Category | Description of Trader | Amount set for License |
|---|---|---|
| CLASS 1 | Men in charge of factories. Prosperous companies, large, substantially built, and do an infinitely better business in every way than any other class. | £10 0s 0d |
| CLASS 2 | Traders taking goods on credit from one or more merchants in Bathurst; or who are employed by merchants in Bathurst at a salary. These men set up large stores at the different wharves in the river. | £5 0s 0d |
| CLASS 3 | Mostly natives, who are supplied with goods by Classes 1 and 2, chiefly the latter, and go by the name of sub-trader. | £1 10s 0d |
| CLASS 4 | Traders, also generally natives, who buy goods from Class 2. They should take out licence for £1 10s 0d but they evade the law by calling themselves the sub-traders of the man who has supplied them with goods. | £1 10s 0d |
| CLASS 5 | Women from Bathurst who sell salt *only* in exchange for corn. | 4s 0d |
| CLASS 6 | Men who travel from wharf to wharf in large canoes, selling dried fish *only* for corn and cotton. | 16s 0d |
| CLASS 7 | Natives who sell kolas only. | 8s 0d |
| CLASS 8 | Traders who come to collect debts *only* and sell nothing. | No Licence |
| CLASS 9 | Clerks or Agents of Classes 1 and 2, who measure nuts only and do not sell anything. | No Licence |

*Source*: CO 87/147, Gambia no. 64, 19th July 1985.

of taxation, which ranged from those in charge of substantial factories, through clerks and agents of the larger traders, to debt-collectors, and natives selling kola.[28]

The accounts of the newly appointed Commissioners on the implementation of the Traders' license fee supports previous ones of how traders operated, as well as new insights into the numbers involved. Ozanne's report of the North Bank in 1893 dwells on relationships between merchants and chiefs, as well as emphasizing the problem of indebtedness.[29] He also described how in the area under the French

---

[28] CO 87/149, Ozanne to Llewelyn, 27th July 1895.
[29] RHL Micro Afr. 485, The Gambia, North Bank Report 1893.

Commandant at Nioro, traders were helped by the chiefs to secure their debts; *alkalos* were expected to detain debtors until they were 'redeemed' by their friends, a practice which underpinned credit-based trade. Failure of the *alkalos* to assist was punished by reporting them to the Commandant who imposed a heavy fine. In the report Ozanne also castigates the traders for giving out too much credit, "as trouble occurs when natives overdraw": but he warned traders that government would only help recover debts up to a certain extent. However, it was agreed that the old method of detaining debtors could continue, but the guilty would be sent to Bathurst until redeemed by their friends, and he believed this threat would prove to be a sufficient deterrent.

Ozanne's first report explains how traders set up their businesses by the creeks, paying dues to the chiefs, and as he wryly remarked "these pickings will be missed under the new Administration".[30] Traders offered cotton goods and tobacco to producers, which they had taken on credit from the Bathurst merchants in return for groundnuts. Alternatively, local cloth currency was offered to producers, which was still widely used on the North Bank. The local cloth currency, comprised strips of cloth known as *pagns* and was a principal reason for the importance of cotton cultivation in the North Bank and its flourishing textile industry: as Ozanne observed, every town has its spinning and weaving sheds.[31] Pagns accumulated by merchants through direct purchase of their goods, along with groundnuts were sent into Bathurst at the end of the season.

Ozanne's report of 1893 gives some indication of the number of traders and sub-traders on the North Bank. He counted some 250 who included "Mandigoes, Jollops (sic) and Sierra Leoneans": in the previous year Goddard, a merchant and member of the Executive Council had indicated he had 600 traders throughout the river.[32] The new arrangements regarding traders licenses were not just intended to raise revenues payable in cash, but to ensure that that chiefs were turned into salaried officials (as in may parts of West Africa), and make them part of the local bureaucracy who were expected to collaborate with the British Administration. This was an

---

[30] Ibid.
[31] Ibid.
[32] CO 87/141, Llewelyn to Chamberlain, 20th May 1892.

integral part of indirect rule, and as we have noted district chiefs in The Gambia were summoned each June to the capital to receive their share of the license fees, when any matters of dispute or appeal could be resolved by the chief magistrate.[33] Also, this was an attempt to keep the chiefs in contact with the Administration and visibly establish the hegemony of British rule. As a result of this and other legislation, indirect rule regularized and legitimized the power of chiefs and headmen, and endowed them with new sanctions and power, the consequences of which at times have proved contentious up to the present day.

The merchants' dislike of the new system led to a vigorous protest: in September 1895 they complained to Chamberlain the Secretary of State for the Colonies that they believed the licenses to be unconstitutional, as two justices of the peace or members of the legislative council were required to give applicants a certificate of good character.[34] The Colonial Office was not impressed, while Governor Llewelyn who was determined on its acceptance advanced the view that the Ordinance was a means of protecting the natives against unscrupulous traders, who frequently were the cause of outbreaks of violence and of pushing trade into French territory.[35] This was one of many future attempts to play-off traders against the producers, and attempts at 'divide and rule'.

In order to assert firmer control over the groundnut trade, as well as trying to increase revenues new arrangements had to be made with respect to Strange Farmers' rents. In 1895 the Governor fixed the rent at 4s 0d per stranger, of which the *alkalos* of the towns were to receive half, and subsequently this became incorporated into the Protectorate Yard Tax Ordinance of 1895.[36] Previously the Strange Farmer had paid three dollars tribute (12s 0d) to the District chiefs, who gave the *alkalos* a share. Under this new arrangement the chiefs lost out, but the Administration argued that chiefs now received stipends, and with rents fixed at reasonably low levels and the *alkalos* receiving their share, the net effect would be to attract more strangers and so increase revenues and groundnut production. This

[33] Ibid.
[34] CO 87/150 Merchants, traders and principal inhabitants of Bathurst to Chamberlain 17th Sept. 1895.
[35] CO 87/150, Llewelyn to Chamberlain, 17th Sept. 1895.
[36] CO 87/149, Ordinance no. 7 1895, 19th Mar. 1895.

new measure was extremely important as it formally gave the *alka-los* a vested interest in the migrant labour system, and a *pro rata* return for taking Strange Farmers into their communities.

The strategy of lowering Strange Farmer rents in order to attract migrant labour from French territory seems to have worked, as the following account shows. From 1890 to 1900 groundnut cultivation in Sine Saloum around Kaolack was encouraged by the French and facilitated by merchants operating out of Bathurst, Albreda and MacCarthy Island. The build-up of the Kaolack area into an integral part of Senegal's peanut basin relied heavily on navetanes, and reports indicate that in one canton south of Kaolack 36 villages comprising some 10–12,000 inhabitants received between 6,000 and 7,000 strangers.[37] But the paramount chief 'le Bour' demanded 20 francs tax (*nangu*) from migrants on arrival, while a variable tax (*namou*) was paid to local chiefs. The result was that some 90% of navetanes left for The Gambia. Eventually the Commandant persuaded 'le Bour' to reduce his tax to 10 francs, but it needed a reduction of the *namou* to 5 francs in Saloum, and 6 francs in Sine to bring back navetanes. Finally in 1902 the French implemented a basic tax per farmer, in common with the British.

After Traders' Licenses and Strange Farmer rents came the Protectorate Yard Tax Ordinance in 1895, which brought all Gambians within the orbit of taxation on the basis of the number of huts within a compound (yard).[38] The impact of taxation on agricultural producers loomed large in the literature during the 1970s and has been seen as the means whereby African farmers were forced into the cash crop economy.[39] It is argued that every tax-payer to meet his obligations either had to sell his labour or some of his produce for the export market; in some cases they sold both. In The Gambia, British taxation did not initiate the groundnut trade, but it may have helped to push it into new areas. In British Kombo taxation had been in place since 1864, but in 1897 the Administration decided to encourage groundnut production in this area by repealing the 1864 Ordinance, and put Kombo as near as possible on the same

---

[37] David, P., 1980, *Les navetanes. Histoire des migrants saisonniers de l'arachide en Sénégambie des origines à nos jours.* Dakar: Les Nouvelles éditions Africaines. pp. 23–25.

[38] CO 87/149, Ordinance no. 7 1895 29th Mar. 1895.

[39] See for example, S. Stichter, *Migrant Laborers*, Cambridge: CUP.

footing as the Protectorate.[40] But we have shown Gambian producers were brought into the world trading economy by the activities
of the merchants, and they were firmly held there by entrenched
systems of credit and webs of indebtedness. And, as we shall suggest later, increased production was not unconnected with the abolition of slavery and slave trading, especially their impact on the
recruitment of Strange Farmers. Manchuelle's views on taxation as
a 'push' on Soninke migration are clear: he believes that producer
prices and access to trade goods were the most important factors,
but this may not have been true for all navetanes, as differential
taxation and government policies between British and French territories certainly affected migration.[41]

There was no doubt that the Gambian Administration believed
the expansion of the groundnut area was not only necessary, but
could also be promoted by taxation. In 1896, when dealing with the
Kombo tax question, Llewelyn stated that taxation was already pushing producers to expand their farming activities,[42] and three years
later Ozanne reported he believed the area of groundnut cultivation
had increased every year, while that under corn, cotton and indigo
had decreased proportionately as farmers grew groundnuts to pay
their taxes.[43] On the South Bank in 1899 Sitwell reported his direc-
tive to the Jolas in Foni to grow groundnuts to pay their taxes,
although it will be recalled they were food crop farmers who traded
their food surpluses.[44] In 1900 groundnuts were being grown in some
measure in every Jola town, but Sitwell amended the Ordinance to
a tax level of one bushel of nuts, and even this was difficult to collect, because "the people are so very wild and so poor".

In a report of 1900 Milne the Agricultural Superintendent for
India and Ceylon quoted a report for the Bathurst Trading Company
in 1893, which estimated that there were 230,000 acres of cultivable
land in The Gambia of which 21,000 acres were under groundnuts,
but by 1900 the area had increased to 32,000 acres.[45] And, in 1902

---

[40] CO 87/153, Llewelyn to Chamberlain, 7th Jan. 1897.
[41] Manchuelle, 1997, op. cit.
[42] CO 87/151, Llewelyn to Chamberlain, 15th April 1896.
[43] CO 87/159, Ozanne to Llewelyn, 1st Aug. 1899.
[44] CO 87/160, Sitwell to Griffith, 14th Aug. 1900.
[45] CO 87/161, W. Milne, Superintendent of Agriculture for India and Ceylon.
General Observations on The Gambia for the Bathurst Trading Company: 1900.

reports from the South Bank reinforced earlier ones about the acceptance of groundnut cultivation by the Jolas, as a means of paying
their taxes. Traders at Kudang, the only South Bank port from
which ocean going ships sailed for Europe reported they were confident
of increased purchases from the Jola country in the next trading season.[46] Expansion of groundnut cultivation was also occurring in Upper
River in Fulladu and Kantora, where the Bathurst Trading Company
opened a large factory in 1903.[47] So one might conclude taxation
was important, but the problem is to know whether there was a
direct relationship between taxation and the expansion of cultivation, or whether it was due more to the rising tide of migrant farmers and settlers.

The Commissioners may have exaggerated the benefits and acceptance of taxation, as the returns shown in the early Blue Books after
the introduction of Yard Tax suggest under-collection, or the avoid-
ance of payment.[48] Also, immediately after the introduction of Yard
Tax, production fell. (Fig. 4.2) And, while taxation did not provoke
resistance on the scale of the Sierra Leone Hut Tax Wars of 1897–8,
there were protests from chiefs on the South Bank, notably in
Sutukung, Dumbutu, Kwinella and Pigni who in 1893 refused to
accept laws affecting traders' licences, slavery and farm rents.[49] Later,
during 1897–99 tax collection became difficult, while traders reported
harassment because of the new system of licenses, and chiefs refused
to declare the number of Strange Farmers. As a result in 1900
punitive expeditions were mounted: a naval force of two hundred
was sent to Dumbuta and Kwinella towns, which were destroyed,
and troops marched throughout the South Bank and the Kombos[50]
(Fig. 4.3).

Some areas however were treated more leniently than others; for
example between 1902 and 1909, the government found it expedi-
ent to allow the powerful rulers of Kantora, Wuli and Sandu to
retain all the revenue collected on farm rents from strangers, as an
inducement to accept the newly established Protectorate system.[51]
These were the hereditary chiefs who had a legitimacy beyond that

[46] CO 87/167, Sangster to Denton, 5th July 1902.
[47] CO 87/167, Stanley to Denton, 9th July 1902.
[48] Blue Books, 1900 and 1920.
[49] CO 87/143, Sitwell to Llewelyn, July 1st 1893.
[50] CO 87/161, Conf. minute no. 40564, 26th Nov. 1900.
[51] BA, Class 77, piece no. 1. 1910.

of the appointees of the British, or chiefs whose authority derived from dubious outcomes of the Soninke-Marabout wars. In 1905, the four important districts of Fulladu East, Kantora, Wuli and Sandu, contributed £1,066 8s 0d in taxes out of a total government revenue of £51,868, the bulk of which was derived from import and export duties.[52]

Although taxation levels were relatively low, payment by households has to be seen in the context of the addition of tax to their existing debts to the merchants, and household incomes which in labour intensive farming systems varied considerably according to the incidence of mortality and morbidity, as well as good and bad rainfall years. New taxation created resistance from chiefs, and to what extent they continued to exact traditional custom or payments is unknown. A frequent grievance of many Gambian households was the mistaken inclusion of kitchens, granaries and stores and animal huts in the assessment for tax.[53] Overall the new taxes formed a small proportion of the Administration's total revenue, and it is hard to believe that taxation was a sufficient condition for the acceleration of groundnut production. Perhaps what is more pertinent is that in 1906 a pitiful £198 was spent in the districts on 'Protectorate development', despite a consistently healthy balance of revenue over expenditure.

Taxation may have played some part in the expansion of cultivation into new areas, and certainly the trend in exports was upwards until the beginning of the First World War. (Fig. 4.2) Judging the effects of taxation on production is difficult because of how to disaggregate this factor from several others. For example, increased production was assisted by the influx of migrants and a general increase in labour mobility related to improved transport and the abolition of slavery, which we discuss below. In addition, one cannot discount the expectations of Gambians and a demand for wage goods supplied by traders on credit And, as the 20th century progressed there is evidence that in the face of falling, or even stable prices, expanding production was the means whereby producers achieved these ends, or simply paid-off their debts while economically 'standing-still'.

An increase in population was also another factor in expanded production. There was an increase in the population of The Gambia

---

[52] Derived from BA Class 77 piece no. 1.
[53] Ibid.

from 1891 onwards, which was due to natural increase, as well as migratory drift from French West Africa, principally from Senegal. In 1891 the population of that part of the Protectorate covered by the census was estimated at 53,849, while in 1901 the total population of the same area was 76,9948. Later in 1907, the population for the Colony and Protectorate was recorded as 90,404,[54] and by 1911 the figure had reached 138,400.[55] These figures are no more than approximations, complicated by double counting, the mobility of the population in general, and the movements of Strange Farmers in particular.

*The abolition of slavery*

Not least in any explanation of the expansion of export crops was the erosion of domestic slavery, which had significant consequences throughout West Africa. Colonial regimes implemented policies aimed at the erosion, if not complete abolition of slavery, either in the belief it would be economically advantageous to labour markets, or from some moral imperative. Whatever the reason it had profound effects on the organization of household labour and their constituent social relationships, and contributed to a surge in seasonal labour migration. This was part of the internalization of the new forces of colonialism that re-shaped households and farming: emancipation was as powerful a push towards migration as taxation, if not more so. The abolition of regional and local slave trading was not without difficulties for Administrations, and in British territories there was an inclination towards a gradualist approach, or the 'slow death' of slavery.[56] Gambian administrators were aware of long standing resistance from slave owners; for example in 1862 during the Soninke-Marabout wars the besieged Soninke leaders at Essau feared that once their people took refuge at Barra the British would free all the slaves.[57] In 1893 the chiefs at Sutukung, Dumbutu, Kwinella and Pigni told the Commissioner they would not entertain laws with

---

[54] Annual Report 1891. This figure excluded the population of British Kombo, the Ceded Mile, MacCarthy Island, and the vast Fulladu districts.

[55] CO 87/155, Census Report 1901: Annual Report 1911.

[56] Lovejoy, P.E. and J.S. Hogendorn, 1993, *Slow Death for Slavery: The Course of Abolition in Northern Nigeria, 1897–1936.* Cambridge: CUP.

[57] CO 87/74, D'Arcy to Newcastle, 22nd May 1862.

regard to slavery, and if they were enforced they would move into French territory.[58]

While the government ignored these threats and passed the Slave Trade Abolition Ordinance of 1894,[59] it was nonetheless aware of the amount of work done by slaves and as the South Bank Commissioner put it; "they are the capital of the people."[60] The Alimami of Kaner, when interviewed, expressed the same sentiment when he said "the slaves are our hands and feet".[61] As we have observed earlier, slaves were used in the establishment of the groundnut trade, and they were an essential part of the relations of production. According to the Commissioners' reports of 1893 slaves were incorporated into families, inasmuch owners would marry female slaves, while all slaves after a certain time were allowed land and the hours to cultivate it on their own account. Every headman had slaves which he fed, but did not clothe who worked for him from 5 am to 3.30 p.m. on five days of the week; the rest of the time they cultivated farms at their own pace on land allocated by owners, or other freemen.[62] Such shared-time systems that involved both slaves and family members were common within households in many parts of the West African Sudan; for example such arrangements were recorded by Lugard in his Political Memoranda for Northern Nigeria.[63] And we have already noted in Chapter Two how such work arrangements provided a pattern for Strange Farmer contracts, while some second generation slaves or 'serfs' enjoyed enhanced mobility as migrant workers under supervision.

The North Bank Commissioner Ozanne advised that abolition must be a gradual process if social discontent and economic disruption were to be avoided, or in other words, it should not disrupt the groundnut trade.[64] Thus the Ordinance declared slave trading illegal, and it stated all slaves imported into The Gambia after 1894 were free, while maltreatment became grounds for emancipation.

---

[58] CO 87/143 Sitwell to Llewelyn, July 1st 1893.
[59] Annual Report 1894.
[60] CO 87/49, encl. no. 1. Llewelyn to SS, July 1st 1893.
[61] Ibid. encl. no. 2.
[62] RHL, Micro Afr. 485, The Gambia, Annual Reports North Bank and South Bank 1893.
[63] Lugard, F.D., 1906, *Instructions to Political and Other Officers, on Subjects Chiefly Political and Administrative.* London.
[64] CO 87/49, Llewelyn to SS, July 1st 1893.

The Ordinance did not institute general emancipation or mass abolition, but did make a provision under British law for slaves to ransom themselves. The ransom was set at £10 for an adult and £5 for a child, and similar ransoms were instituted in Senegal in 1892 and Sierra Leone in 1896. Furthermore, the Ordinance outlawed the transfer of slaves, and declared that a slave was automatically free on the death of his master. Finally, the Governor had discretion to free an individual, or all slaves in a particular district. Therefore the legal status of slavery was altered by British law and the control of owners irrevocably weakened.

In addition to any moral imperative concerning abolition, there was the economic advantage that released slaves could sell their labour in the market place. And although many West African administrators were fearful of the flood of slaves into the towns, and the creation of lawless vagrants, they were attracted to the idea that abolition was essential for the creation of a wage labour force and expanded production. It is difficult to estimate to what extent slaves left former masters and contributed to a free labour force, and if they did leave was it seasonally or permanently? In the case of The Gambia, there already existed a wage labour market, albeit a shallow and expensive one. In the period 1881–1891 the merchants continually complained of labour shortages in the trade season, grumbling about the cost of labour and having to pay rates of 1s 0d to 1s 6d per day for unskilled workers,[65] while much earlier in 1851 rates of 1s 0d had been quoted in Bathurst by MacDonnell.[66] In 1892 Llewelyn complained that proprietors of slaves would not hire themselves, or their slaves to the steamer owners loading groundnuts at Ballangar, so they had to send for labour from Bathurst.[67]

By the late 19th century Bathurst seems to have become an establish centre for young men looking for casual work in the 'hungry season', and in 1904 the Commissioner of the North Bank observed that this practice was increasing,[68] while in 1905–6 the Commissioner added that Kaolack and other places in French Territories were attracting young men in the dry season.[69] This apparent increase in

---

[65] CO 87/139 Carter to SS, 11th Mar. 1891.
[66] Annual Report 1851.
[67] CO 87/142 Llewelyn to Ripon, 27th Dec. 1893.
[68] RHL Micro Afr. 485, The Gambia, Annual Report for the North Bank, 1904.
[69] RHL Micro Afr. 485, The Gambia, Annual Report for the North Bank, 1905–6.

dry season migration may well have reflected the increasing ground-nut tonnages being exported in good years, together with increased mobility of former slaves, who were now looking for work as they were no longer provided for by their masters in the dry season when food was short. Some measure of the labour shortages in The Gambia are shown by the Administration's alarm, when British Honduras asked for manpower, and although this failed, the Congo Free State managed to recruit 200 labourers in 1893.[70] The upshot was an Ordinance passed later in 1893 to Regulate and Protect the Emigration of Labourers from The Gambia.[71]

The impact of the 1894 Abolition Ordinance appears to have been considerable, especially in areas such as the North Bank the historic core of the groundnut trade, where slaves outnumbered freemen by two to one.[72] In the same year there occurs the first report by the Commissioner of the North Bank of the emancipation of 68 slaves and, in 1895 and 1896 both North and South Bank Commissioners emancipated 97 and 210 slaves respectively.[73] In The Gambia there is evidence that when ex-slaves bought their own freedom they settled alongside former masters and took up unused land with the approval of the *alkalos*, although this was not necessarily of good quality.[74] But self-redemption accounted for relatively small numbers, and in a majority of cases slaves refused to continue working for their masters: the Annual Report for 1897 observed that "hundreds of slaves are running away from their masters and returning to the villages where they were captured."[75] These runaways were those captured towards the end of the Soninke-Marabout wars, and they reflected a general trend in West Africa when after abolition those recently captured de-camped and returned home.[76]

In Wuli, in Upper River, studies by Weil have shown that by the last decade of the 19th century the royal-commoner caste began to decrease their overheads by reducing the number of work-days of slaves to whom they had access, and likewise the number of days

---

[70] CO 87/144, Llewelyn to Ripon, 27th Dec. 1893.
[71] CO 87/144, Renner to Maxwell, 31st Dec. 1893 Ord. No. 7 of 1893.
[72] CO 87/146, Ozanne, 25th June 1894.
[73] Annual Reports, 1894, 1895, 1896.
[74] Annual Report, 1900, and field interviews, 1977.
[75] Annual Report, 1897.
[76] See for example, P.E. Lovejoy, 1983, *Transformations in Slavery*, Cambridge: CUP. ch. 11.

worked by personal slaves was reduced.[77] These changes were in
large measure brought about by taxation, since yards were taxed
according to the number of huts and their inhabitants. Given that
slaves resident within compounds had to be fed, even on days when
they worked on their own plots, taxation increased the costs. Stanley
the Travelling Commissioner for Upper River, remarked in 1902
that the suppression of the trade in domestic slaves under gradualist measures had also improved the lot of existing ones; they now
worked 4 or 5 days per week instead of the 6 days formerly required.[78]
Therefore, it was this kind of partial disengagement which accelerated the drift of slaves into periodic or circulatory wage labour, or
share-cropping.

By 1903 the Governor in his Annual Report believed that in the
past decade the slave trade had been brought under control, and,
if there were still some slaves in captivity and surreptitious trading
continued, it seemed fair to assume many slaves had been freed.[79]
One important aspect of the change in status and condition of slaves
which concerns us was its effect on labour supply and production
within The Gambia. Writing of Senegal, Klein believed the break-
down in the slave system had no negative effects on commercial
growth but encouraged rapid and more efficient forms of labour as
well as increasing the use of migrant labour.[80] This is a position we
would generally support, but two questions in particular arise in
assessing changes: first, what was the effect on households of emancipation, and second how did emancipation relate to Strange Farmers?

In the case of household production, it is necessary to understand
that although slaves and free-born worked on farms together doing
similar kinds of work, the slaves generally worked the harder. Therefore,
when a household lost its slaves its likely effect was to either require
their replacement by some form of free labour, or increase the work
loads of remaining members. Whether women were called upon to
do more work after abolition is something that is not revealed by
the records. However, Wainwright was moved to write to Governor

---

[77] Weil, P., 1984, 'Slavery, Groundnuts and European Capitalism in the Wuli
Kingdom of Senegambia, 1820–1930', *Research in Economic Anthropology*, 6, 77–119.
[78] CO 87/85, encl. no. 4. Denton to SS 3rd June 1902.
[79] Annual Report 1903.
[80] Klein, M.A., 1977. In S. Miers and I. Kopytoff, *Slavery in Africa: a Historical
and Anthropological Perspective*. Madison.

Llewelyn in 1897 that" one now sees headmen going to work on their farms, a thing which I am informed was never before seen".[81] Commissioner Ozanne in 1898 was equally convinced that people had to work harder with young men and boys doing more work, as well as using more and more migrant labourers.[82] Such observations by colonial administrators have been subsequently backed-up by interviews with elderly Gambians conducted in 1977 in Upper River. One corrolorary of abolition was the re-direction of capital formerly invested in slaves: it appears that surplus capital was being invested in cattle rather than slaves, which Ozanne believed were highly valued for their milk and manure.[83] Consequently one can assume the cattle population increased as a result of abolition.

### Strange Farmers and abolition

The abolition of domestic slavery and the suppression of the internal slave trade arguably had a substantial impact on the demography of West Africa: household formation was altered, and the changing conditions and age of marriage affected fertility.[84] These topics require much further research, but it is apparent that changes were neither universal, nor uni-directional; for example, Manchuelle's account of the Soninke indicates many ex-slaves stayed with their masters, unlike the Mandinka in Mali who left them. And while the end of slavery allowed new freedoms and greater mobility, it did not always provide an ex-slave with land or good land, hence the attraction of becoming a seasonal migrant farmer. Abolition also shook the foundations of domestic groups and many freeborn juniors loosened the shackles of authority and they became seasonal migrant farmers too.

David's account of the navetanes in Senegal point to the importance of abolition in French West Africa and the construction of the Dakar-Bamako railway, which by 1911 had been extended beyond

---

[81] CO 87/154 Wainwright to Llewelyn, 5th July 1897.
[82] CO 87/156 Ozanne to Llewelyn, 19th July 1898.
[83] CO 87/154 Ozanne, 5th July 1897.
[84] See K. Swindell, 1981, 'Domestic production, labour mobility and population change in West Africa' in *African Historical Demography* vol. 2, Centre of African Studies, Edinburgh Univ. Also, K. Swindell, 1984, 'Farmers, Strangers and Labourers', *Africa* 54 (1), 1–19.

Kaolack and Thiès towards Tambacounda.[85] The railway workshops
and construction teams were made-up primarily of permanent migrants,
especially Soninke from Upper Senegal whose presence facilitated a
second wave of seasonal migrants, many of whom were ex-slaves.
David cites reports for French West Africa in 1911, which describe
former slaves of the Sahel travelling in bands along the railway track
to farm in Senegal, who when the season was over returned home
intending to return the next season.[85] The railway was an important
link to the upper Niger valley and it encouraged the spread of commercial groundnut farming in the Upper River district of The Gambia,
as Tambacounda was only some 40km distance from the eastern
border. It became the means of attracting migrants and Strange
Farmers from eastern Senegal and Mali, and it was at this time that
Basse was established as the major up-river trading centre. David
estimates that after 1910 perhaps 10,000 slaves were liberated quite
suddenly, and most went into the groundnut areas of Senegal and
The Gambia in the hope of achieving an easier and better life. This
new wave of migrants comprised what David refers to as 'part-up-
rooted people', and quite the opposite of the migrant farmers of the
19th century, the 'voyageurs chevronnés', who were pioneers cultivating groundnuts in the midst of a local population often indifferent
to the new crop.[86] As we have suggested these pioneer migrants were
a devolution from the old trading networks who were attracted by
the new opportunities offered by groundnut farming. The 20th century wave of Strange Farmers were more a result of the social and
economic dislocation arising from abolition in the interior, and the
increasing marginalization of this area which resulted in more of a
'push' towards seasonal groundnut farming.

The new status of former slaves within their own independent
households exerted new demands and pressures. The question of
food is crucial here as former household slaves were fed according
to various arrangements between masters and slaves, but importantly
they were fed during the dry season. Now emancipated slaves were
faced with reproducing their own households throughout the year
by their own labours on any land they may have acquired, as well
as a variety of dry season jobs. In addition, ex-slaves as independent

---

[85] David, op. cit. 1980.
[86] Ibid.

households were subject to colonial taxation. Given the marginality of their new status, they sought a wide range of income earning opportunities, and the Strange Farmer system offered access to cash, trade goods and free feeding during the time spent with one's host. In addition, seasonal migration allowed young men in general to accumulate money for bridewealth, which became their responsibility as the economy became more commoditized and social ties between seniors and juniors loosened. As for the host farmers, the Strange Farmer system after abolition offered the chance to replace lost slaves, or take on extra labour without recourse to cash wages. As we have suggested the similarities between the work regimes of former slaves and strange Farmers seems unmistakable: and slaves and strangers frequently gave a tenth of their crop to their masters or hosts, so an elision from one system to the other was relatively simple. But the *status* of the migrant workers was different: unlike slaves they entered into a free contract, and unlike a slave or junior member of a compound they were always assured of a groundnut farm and full access to their earnings.

The erosion of slavery in Weil's opinion gradually led to the emergence of ex-slaves as a capitalized market-orientated class of farmers, as they became involved in groundnut production.[87] Abolition increased the flow of Strange Farmers on an unprecedented scale: migrants as groundnut farmers on their own plots as well as being labourers for their hosts became essential for the further expansion of the groundnut trade. Earlier in 1894 Ozanne estimated that over 1,000 migrants were on the North Bank, principally around the wharf towns such as Katchang, Kaur, Ballangar, Ker Alieu and Niamaru, and these strangers were estimated to have produced 1,250 tons of nuts in the 1893–94 season.[88] Ozanne went on to estimate the value of these migrants to The Gambia, and in doing he gives further insights into the way the merchants and traders operated.[89] Ozanne noted that the 2s 0d per bushel they received was paid half in local pagns and half in imported goods on which duty had been paid. If one took the duty paid on imported goods, together with the export duty on nuts and Strange Farmer rents, then each stranger was worth 9s to the government. But Ozanne observed traders

[87] Weil, 1984, op. cit.
[88] CO 87/146 Ozanne, 6th Jan. 1894.
[89] RHL Micro Afr. 485, The Gambia Annual Report for the North Bank, 1893–4.

doubled the price of their imported goods, so payment for a bushel in fact was only 6d, plus the balance in *pagns*. As elsewhere in West Africa this was the reason why merchants liked the barter trade; goods avoided cash advances from banks, while the export of nuts was a means of repatriating their profits on imported goods without the necessity and cost of exporting specie or using bank transfers. The use of barter goods and the prices they fixed vis à vis ground-nuts gave them considerable latitude compared with using specie. However barter and cloth currency were nearing extinction as a medium of exchange, assisted by the demand for licenses and taxes to be paid in coin, and the Strange Farmers' long held preference for the 5 franc piece.

The Administration's view of Strange Farmers as a means of expanding production is re-iterated by Sangster, who in 1898 reported some 700 Strange Farmers in the South Bank whom he believed were of "considerable significance, more so since the people have in large measure lost their slaves": he went on to estimate strangers had grown at least 1,700 tons of nuts.[90] Later in 1903 the Annual Report suggests that The Gambia was receiving on average 6,000 migrants every year, and from this point onward an annual estimate was made of the number of Strange Farmers based on the rents received.[91] The numbers of migrants from 1903 up to the First World War varied between 4,000 and 6,000, and in 1904 Griffith com-mented that strangers took about double the quantity of land culti-vated by local farmers.[92] Once again, again these comments are a salutary reminder of one of the deficiencies of theories which assume that the export trade developed without significant increases in pop-ulation. Migrant labour systems throughout West Africa, of which the Strange Farmer system was one of the oldest, were the means of an effective seasonal (and often permanent) transfer of population from the interior non-commercial areas towards the coastal margins and valleys, where export crops were being expanded.

But the Strange Farmer system was not just expanded by the inward movements of men from Senegal, Mali and Guinea, but also by increasing numbers of young Gambian men; and here there was no net gain of labour, but rather a redistribution of labour. We have

---

[90] CO 87/156 G.H. Sangster, 29th July 1898.
[91] Annual Report, 1903.
[92] CO 87/171 Griffith, 13th June 1904.

Fig. 4.5: *Local groundnut prices 1903–1909*

| Trade Season | Price per Bushel Wharftowns+ | Price per Bushel Non-wharf Towns |
|---|---|---|
| 1902–3 | 1s. 6d. | 1s. 3d. |
| 1903–4 | 1s. 1½d. | 9d. |
| 1904–5 | 1s. 4½d. | 1s. 2d. |
| 1905–6 | 1s. 11½d. | 1s. 5d. |
| 1906–7 | 1s. 8½d. | 1s. 4d. |
| 1907–8 | 1s. 10½d. | 1s. 4d. |
| 1908–9 | 1s. 5½d. | 1s. 2½d. |

+ Places where ocean steamers can go—Bathurst, McCarthy Is., as well as Ballangar, Kudang, Kaur, Kuntaur, Nianimaru, Tendaba, Tubacolon, Albreda, Jowera.

already noted the local migration of 'Jollofs' and liberated Africans into wet season groundnut farming around Bathurst in the 1860s, but as the 20th century progressed reports makes more mention of the numbers of Gambians who shifted from their home areas to farm groundnuts. It would appear the loosening of domestic ties was not just confined to slaves, but had a knock-on effect to include unmarried males, who went farming to secure control over the returns to their own labour. And, importantly, an increasingly monetized economy, together with seasonal absence meant many young men both Gambians and non-Gambians gave money rather than labour as bridewealth. Thus it would appear that in the early years of the 20th century there was a general increase in labour mobility, greatly influenced by abolition, partly by taxation and the wider use of specie, which seasonally shifted workers towards the most prolific areas of production, especially those close by the wharf towns where prices for nuts were higher. The Annual Report for the North Bank for 1907 noted that Strangers preferred to plant around the factories, especially Ballangar and Kaur, where prices were 1s 6d per bushel, compared with 1s 3d elsewhere.[93] (Fig. 4.5)

The extension of colonial rule by the establishment of the Protectorate, as well as the formation of French West Africa created conditions for the expansion of the groundnut trade, and a further shift towards a dependency on one export crop. But economic and political forces did not exist within an environmental vacuum; climate

---

[93] RHL Micro Afr. 485, The Gambia, Annual Report for the North Bank, 1907.

and ecology cannot be ignored. Yet neither can climate be seen as
an independent variable; it was mediated through the larger structural forces affecting the groundnut trade as well as colonial policies. As we have mentioned before, it was the interaction of the
market for groundnuts, labour supply, credit, food importing and
environment which were crucial for the groundnut trade; and the
pace and incidence of change were often geared to specific moments,
or periods when there was either a positive or negative convergence
of these forces.

*Groundnut production and environmental disturbance*

The opening years of colonial rule from 1893 to 1913 give a good
indication of the way groundnut production and environmental circumstances were inextricably linked, which at times were further
complicated by price-fixing and the suspension of credit by the merchants. In the mid-19th century, reports, minutes and memos had
observed the effects of poor rainfall years, but by the late 19th century it is clear that annual rainfall variability was not the only concern. The annual rainfall of The Gambia was certainly erratic, but
it was gradually realized that the *seasonal* distribution of rainfall, and
the *geographical* variability along the river also mattered, as well as
the problem of floods. In general this is an important point that is
frequently overlooked when assessing rainfall totals, as well as the
difference between meteorological drought and agricultural drought.
Also, pests importantly affected both food and groundnuts and, as
with rainfall crops were affected differentially which was why farmers refused to abandon totally their crop mixtures geared to specific
local ecological niches. Clinging to trusted methods and traditional
crops was as much a form of resistance as groundnut hold-ups. But
the effects of environmental disturbance became magnified as the
Gambia moved to a greater dependence on groundnuts.

By the 1890s the better than average rainfall years that began in
1875 were coming to an end, and in 1892 producers experienced
moderate rains, as well as a cattle epidemic which reduced manure
inputs. In the same year locusts destroyed huge quantities of rice
and corn,[94] while in 1893 the worst damage that farmers experienced

---

[94] CO 87/143 Llewelyn to Ripon, 23rd March 1893.

came from excessive rains; in particular quite unexpected downpours occurred in December of that year. At Bathurst 0.43 inches (10.75 mm) of rain was recorded for December and there was an even higher rainfall up River, where Basse had 8 days of continuous rain.[95] The late rains destroyed large amounts of groundnuts after they had been pulled, which reduced the 1893–94 crop to 20,010 tons. The Administration blamed the farmers for lifting the nuts too early, whereas farmers traditionally erred on the side of caution, as when nuts were left in the ground too long they became difficult to pull, which reduced the yield. The season's groundnuts were of poor quality, and the traders refused to buy spoiled nuts so many farmers sowed them in the 1894 planting season: only half the seeds germinated and the rains stopped too soon, which consequently depressed the 1894–95 output to 10,006 tons, an all time low.[96] In response to a petition from the merchants, the government reduced the export duty in 1894 from 6s.8d to 4s per ton, which was an example of the government tinkering with tariffs (as in 1880), and it simply led to an increase in import duties to off-set lost revenue.[97]

Meanwhile in both the North and South Bank, the Commissioners reported that locusts had destroyed the first two sowings of corn, although in South Bank the rice seemed to be fair.[98] The combination of a failure of corn and groundnuts in 1894 saw many people suffering distress, and Ozanne reported that in North Bank people were reduced to living off roots and berries in the rains, until they could harvest the first corn crop.[99] People also resorted to selling their jewelry, which they were taking to Bathurst together with any *pagns* they had left, and used the proceeds to buy small quantities of rice at hugely inflated prices. As Ozanne remarked, "the traders are stocking-up on pagns at very low prices and in due course will make a killing".[100] People were literally living from hand to mouth, as they sold household resources little by little. The knock-on effect of food shortage meant that many were too weak to plant groundnuts and cotton in the later part of the wet season. Sitwell on the

[95] RHL Micro Afr, 485, Annual Reports for North Bank and South Bank, 1894.
[96] Annual Report, North Bank, 1895, op. cit.
[97] CO 87/125 Llewelyn to Ripon 1094: 13th April 1895.
[98] RHL Micro Afr. 485, Annual Reports for the North Bank and South Bank, 1895.
[99] Ibid.
[100] Ibid.

South Bank observed that many small towns were near starvation, and one encountered bands of women and children looking for work, including some who had come in from Senegal.[101] Total disaster was averted, as on a number of occasions, because Gambians were able to fall back on foraging, and had sufficient entitlements through the sale of personal possessions and animals to ensure they could stave-off famine. However, on the South Bank there were signs of adaptation by producers, as they diversified food crops in the face of two bad years, and Sitwell noted considerable amounts of cassava being planted.[102] Cassava was adopted because it is a root crop and considered immune to locusts, as well as growing under a wider range of rainfall conditions.

The situation was slow to improve, and in 1895–96 Ozanne estimated that groundnut yields were 40% down in North Bank, where losses were especially large in some areas as increased amounts had been planted to try and compensate for last year's losses. The situation for a majority of households in North Bank was serious: they had sold many of their assets in the previous year, and now the merchants and traders were unwilling to advance credit as they had made heavy losses on the previous crop. Ozanne reported that most people were living on one meal per day until the first *coos* (millet and sorghum) was ready.[103] Food was available, in the form of imported rice, but few had sufficient entitlements to access it, and those who had saw them dwindle as shortages persisted. Meanwhile the Administration had decided to try and improve the quality of the groundnut crop by importing 40 tons of seeds from Rufisque in Senegal, and distributing them to farmers on the basis of one measure of 42 lbs being repaid at the rate of 64 lbs.[104] The Governor impressed upon the headmen that this was *not* to be seen as a precedent, and he ordered farmers in future to deposit seed nuts in barns under the headman's custody before selling commenced. Apparently the normal practice was for traders to take the last 'handful' of nuts from farmers at 2s 0d per bushel, and then sell them back next season at 6s or higher.[105] But most producers ignored the injunction

[101] Annual Report, South Bank, 1895 op. cit.
[102] Ibid.
[103] RHL Micro Afr. 485, The Gambia, Annual Report for the North Bank, 1896.
[104] CO 87/149 min. no 6248 11th April, 1895: CO 87/149 Ozanne to Llewelyn, 27th July 1895.
[105] CO 87/149, Llewelyn to Ripon, 13th April 1895.

and kept their own seeds, and the seed storage scheme did not really take-off until 1901.

The large surge in planting in 1895–6 according to Ozanne proceeded "to the exclusion of food supply".[106] Confidence had been restored partly in the belief that another bad year was unlikely, and merchants and traders began to give out credit. The groundnut crop struggled to reach 12,101 tons, but this was further improved in the 1896–97 season when 20,279 tons were exported. In 1897 Ozanne was able to report that for the first time since 1892 all crops were good, and there was probably sufficient *coos* (millet and guinea corn) to last over, and he added that more time could be spent on nut production.[107] Because the *coos* harvest was so good, merchants were giving-out big advances of food for Strange Farmers, together with seed nuts and mosquito curtains, although the government warned traders they would receive no help if they couldn't recover their debts.[108] In order to improve production further, the government gave strict orders to the chiefs that groundnuts were not to be pulled until the Travelling Commissioner had arrived back after the rains, so avoiding damage from late rains.[109]

By 1897 conditions seemed to have improved and groundnut exports gradually climbed to 35,085 tons in the 1899–1901 season, but any general improvement hides sporadic localized difficulties experienced by producers along both banks of the river. For example, locusts struck again in the North Bank in 1898, where Ozanne recommended that trenches should be dug into which the hoppers could be driven, and then burnt.[110] Ozanne also reported that corn and rice were short in some districts and merchants were supplying whole towns with rice at 16s per 90 lb bag. If farmers had no cash, then they repaid their rice debt next season in groundnuts with the *alkalos* and headmen accepting responsibility for repayments.[111] Locusts were not necessarily a universal menace as they did not attack groundnuts, a fact which was seized upon by the Administration in order to promote the expansion of the crop. The Administration's real

---

[106] Annual Report for the North Bank, 1896, op. cit.
[107] RHL Micro Afr. 485, The Gambia, Annual Report for the North Bank 1897.
[108] Ibid.
[109] RHL Micro Afr. 485, The Gambia. Annual Report, North Bank, 1902–3.
[110] RHL Micro Afr. 485, The Gambia, Annual Report for the North Bank, 1898.
[111] Ibid.

concern about food shortages were expressed by Ozanne in his report
on the prospects for 1898–99, when he observed that the affected
districts were unlikely to be able to take as many Strange Farmers
as usual.[112]

Matters came to a head once again in the 1900–1901 season. In
the previous trading season of 1899–1900 the prices offered to producers were particularly good, between 2s and 3s per bushel, principally because the nuts were of good quality, while at the same
time the Senegalese crop was small.[113] This was the highest price
paid for 20 years and it encouraged producers to cultivate and plant
large areas, but alas the rainfall was less than average and a large
crop with light shells fetched much lower prices, as little as 1s 0d
per bushel. The 1900–1901 season was also affected by locusts and
large amounts of corn were destroyed, a situation exacerbated by
the traders refusing to give rice on credit, and many people were
short of food.[114] The refusal of the merchants to give credit was
another blow for producers, which together with the holding of prices,
was an integral part of the formation of the Merchant Combine in
1900, which we describe shortly. Once again people pawned household goods, took to wearing rice bags, as they sold their clothing
and relied on the bush for roots and berries to supplement their
meager diets.[115] As the merchants refused to help, so the government stepped in and countered the effects of the Combine by distributing 4,000 bags of rice on credit, as well as groundnut seeds.[116]
This intervention was a momentous turning point in the groundnut
trade; rice imports jumped to 86,000 cwts, and imports continued
at high levels in subsequent years to offset environmental disturbances and to feed the rising number of Strange Farmers. (Fig. 4.6)
The government distribution of rice and seeds added a new dimension to the credit system as a means of underpinning exports in
times of crisis, and arguments about rice and seed nut distribution
began to dominate the Administration's thinking on agricultural policies, for example, the possibility of irrigated agriculture was discussed.

The 1902–03 season saw a return to better conditions and the
groundnut crop rose steeply to 45,477 tons in 1903, but the old

[112] Ibid.
[113] Annual Report, 1900.
[114] Annual Report 1901.
[115] Ibid.
[116] Ibid.

Fig. 4.6: *Gambian rice imports by value, amount and source 1890–1912*

| Year | Amount cwts | Value £ Sterling | Source |
|------|------------|------------------|--------|
| 1890 | 16,373 | 7,823 | Great Britain; France |
| 1891 | 28,833 | 13,919 | Great Britain; France |
| 1892 | 26,912 | 14,762 | |
| 1893 | 40,840 | 20,471 | |
| 1894 | 51,401 | 24,409 | |
| 1895 | 26,000 | 10,656 | |
| 1896 | 24,297 | 9,904 | |
| 1897 | 29,426 | 13,460 | |
| 1898 | 79,208 | 38,222 | |
| 1899 | 35,662 | 16,050 | |
| 1900 | 53,507 | 25,136 | France; Great Britain; Germany |
| 1901 | 86,636 | 38,372 | France; Great Britain; Germany |
| 1902 | 39,481 | 15,776 | France; Great Britain; Germany |
| 1903 | 49,841 | 22,463 | France; Great Britain; Germany |
| 1904 | 54,015 | 22,699 | France; Great Britain; Germany |
| 1905 | 52,769 | 23,185 | France; Great Britain; Germany |
| 1906 | 121,235 | 52,364 | France; Great Britain; Germany |
| 1907 | 141,776 | 71,813 | Great Britain; Germany; France |
| 1908 | 68,234 | 31,584 | France; Germany; Great Britain |
| 1909 | 138,532 | 85,618 | Germany; Great Britain; France |
| 1910 | 101,121 | 46,006 | France; Germany; Great Britain |
| 1911 | 125,681 | 62,358 | Germany; Great Britain; France |
| 1912 | 138,532 | 85,618 | Germany; Great Britain; France |

*Source*: Blue Books

problems of groundnut crop failure and food shortages re-appeared in 1906 and 1908. By this time, food distribution, the control of groundnut farming and trading required further Travelling Commissioners, and new administrative areas. (Fig. 4.3) In 1905–1906, the new Commissioner for MacCarthy Island was reporting groundnuts were affected by widespread December rains: in Georgetown 2.72 inches of rain fell in December while in South Bank rain was almost continuous from December 2nd to the 8th.[117] These late rains spoiled a very large groundnut crop after it had been lifted, and prices dropped by 50%. At the end of 1906 late rains again proved a problem, especially for the early millets in North Bank, which

---

[117] RHL Micro Afr. 485, The Gambia, Annual Reports for the South Bank and M.I.D. Provinces, 1906.

began to sprout after they had been cut and laid on the ground awaiting collection. On the other hand the late rains benefited the rice crop which was good, but the Commissioner lamented that, "so little is grown, as it is a women's crop and unfortunately extremely labour intensive".[118]

The failure of groundnuts and corn in 1906–7 due to a very low rainfall at a time when merchant credit had been suspended, prompted the government to issue a huge amount of rice on credit; 8,500 bags.[119] In MacCarthy Island alone 2,303 bags of rice were distributed at 12s 6d per bag, while the groundnut failure led to a demand from the chiefs for double the quantity of seed nuts being issued (9,460 bushels).[120] The issue of seed nuts seems to have paid-off, as the 1908–09 crop was the highest on record for The Gambia, some 53,000 tons. Thus despite the warning in 1894 that producers must not expect assistance in times of distress, the Administration from 1908 to 1931 annually issued seed nuts as a matter of policy to try and produce a bigger and better crop, which further expanded the credit system. The heavy December rains of 1906 also led to the introduction of new legislation regarding the lifting and storing of groundnuts. All producers after harvest had to stack unbeaten groundnuts on platforms one foot above the ground thatched with palm leaves and grass: failure to do so led to fines, and or imprisonment, and some initial resistance was reported from North Bank.[121]

From 1908 to 1912 climatic conditions were not unduly adverse, and the outbreaks of pest and plague were localized. While it was true that prices fluctuated, record exports of groundnuts were being achieved which peaked at 67,404 tons in 1913, when the South Bank Commissioner also reported record corn harvests.[122] Some localized damage to corn occurred in McCarthy Island Division due to a previously unknown insect locally called 'lem' and rice had to be issued in 1911–12.[123] But in general food crops were good, and if rice was poor this was offset by excellent corn crops.

---

[118] RHL, Micro Afr. 485. The Gambia. Annual Report for the North Bank Province, 1907.
[119] Annual Report, 1906.
[120] RHL Micro Afr. 485, The Gambia, Annual Report for M.I.D., 1907.
[121] Annual Report, 1908.
[122] RHL Micro Afr. 485, The Gambia, Annual Report for the South Bank Province, 1913.
[123] RHL Micro Afr. 485, The Gambia, Annual Report for South Bank Province 1912.

*The Merchant Combine*

A slight improvement in environmental conditions, especially a better seasonally distributed rainfall around 1908 may have been propitious, but the boom in groundnut exports from 1909 onwards was not simply a product of the weather; the weakening of the Merchant Combine also helped it. The Combine had been in operation since 1900 and it was at its strongest from 1902–1909, finally ending in 1913. It was a mutual agreement among French and English firms to fix prices and check competition, which they claimed, "was enriching sub-traders and Natives only".[124] The five largest traders, The Bathurst Trading Company, Maurel et Prom, Maurel et Frères, Compagnie Française d'Afrique Occidentale and J. Barrrière agreed in effect to abandon the 1857 Anglo-French(trade) Convention, and in addition to price fixing they stopped giving credit to producers, employed traders only at wharf towns, as well as 'abolishing all presents to natives'. The Combine was a reaction to the implementation of *tong* by native producers, which made the collection of debts very difficult, especially if they were paid in groundnuts The merchants in effect tried to coerce producers into accepting their prices, as well as reducing the risks associated with the credit system operated by a multitude of small traders.[125]

The 'ring' or Combine had diverse consequences for producers, and should be contextualized within the run of adverse environmental conditions and low groundnut prices discussed above, which obtained from 1900 to 1907. As the Combine stopped large-scale credits the Governor used the merchants' initiative to further push for the abandonment of cloth currency in favour of specie. And while the merchants now agreed with the Administration on this point, it is clear barter was not entirely stopped. The Administration wished to push the specie issue as it wanted taxes paid in coin not produce, as frequently they either had to take produce or wait for cash. The suspension of credit inevitably increased the amount of specie

---

[124] CO 87/163 Ozanne to Denton, 27th June 1901.
[125] Government intervention in export markets, traders 'pools' and 'rings' were considered during the slump of 1930–31, especially after the cocoa hold-ups in the Gold Coast, which led to the Bartholomew Plan of 1931 and Nowell Commission of 1938, although no action was taken until after the Second World War.

in circulation, and imports of specie rose from £19,266 in 1896 to £155,304 in 1903.[126]

The decision not to employ traders except at wharves and wharf towns meant a reduction in the number of native traders, and in places bereft of their services the producers were faced with taking their groundnuts to the nearest point of sale, or if traders were still operating in the remoter areas they had to accept lower prices. As Ozanne remarked in 1901 this was "a sudden blow to the Natives, as not only were they deprived of 'presents' on delivering their produce, but they had to transport nuts to the wharf, in some instances at a cost of 6d per measure".[127] By 1902 the number of traders' licenses had been reduced, and the sub-trader had almost disappeared. In Upper River, Stanley reported that farmers were looking around for donkeys to partially solve their transport problems, while Denton the governor fearing the effects on the groundnut trade produced an abortive scheme for the use of wheeled carts.[128]

The most important effect of the Combine for farmers was the lowering of groundnut prices, and a fall in incomes to levels less than under conditions of active competition. At the same time that nut prices were lowered, a run of bad rains required the purchase of imported rice at exorbitant prices, either for Strange Farmers or to supply domestic needs. This underpins the contention that under certain conditions having largely neglected food crops in favour of groundnuts, producers derived limited material gain after being drawn into the overseas export economy. The terms of trade had now significantly shifted against producers, and in addition they were paying newly implemented taxes.

The response of producers to poor prices initially was one of resistance. The dispatches and Commissioners reports from 1902–1909 contain many references to complaints from chiefs and their people about poor prices, measures, and overcharging for rice. From 1902 to 1909 the prices of groundnuts varied locally from 9d to 1s 11½d. (Fig. 4.5). Not only were prices a source of contention, but, as in the past, the size of the measure used. Complaints were recorded by the Commissioner of MacCarthy Island in 1901, that were confirmed when he measured the size of the 'bushel': it measured

---

[126] BA Class 54/157, Administrator's reports: 1899 and 1904.
[127] CO 87/163, Ozanne to Denton, 27th June, 1901.
[128] CO 87/169 Denton to SS 18th July 1903.

17 by 15 inches for the payment of nuts in goods, and 18 by 18 inches for payments in cash. Thus it would appear traders and their agents were still pressing for barter trade, rather than the government's preferred coinage, because the former was more profitable and a greater surplus could be extracted from producers. Complaints were withdrawn when the weighing scale replaced the bushel: at first it appeared a fairer method of purchase, until it became clear many producers did not understand the weighing scales and could be cheated. When producers became aware of the way in which scales could be used to cheat them, they responded by adding soil and gravel to the nuts to increase the weight.[129]

As to prices, a rough indication of the relationship between local and international levels is given in a report of 1899 sent by Llewelyn to Chamberlain, the Secretary of State in London.[130] It appears most groundnuts went to France, with some being sold in Holland, but the burden of the dispatch was the profitability of the trade to foreign oilseed mills which Llewelyn thought might be replicated with advantage in England. Apparently Gambian nuts bought from producers at £6 per ton (1s 5 ½d a bushel) gave 80 gallons of oil which was worth 2s to 3s per gallon, (equivalent to £8–£12 per ton), which together with the sales of oil cake for fodder led Llewelyn to believe this was a profitable trade. Later in 1905 Governor Denton commented on the price of £5 10s 0d per ton, noting that large quantities of nuts had been sold to be delivered at Marseilles and Bordeaux at £10 0s 0d per ton. Merchants paid £1 per ton freight which "still leaves them with a profit on the face of it of £3 10 0d on the local price of £5 10s 0d per ton".[131]

These reported prices were based on the highest paid during the buying season, something unknown to producers at the beginning of the season, so they had to decide whether to accept opening-prices or wait for an improvement and ultimately risk lower ones. Such was the case in Sandu in 1903 when opposition to a price of 1s 4 ¼d turned into forced sales later at lower prices.[132] The Strange Farmers ever anxious to return home, or move on to other employment generally accepted opening-prices, and in Fulladu in 1903

---

[129] RHL Micro Afr. 485, The Gambia, Annual Reports for MacCarthy Island Division, 1901 and 1913.
[130] CO 87/158, Llewelyn to Chamberlain, 26th April 1899.
[131] CO 87/168, Denton to SS, 14th Jan. 1905.
[132] CO 87/169 Stanley to Denton, 18th July 1903.

Strange Farmers did well considering prices dropped to 9d by the end of the season.[133] In Upper River in January 17th 1903, traders complained to the Commissioner *tong* had been in force at Kanube for 22 days in an attempt to try and force prices up to 1s 5p per 28 lbs, and he was shown a letter from the houses in the Combine instructing no price rises; the fixed price was to be maintained. By January 25th trade had stopped in Wuli, Faraba, and Madina. At Fattatenda the traders begged the Commissioner to induce sales, but he refused; instead he called meetings of chiefs, traders and people where he had some limited success in persuading producers to sell.[134] This situation appears many times in dispatches and indicates that the Commissioners attempted to act as brokers between producers and the firms. But in the long run the firms usually won.

The institution of *tong* was the most immediate and obvious response to the Combine, although it had been one of the reasons the Combine was started. Denton had some sympathy with the producers: when writing to the Secretary of State in 1904 he deplored the low prices, as he knew the pooling of the crop by the five principal firms in the Combine deprived the producer of competition, and forced down prices to the extent that people were getting only 75% of what might have been achieved.[135] It appears that the Combine was a calculated 'squeeze' on the terms of trade. No doubt the Administration's sympathy was partly motivated by the possible effects of low prices on government revenues, and it is difficult to decide whether they actually depressed production. Hitherto we have suggested that low prices and adverse terms of trade were compensated for by increased acreage, but in the absence of credit under the Combine it seems likely local producers were reluctant to commit more land and energy to increased areas of cultivation to offset low prices. But this was not necessarily so for Strange Farmers, who by now were a key element in production. Their efforts kept production around 35,000 tons during the years of the Combine, however there is no doubt (as we shall see later) once competition was resumed production surged.

Between 1905 and 1907 the merchants were extremely unpopular: a report of 1905 shows that farmers were linking low groundnut prices, tax demands, and the need to buy increasingly expensive

---

[133] GNA 2/40, Upper River District: Commissioner's Diary for 1903.
[134] Ibid.
[135] CO 87/171, Denton to SS 17th Feb. 1904.

imported rice from merchants, despite the amounts distributed by
the Administration which was never enough to cover all requirements.[136] The same report indicates that disenchantment and resistance were leading to violence and robbery against traders at wharf
towns, which was not surprising given the escalating costs of rice
and fixed groundnut prices.[137] Outbreaks of violence caused Denton
in January 1905 to address possibly the biggest meeting ever held
in North Bank, when people from 23 villages assembled at Albreda.
Denton in his report to the Secretary of State, admits in defense of
their criminal acts that a 100 lbs net bag of rice costing 9s 9d at
Bathurst was being sold by Maurel et Prom's agent for 15s 3d, compared with the government price of 11s 0d.[138] And, in a few instances
credit was being offered at the rate of a 90 lbs net bag against
groundnuts repayable from between 24s to 32s, Yet once again
Denton warned about the dangers of *tong*, and that although he
would not intervene *tong* should not be forced upon people by the
chiefs.[139] After the meeting the warning on *tong* was accepted and
producers began taking 1s 3d per bushel, but this price was rejected
in Upper River. Furthermore, in December 1906 the chiefs also
decided to prevent groundnuts being brought in from Senegal, where
there was also *tong*.[140] Thus in Upper River there were signs of solidarity and resistance, but interference with trade was intolerable to
Denton, who again warned the chiefs about the prevention of sales,
and the fining of those who did so.[141]

Frequently the Administration's attitude was seen as being anti-
*tong*, especially Denton's opposition to anything which smacked of
coercion, yet Denton remained a popular governor because of his
perceived generosity in distributing seed nuts, giving out rice, and
his scorn for the Merchant Combine. A measure of his popularity
and the regard in which he was held was shown in 1907, when the
Gambian chiefs wrote to 'the King of England' confirming their view
of Denton, especially on his distribution of rice which attempted to
undercut the traders' inflated prices.[142] Indeed, it may have been

---

[136] CO 87/173, Stanley to Denton 2nd Jan. 1905.
[137] Ibid.
[138] CO 87/173, Denton to SS, 3rd Mar. 1905.
[139] Ibid.
[140] CO 87/177, Denton to SS, 6th Feb. 1907.
[141] Ibid.
[142] CO 87/178, 12th Sept. 1907. Translation of Arabic letter received by the
Governor from the Head Chiefs and Headmen in The Gambia.

government rice sales during this period, which kept the population not only from starvation, but also politically in check.

During the early 1900s *tong* was imposed frequently, but never long enough to have the desired effect of improving prices, and the government while strong on rhetoric and remonstration had no intention of intervening directly in trader—producer conflicts. Inescapably, revenues ultimately depended on the evacuation of groundnuts by the merchants, whose position was far stronger than the producers. The government's position was equivocal: it deplored the Combine's actions, yet liked the removal of merchant credit as it was consonant with a belief that the poor should live within their means. And, stopping credit was an integral part of the agreement on price-fixing. Unlike the credit crisis of the mid-1880s, merchants were owed relatively small amounts, which were not at risk if prices were low: on the other hand producers had few debts and could hold back groundnuts without fear of non-payment of credit arrears, but the weakness in their position was they had to buy rice and pay taxes.

The government's intervention through the distribution of rice was crucial, and the Combine may have been ultimately undermined by this action. Food distribution was certainly emerging as an important method of political and economic management by the government, and in the sphere of food distribution at moments of crisis it was prepared to act in its own interests, not the merchants. But it must also be remembered too that the merchants made handsome profits from credit sales of imported goods, which were dampened by low producer prices, thus for them it was a 'trade-off' between the profits on groundnuts, and profits on imported goods. However, from the early 1900 onwards *tong*, food distribution and price-fixing had become established as part of the groundnut trade. (Fig. 4.7)

If the Combine had failed, so had the hold-ups; moreover production was maintained and at times increased, while as we have shown new areas were opened-up for groundnut farming. Of particular importance was the role of Strange Farmers, whose numbers were substantial by the end of the 19th century, and a majority of whom came from remoter areas where groundnuts were not cultivated commercially, or where prices were lower. These migrants demonstrate the ability of capital to benefit from a mobile semi-casual labour force, which was the means of keeping prices low. In 1903–4 trade season Strange Farmers ignored *tong* and sold nuts early, well aware of the Governor's stand on the freedom of producers

Fig. 4.7: *Producer resistance, Government and Merchant Interventions, 1867–1932*

| Year | Producers | Government | Merchants |
|---|---|---|---|
| 1867–68 | *Tong*-Casamance | | Bushel size reduced |
| 1873 | *Tong*, N. Bank | | Bushel size reduced |
| 1884/6 | *Tong*, N. Bank<br>S. Bank | | |
| 1884 | Nuts taken to Senegal: better prices | | |
| 1894/5 | | | Credit suspended |
| 1894/5 | | Seed nuts distributed | |
| 1897 | | | Credit restored |
| 1900 | | Rice distributed | Price fixing<br>Credit suspended |
| 1903 | *Tong*. Upper River | | Combine formed |
| 1905 | *Tong*. Upper River<br>Outbreaks of violence | | |
| 1906/7 | | Rice/seed nuts distributed | |
| 1913 | | | Combine collapses<br>Price fixing ends<br>Credit restored |
| 1914 | | Rice/seeds distributed | |
| 1918/19 | | Rice distributed<br>Floods | |
| 1921/22 | *Tong*<br>Outbreaks of violence | De-monetization | Credit suspended<br>Price fixing |
| 1923 | | Trading season prescribed | |
| 1925 | | Rice debt cancelled | Intermittent price fixing until 1933 |
| 1927/28 | *Tong* | | |
| 1927 | | Rice distribution | |
| 1928/29 | | Rice/seeds distributed | |
| 1929/31 | *Tong* | | |
| 1932 | | Yard Tax increased | |

to accept or ignore *tong*. The Annual Report for 1903 believed strangers cultivated double the amount of groundnut land compared with local farmers, and in 1907 Sproston in Upper River suggested that Strange Farmers did most of the planting.[143] However, Sproston feared depressed prices might turn away migrants, but the figures show that no such thing happened: in Fulladu West in 1908, some 3,016 came compared with 1,500 in 1907.[144] Fluctuating numbers were also related to food availability and environmental conditions, but the attitudes of Strange Farmers tend to confirm the view that under certain conditions such as the Combine, migrant workers worked in the interests of capital, as they undercut producer prices and lacked any solidarity with local peoples. Despite the supportive behaviour of Strange Farmers the Combine failed; not because of producer resistance, but arguably because of government rice distribution which lessened the effects of low prices and bad weather. And, the Administration was aware of the valuable role of Strange Farmers, whose presence depended on an adequate supply of food.

By the early 19th century the position of Gambian producers was clear: they were in the market, but not of the market. As producers they lacked knowledge and information about world commodity markets and prices, on which to base decisions: information came via the merchants and the government, both of whom had their own agenda. The merchants sought to maximize profits, the government to secure revenues and minimize the costs of administration. Producer prices varied from year to year and within any one season which made production a 'hand to mouth' affair. Farmers suffered the consequences of bad rainfall years and low prices especially when they coincided: in marginal years they experienced indebtedness, in the worst years severe undernourishment. The groundnut economy did alter farmers' access to exotic goods, and spasmodically raised their standard of living rather than leading to sustainable improvements. The episode of the Merchant Combine exposed the weak position of producers as well as the temporizing and ambivalent attitude of a government, whose investment in the colony was minimal.

---

[143] CO 87/178, Sproston to Denton, 14th July 1907.
[144] Ibid.

*Attempts at diversification*

Sensing the problems facing groundnut production the Administration made some effort to improve agriculture, primarily to the groundnut crop on which the colony's financial base rested. The importation of seed nuts and their distribution, together with injunctions on lifting and stacking groundnuts formed the chief thrust of intervention in the opening years of British rule. There was limited concern about the problems of plagues and pests, which so frequently affected the corn crop, and it is a matter for some speculation as to the extent to which the intensification of groundnuts actually contributed to these problems. The Commissioner for the South Bank in his Report for 1906 pointed out that long stretches of uninhabited bush in Central and Eastern Jarra limited the spread of plant disease;[145] and on another occasion similar comments were made about the spread of cattle epidemics.[146]

Apart from any environmental damage, the government as well as the merchants expressed their concern about the financial dependence of the colony on groundnuts and the associated imports of foodstuffs. Thus some attempts were made to diversify export production and food supply. In 1895 the merchants wrote to Governor Llewelyn (prompted by the abnormally heavy rainfall of 1893) pointing out the variability of output combined with price fluctuations on the world market demanded some attention be given to other products of commercial value.[147] In 1897 Llewelyn wrote to the Secretary of State about the lack of merchant interest in investment in agricultural production, despite the law and order brought by the Protectorate and suggested they should begin by considering the potential of the large tracts of river land suitable for rice, and that indigo and cotton had long been cultivated by local farmers.[148] Between 1897 and 1899 Llewelyn persisted with this theme, but the merchants were cautious: only the Bathurst Trading Company took up the challenge and in 1901 planted 3,500 coconut trees.[149] The idea seemed sound as prices for copra were good, but little came of

---

[145] RHL, Micro Afr. 485, The Gambia, Annual Report, South Bank Province, 1906.
[146] Ibid. Annual Report, South Bank Province, 1918.
[147] CO 87/145, Bathurst merchants to Llewelyn, 13th April 1895.
[148] CO 87/153, Llewelyn to Chamberlain, 24th May 1897.
[149] CO 87/165, Bathurst Trading Company to SS, 1901.

the scheme and marked the limit of mercantile investment in the
Gambia.

Cotton production as in many parts of West Africa had long been
a favourite scheme of Administrators. As early as 1862 Governor
D'Arcy sent samples of Gambian cotton back to London,[150] while
in 1902 the Governor reported the visit of an expert from the British
Cotton growers Association to advise on improved production.[151]
Despite the high hopes of the government, the extension of cotton
foundered on a misunderstanding of local markets; such as its price
vis à vis groundnuts, and the amount and timing of labour inputs.
As Stanley the Upper River Commissioner noted in 1903, groundnuts were more profitable in terms of the returns to labour per
acre.[152] And, the Annual Report for 1905 explained that local traders
paid 3d per lb for cotton compared with the merchants' offer of 1d
per lb.[153] The merchants price of 1d meant an income of £1 5s 0d
per acre from cotton, compared with £4 10s 0d per acre for groundnuts which involved approximately the same amount of work. What
the Administrators also seem to have misunderstood was that cotton not only competed with groundnuts, but also it hindered the
production of millets and sorghum the basic upland food crops. If
cotton is to be grown satisfactorily, it must be planted by July and
harvested in December, which means planting must have been com-
pleted on millets. Also, improved varieties of cotton were grown in
pure stands, which inhibited attempts at intercropping. Such misunderstandings were repeated subsequently in The Gambia, as well
as elsewhere in West Africa.

A longer term consequence of the move towards diversification
was the investigation of the possibilities of irrigated farming along
river Gambia. The idea of perennial cultivation using irrigation was
mooted in 1903, and represents the first exploration by the Gambian
authorities of a technically based development scheme as an answer
to the problem of how to increase groundnut production. Although
The Gambian scheme never went further than preliminary investigations, it represents the first irrigation initiative in British West
Africa. The authorities were aware of the indigenous irrigation of

---

[150] CO 87/74, D'Arcy to Newcastle, 24th Nov. 1862.
[151] Annual Report, 1902.
[152] CO 87/169, Stanley to Denton, 18th July 1903.
[153] Annual Report, 1905.

dry season crops in West Africa, which had a long history along the Niger and Senegal valleys and in Northern Nigeria. In addition to their knowledge of indigenous irrigation, Colonial administrators were well aware of the development of large barrages in the Sudan, India and Ceylon. By the 1900s the notion of introducing modern irriga-tion was a persistent feature of British and French policies in Africa, and was still extant in the post-colonial era.

It was Chamberlain as Secretary of State for the Colonies in 1900, who wrote to Denton suggesting that some of the Gambia's surplus revenue might be spent on irrigation.[154] The outcome was that Mr. Parker, an Irrigation Assistant from Ceylon visited The Gambia in 1902, and submitted reports during 1903.[155] The Gambian govern-ment initially hoped that irrigation might secure a second crop of groundnuts, but Parker reported that rice might be the thing, as local informants had told him that groundnuts occupied too much time to allow for a second groundnut crop in a year. Parker also reported that in the villages he visited there was a readiness to grow more rice if water could be supplied, as people wished to eat it, although they could not afford to buy it. On the other hand Governor Denton felt that if rice was the only product to benefit from the scheme, then "irrigation is not worth the candle"; pumping water as suggested from either side of the river above Ballangar would be too expensive.[156]

As a result of Denton' objections, Parker prepared another report based on a visit to Asyut in Egypt, which explored the possibilities of cotton and rice irrigation.[157] Parker observed that in The Gambia low yielding local varieties of cotton, which suffered from the effects of the dry season might be replaced by heavy yielding varieties of foreign cotton that in Egypt were cultivated on the same soils as Gambian millets. But the problem in The Gambia was that such fields were too high above the water level. However, in Egypt on saline soils along the river margins rice and cotton were grown on a three-year rotation in conditions similar to those found in The

---

[154] CO 87/161, minute no. 37951, 21st Nov. 1900.
[155] CO 87/168, Parker to Denton, *Report on Proposed Irrigation at The Gambia*, 31st Mar. 1903.
[156] Ibid. Encl. to Antrobus, minute no. 14935, 22nd May 1903.
[157] CO 87/228/5, Irrigation File: H. Parker, *Second Report on Irrigation in The Gambia*, 23rd Nov. 1903.

Gambia. Were such a scheme adopted in the lower Gambia, then a new cultivation system would have to be introduced for which an adequate labour supply would be essential, and the government might have to prepare the land and impose an irrigation levy, and employ local villagers as labourers. Parker identified the wetter end of MacCarthy Island as a possible site, and suggested three methods of irrigation; damming the river, reservoirs, and tanks and pumps. He concluded the latter the best option, with steam pumps on floating pontoons costing £78 7s 4d per 100 acres of rice and £106 5s 4d per 100 acres for cotton. Again nothing happened, as it was considered too expensive.

*Summary*

The establishment of the Protectorate in 1893 led to a number of changes along the river; principally new forms of taxation, and measures to speed the erosion of domestic slavery that need to be judged along with similar measures introduced in French West Africa. The decay of domestic slavery and the development of the Dakar-Bamako railway gave a major boost to the number of migrant farmers in Senegambia, which together with taxation stimulated the spread of groundnut cultivation into hitherto un-exploited areas. The British authorities were certainly aware of the necessity of sustaining, and if possible expanding groundnut production: this was the basis of The Gambia's financial self-sufficiency, and the crucial decision to distribute imported rice when producers were in difficulties bore witness to this concern.

By the first decade of the 20th century The Gambia was a primary export producer, heavily dependent on merchant credit and migrant labourers to supplement low population densities, albeit at the expense of rising food imports. Gambian producers were now embarked on a "roller coaster" economy, whose undulations were shaped by the world markets and environmental vicissitudes. Groundnut production had become something of a 'contested terrain' due to divergent perceptions and interpretations of what the groundnut economy constituted. For the Administration groundnuts were the basis of financial solvency, underpinned by a faith in the benefits of British commerce and justice. For the producers, the groundnut trade had led to transformations of work and household consumption, albeit in the face of uncertain groundnut prices, especially under the Merchant Combine. As for the migrants from the interior, the groundnut trade was a means of coping with the marginal economic conditions in their homelands. For the merchants the groundnut trade and the associated imports of food and trade goods were a particular niche for profit. And more often than not, merchant interest triumphed, albeit with peripheral trimming by the Administration.

CHAPTER FIVE

SUCCESS AND DISASTER, BOOM AND SLUMP:
THE GROUNDNUT TRADE, 1913–1922

The First World War has been regarded as a watershed in the social
and economic life of Britain, marking the ending of a Golden Age
of peace and stability. But more dispassionate analyses suggest that
pre-war Britain contained the seeds of social change, while the economy had begun to decline in the late 19th century in the face of
German and North American competition.[1] Yet the war was a cata-
clysmic event, which triggered transformations of political structures
and social attitudes that had an impact on British possessions not
directly involved in the conflict. Also, the colonies and their administrators began to feel the winds of change generated by the gath-
ering pace of 20th century science and technology, which led to the
emergence of new kinds of expertise and ideas about agriculture.

In The Gambia, the war and the aftermath significantly altered
the groundnut economy through their effect on international trade.
Initially the war disrupted the revival of trade following the end of
the Merchant Combine, and although production surged in 1915 to
a record, it was accompanied by low producer prices depressed by
the shortage of shipping and the disturbed state of the market. (Figs.
5.1 and 5.2). Not surprisingly in 1916 production was poor, but the
price of groundnuts rose and thereafter climbed to an all time high
in 1920, which reflected the post war shortages of oilseeds as well
as new sources of demand. Throughout the period 1913–1922 exports
reached new highs averaging 70,000 tons per annum, which were
achieved with the assistance of an unprecedented number of Strange
Farmers, some of whom were escaping conscription in French territories. The war also saw the collapse of the hegemony of the French
firms due to their inability to continue trading during the opening
months of the war. By 1919 Great Britain received 91% of Gambian
groundnuts by weight, compared with 2% in 1913.

---

[1] Thomson, D., 1981, *England in the Twentieth century*. Second Edition. London:
Penguin.

Fig. 5.1: *Volume of Gambian groundnut exports and value, together with local (f.o.b.) and UK (c.i.f.) prices and government finances, 1913–1923*

| Year | Groundnuts: Total Export | Total Value of Ground-nut Exports (F O B) | Approx price per ton (F O B) | UK (C I F) Price per ton | Reve-nue | Expen-diture |
|------|------|------|------|------|------|------|
| | Tons | £ | £ | £ | £ | £ |
| 1913 | 67,404 | 622,098 | 9.22 | 23.1 | 124,995 | 97,405 |
| 1914 | 66,885 | 650,461 | 9.72 | 15.8 | 85,421 | 120,921 |
| 1915 | 96,152 | 400,435 | 4.16 | 16.5 | 92,217 | 89,028 |
| 1916 | 46,366 | 506,098 | 10.91 | 28.0 | 103,019 | 83,217 |
| 1917 | 74,300 | 869,790 | 11.70 | 20.8 | 117,962 | 94,519 |
| 1918 | 56,490 | 800,319 | 14.16 | 32.0 | 113,304 | 88,703 |
| 1919 | 71,677 | 1,172,843 | 16.36 | 41.0 | 180,585 | 143,451 |
| 1920 | 84,037 | 2,322,032 | 27.63 | 45.0 | 268,788 | 171,160 |
| 1921 | 59,175 | 628,901 | 10.62 | 20.4 | 183,201 | 225,461 |
| 1922 | 64,800 | 780,889 | 12.05 | 21.7 | 204,244 | 430,312 |
| 1923 | 64,178 | 864,885 | 13.47 | 23.1 | 407,851 | 211,316 |

Fig. 5.2: *Gambian groundnut exports (tons) 1912–1923*

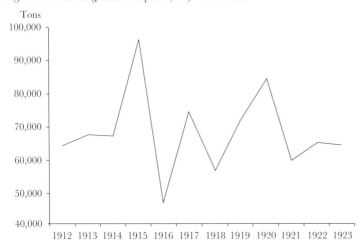

*Source*: Blue Books

The war was one of a cluster of structural and contingent events between 1913 and 1922, which shaped the fortunes of this small colony for many years afterwards. For example, this period saw a number of local and regional catastrophes which had immediate consequences for the groundnut trade: the great drought of 1913, the cattle epidemic of 1917, the influenza pandemic of 1918 and the climatic disturbances in 1918–1919. Collectively these events left their mark, especially on local food production. After the war the boom in groundnut production continued assisted by the extension of credit and food imports, but when prices collapsed in 1920 the groundnut trade fell into disarray culminating in a costly de-monetization of the currency.

These events from 1913–1922 provide the focus of this chapter, and illustrate how they accentuated the fluctuations in The Gambian economy, and the linkages between increased production, migration, credit and climate. Historically the general trend in production was upwards, but the experiental reality for many producers was the uncertainty of one year to the next. A sufficiency of food might be followed by a shortage of food; good prices were often quickly succeeded by low groundnut prices; credit and indebtedness were pervasive; and the government swayed between exhortation and censure to encourage or control producers. Meanwhile the merchants managed to steer a successful path amidst the pitfalls of world market prices and local contingences. This period was one of the most dispiriting episodes in the groundnut trade: it was marked not only by natural disasters, but also by commercial opportunism of the worst kind. In addition there were outbreaks of violence and administrative incompetence and temporizing: it was at some remove from the pious hopes of the early 19th century whereby commerce would inevitably promote civilization and the betterment of mankind.

### The 1913 drought

The outbreak of the Great War was preceded by one of the major droughts of the 20th century, which was widespread throughout Africa and Asia; and although The Gambia lies at the wetter Atlantic margins of the West African savanna, crops and cattle were seriously affected. Drought can be defined in three ways: meteorologically when there is a percentage departure from the expected amount of rainfall, hydrologically when surface or groundwater levels fall below average, and agriculturally when there is a shortage of water which inhibits crop growth.[2] In 1913–14 The Gambia, in common

---

[2] Mortimore, M., 1989, *Adapting to Drought*. Cambridge: CUP. Ch. 1.

with other parts of West Africa qualified on all three, but in terms of food shortages and famine which are processes rather than statistical events, it fared better than some of its neighbours. For example, detailed studies in Bakel in the middle Senegal basin have shown that people make distinctions between the short 'hungry season' of up to two months, famines which last 3 to 8 months and grand famines, which last over 12 months and affect two agricultural seasons.[3] In Bakel the abnormally low rainfall of 1913 affected two seasons, but evidence from The Gambia suggests there was a quicker recovery, an essential element in judging the severity of abnormally low rainfalls. Unlike the Bakel region The Gambia was not an area of out-migration; on the contrary historically it received migrant labour from Bakel, where the impact of the famine was exacerbated by the absence of males and consequently the elderly and young took longer to rehabilitate their farming systems and food stocks.

The details of the drought, its progression and aftermath are logged in the various reports and diaries of the Commissioners, and reflect better reporting as the Administration became established. This increased level of information makes it possible to catalogue environmental hazards and agricultural performance, which are shown from 1912 to 1934 in Fig. 5.3. All the accounts indicate the 1913 drought was a serious event, which affected the rice crop rather than groundnuts, leading the government to distribute rice to alleviate widespread food shortages. In the North Bank in 1913 the first planting of nuts was good, but thereafter the lack of rain affected food crops, and although in some areas corn, (especially sorghum) did fairly well, rice was a complete failure. By December the North Bank reported wells and swamps were drying up fast, while in Senegal water was being sold to non-locals as they passed through the villages.[4] In MacCarthy Island the story was the same; nuts were light, and rice and corn were failures. Once again, the people were living from hand to mouth and the rice advance of 5,400 bags at 11s 0d per 90lb bag saved the day.[5]

The most graphic account of the famine was given by Hopkinson, from South Bank, who alerted the Governor of likely food shortages

[3] Chastanet, M., 1983, 'Les crises de subsistances dans le villages Soninke du cercle de Bakel, de 1858–1945', *Cah. d'études Africaines*, vol. 23: 5–36.
[4] GNA 2/167, Travelling Commissioner's Diary, North Bank Province, Dec. 1913.
[5] RHL Micro Afr. 485, Annual Report, MacCarthy Island Province, 1913–14.

Fig. 5.3: *Harvests, Pests and Rainfall in The Gambia, 1912–1931*

| Year | Crop Millet | Sorghum | Rice | Groundnuts | Rainfall (inches) | Pest | Comments |
|------|------------|---------|------|-----------|-------------------|------|----------|
| 1912 | Very good | n.a. | Excellent | Very good | 33.39 (low) | | |
| 1913 | Good | Poor | Failed | Poor | 23.68 (very low) | Blight | |
| 1914 | Failed | n.a. | Very good | Good | 48.92 (early) | Caterpillars | |
| 1915 | Very good | n.a. | Fair | Good | 47.64 | | War, trade depression |
| 1916 | Poor | n.a. | Poor | Good | 38.02 (low) | | Trade revives |
| 1917 | Good | n.a. | Fair | Fair | 37.68 (low) | | |
| 1918 | n.a. | Failed | Failed* | n.a. | 54.03 (floods) | Blight | Influenza pandemic |
| 1919 | Failed | n.a. | Failed | Good | 39.23 (low) | Blight, caterpillars | Post-war boom |
| 1920 | Good | n.a. | Fair | Good | 34.22 (low) | | |
| 1921 | Poor | Poor | Poor | Good | 35.12 (low) | Aphids | Price collapse† |
| 1922 | Poor | Poor | Poor | Good | 45.71 | | Trade depression |
| 1923 | Good/fair | Poor | Good/fair | n.a. | 65.53 (floods) | | |
| 1924 | Good | Good | Good | Good | 54.46 | | |
| 1925 | Best in memory | Good | Good | Good | 44.77 | | |
| 1926 | Excellent | n.a. | Failed | Good | 35.05 (short) | | |
| 1927 | Failed | Failed | Very good | Poor | 60.55 (heavy, late) | Mildew | |
| 1928 | Poor | n.a. | Very good | Fair | 57.02 (late) | Mildew | |
| 1929 | Modest | n.a. | Good | Good | 52.30 | Locusts | |
| 1930 | Satisfactory | Failed | Very good | Poor | 47.86 (late) | Locusts | No trade† (tong) |
| 1931 | Good | Failed | Poor/fail | Poor | 30.95 (low, early) | Blight, locusts | No trade† (tong) |

*Notes:*   * This comment refers to Upper River rice only, as production of Lower River rice was moderate.
† These comments refer to groundnuts only.
n.a. No data available.

*Sources:* Public Record Office (Kew) *Annual Report on The Gambia*, 1912–33; Gambia National Archive (Banjul) *Commissioners' Annual Provincial Reports*, 1912–31 (some years are available at Rhodes House, Oxford).

in December 1913 when it was evident that summer rainfall had been insufficient.[6] Hopkinson, a doctor by training, joined the Gambian Administration in 1904, and on numerous occasions proved to be an acute observer. In his report of 1913–1914, he noted that:

> A very large proportion of the rice grounds were never under water at all for more than a few hours at a time immediately after rain, and that at only long intervals. In the Kiangs and Western Jarra I do not believe a grain was harvested, very little in Central Jarra and certainly not half the proper quantity anywhere else. . . . In the Upper River Province, I found the deficiency was much less, in some places negligable, owing no doubt to the fact that there all rice is grown close to the river and flooded directly from it, whereas throughout the greater part of the South Bank, it is the landward margin of the swamps which forms the rice fields, as the river is salt right up to Niamina. The crop therefore depends entirely on the swamps being filled directly by rainfall not an overflow of the river.[7]

Hopkinson went on to observe that "the grass was poor and as a dry as would be expected normally in two months time hence" (late February), which meant a decline in the cattle population and reduced manure inputs for the following season.

The impact and recovery from the drought was softened by four factors; first, the ending of the Merchant Combine, second, through government intervention, third a quick return to good harvests of foodstuffs and fourth the limited effect of the drought on groundnuts. The food situation in The Gambia was ameliorated to some extent by the weakening of the Merchant Combine that was already apparent in 1909, allowing the renewal of rice imports, which by 1913 had reached 109,369 cwts when the Bathurst merchants advanced huge amounts on credit. (Fig. 5.4) What was less fortunate was that they also advanced substantial amounts of manufactured goods, and by December 1913 indebtedness was a major problem, especially in MacCarthy Island where large quantities of nuts had been promised against advances in the previous season.[8] The drought of 1913 was so severe that the food supply for the dry season of 1914 could only be secured adequately by the government also distributing rice and groundnut seeds, and in 1914 rice imports increased to a record

---

[6] RHL Micro Afr. 485, Annual Report, South Bank Province, 1913–14.
[7] Ibid.
[8] RHL Micro Afr. 485, Annual Report, MacCarthy Island Province, 1913–14.

Fig. 5.4: *Gambian rice imports by value, amount and source, 1913–1933*

| Year | Amount cwts | Value £ Sterling | Source |
|---|---|---|---|
| 1913 | 109,369 | 62,409 | Germany; France; Great Britain |
| 1914 | 252,591 | 78,405 | Germany; France; Great Britain |
| 1915 | 42,922 | 26,968 | France; Great Britain |
| 1916 | 21,067 | 19,589 | Great Britain; France; India |
| 1917 | 46,150 | 60,353 | Great Britain; USA; France |
| 1918 | 36,661 | 70,451 | USA |
| 1919 | 57,680 | 103,866 | Great Britain; USA |
| 1920 | 157,811 | 329,069 | Great Britain; USA |
| 1921 | 59,462 | 56,498 | Great Britain; France |
| 1922 | 71,562 | 60,574 | Great Britain; France; Germany |
| 1923 | 91,827 | 69,840 | Germany; France; Great Britain |
| 1924 | 149,802 | 126,982 | Germany; France; Great Britain |
| 1925 | 132,133 | 102,171 | France; Germany |
| 1926 | 92,239 | 72,270 | France; Holland; FWA |
| 1927 | 158,772 | 124,457 | France; Germany; USA |
| 1928 | 228,797 | 156,939 | France; Germany; Great Britain |
| 1929 | 174,108 | 117,844 | France; Germany; Great Britain |
| 1930 | 180,905 | 114,578 | France; China; Germany |
| 1931 | 105,906 | 49,436 | France; Great Britain; India |
| 1932 | 75,002 | 36,101 | India; France; Great Britain |
| 1933 | 84,128 | 30,031 | India; France |

*Source*: Blue Books

high of 252,591 cwts. (Fig 5.4.) But rice distribution was problematic, and in December 1914 the Upper River Commissioner noted in his diary that District heads were taking disproportionate amounts of rice and seed to sell them on in Senegal where conditions were worse.[9] Such occurrences (repeated at other times) are reminders that Bathurst served a population beyond the confines of the colony, while they also appear to prefigure the contemporary problems of food distribution through aid and food distribution schemes.

The impact of the poor harvests of 1913–14 was suddenly ameliorated, when in the 1914–15 season the rice crop was tremendous in both the South Bank and MacCarthy Island. Corn was good except in North Bank, where swarms of caterpillars destroyed the millets, and in South Bank sorghum was affected by blight.[10] (Fig.

---

[9] GNA 59/2, Travelling Commissioner's Diary, Upper River Province, Dec. 1914.
[10] RHL Micro Afr. 485, Annual reports for 1914–15, North Bank, South Bank and MacCarthy Island.

5.3) By now reports suggested that the local variety of sorghum (*basso*) had a three year cycle, and could not be sustained over a longer period, but Hopkinson believed rice was up 100%, corn 40% and nuts by 30–35%.[11] Thus the immediate effects of the drought of 1913 were quickly resolved and while Gambians may not have suffered as much physical deprivation as their Bakel counterparts, for many producers its impact was prolonged, because the large rice advances made by the government and the merchants could only be paid off slowly. The Gambian case is a reminder that drought cannot be considered only in terms of its meteorological, hydrological or agricultural status, as it is mediated by social and economic structures such as levels of household expenditure and indebtedness.

## A deteriorating climate?

The drought of 1913 created widespread concern in West Africa about the climate, but it was not until 1917 that a special report was prepared for The Gambia on 'The Reported Decrease in Rainfall in Gambia.'[12] This report was written by Napier Shaw of the Royal Meteorological Service in London in response to another report on the Gambia's trade, which suggested that over the past 30 years there had been a progressive and detrimental decline in rainfall affecting the whole of Africa. While Shaw's report is specific to The Gambia, it does reveal general environmental concerns being expressed in the early 20th century that anticipate more recent ones, including Global Warming. Napier Shaw examined rainfall records for The Gambia from 1884–1915 and plotted rainfall against sunspot activity. (Fig. 3.1) Sunspots and climatic change in the early 20th century were a source of some speculation, and were the rough equivalent of contemporary concerns about ozone and greenhouse gases. Shaw's analysis of Gambian conditions showed a downward trend of rainfall, and a remarkable correspondence with sunspots. Statistical investigation showed good correlation coefficients and it was suggested that on the evidence the rainfall was decreasing at a rate of 0.35 inches (8.75 mm) per year.

---

[11] Ibid.
[12] GNA 2/238, Napier Shaw to the Colonial Secretary, The Gambia, *The Reported Decrease of Rainfall in Gambia*, 11th June, 1917.

The sun spot theory rested on assumptions that in periods of high activity, increased solar radiation from sunspots increased evaporation over the tropical and sub-tropical oceans. Believing the effect was a general one Shaw extended his investigation beyond The Gambia (as G.T. Walker had done in 1905), where he found similar effects could be detected in Sierra Leone, Cape Verde and the Azores, but not in Accra and Gibraltar. The upshot was that Shaw decided that widespread deterioration was due to there being much larger climatic cycles at work, although a progressive decline in rainfall might be due to "the cutting of the West African forest as part of agricultural clearing". Shaw referred to work on vegetation and climate done by Walker in Mauritius in 1908, but admitted he knew little about "déboisement" in West Africa.[13] However, Shaw did point out that that there were 5,000 more farmers in The Gambia in 1914 than in 1913, by which he meant the upsurge in the number of Strange Farmers. Shaw's comments were taken-up in an unsigned memorandum which added that increased agricultural activity was also influenced by natural population increase, while the consequent removal of forest cover along the river tract might also affect the climate.[14] Whatever the scientific merits of Shaw's report, it set an agenda for The Gambian government as well as pre-figuring a debate that has continued right up to the present. In essence this argument is as follows: that the progressive rainfall decline is either the result of external climatic changes, or the outcome of over-exploitation by farmers, while for some observers it is a mixture of both.

The issue of desertification was highlighted in 1920 when the Comité d'études de l'Afrique Occindentale reported on 'désechement progressif' in West Africa, and thereby established the idea of the southward advance of the Sahara.[15] The report written by Hubert put the blame on European and indigenous woodcutting, and a diminishing rainfall with long term diminution of water levels. This report was influenced by the low rainfall experienced from 1905 to 1920, and as in the Gambian report, the 1913–14 drought was a warning of climatic deterioration threatening the economic future of

[13] Walker, G.T. 1915, 'Correlation in seasonal variations of weather, sunspots and rainfall', *Indian Meteorological Memoirs (Simla)*, vol. 21, pt. 10.
[14] GNA 2/238, Memo on Napier Shaw's report, unsigned and dated April, 1918.
[15] Hubert, H., 1920, "Le desechement progressif en Afrique Occidentale' *Bull de Comite des Etudes Historiques et Scientifiques d'AOF*, 401–67.

export based economies. The advancing Sahara thesis was enthusi-astically taken up later in 1935 by Stebbing, a forester with Indian experience, and subsequently in 1949 by another forester, Aubreville.[16] The colonial forestry school was unanimous in condemning forest burning and bush fallowing, and were quick to convert spatial order-ings of the environment (often temporary or localized) into a sequen-tial hypothesis.

The advance of the Sahara is now known to be variable and patchy rather than uniform, while the concept of desertification is a difficult one to handle. For example, work on the vegetational his-tory of the Futa Jallon in Guinea around Kissidougou has shown how French administrators took patches of forest to be relics of a once humid forest: they 'read history backwards', whereas a forest-savanna mosaic was the norm. The turning of forest into savanna was a major policy concern because it was seen as a threat to local agriculture and tree crops, as well as to climate and hydrology. But the direction of vegetation change now seems open to question: other readings of the landscape are possible and local people see the land-scape as 'half-filled' rather than 'half empty'.[17]

### The War and the groundnut trade

The outbreak of war disrupted the opening months of the 1914–15 groundnut trading season, as the French were unable to find any shipping, partly because of the fear of German raiders and also because ships were being used for colonial troop movements.[18] At the same time, the demand for Gambian groundnuts fell drastically as the Germans invaded north eastern France where much of the French oil-crushing industry was located. The price of nuts in Europe fell by amounts ranging from £2 0s 0d to £4 0s 0d per ton, but the drop was even greater in The Gambia where prices fell from

---

[16] See E.P. Stebbing, 1935. "The encroaching Sahara: the threat to West African colonies", *The Geographical Journal*, 85:506–24. Also, A. Aubreville, 1949' *Climats, forets et desertification del'Afrique tropicale*. Paris: Societe d' Editions Geographique, Maritimes et Coloniale.

[17] Fairhead, J. and M. Leach, "Contested forests: Modern conservation and his-torical land use in Guinea's Ziama Reserve" African Affairs 93 (373), 481–512.

[18] M. Crowder, 1968 "West Africa and the 1914–18 War", *Bull de l'IFAN*, vol. 30 ser. B, no. 1:226–247.

£9 14s 4d to £4 3s 2d per ton f.o.b.[19] (Fig. 5.1) Thus the war years opened on a low note for The Gambian groundnut trade, as well as presaging important changes in the direction of trade.

Prior to the 1914–15 season almost all Gambian nuts were sold in France, but with the demands of war the French market virtually disappeared, and all French shipping to The Gambia was suspended. The Board of Trade in London was sufficiently concerned to consider whether Britain should take Gambian nuts in preference to Northern Nigerian ones, as The Gambia depended entirely on groundnut exports; furthermore it was nearer to Britain and railway freight costs in Nigeria could be avoided.[20] But this proposal never came to fruition when it was realized that it was impossible for Liverpool merchants suddenly to enter a new market in The Gambia. The Gambia suffered a further blow when the Colonial Office rejected a request from Denmark to enter the trade, as it believed processed oil could be re-exported into Germany.[21] The Colonial Office after internal discussion did allow The Gambian government to take a loan from the West African Currency Board to ease the situation, which some thought was against orthodox Treasury practice.[22] This was one of several issues concerning The Gambia's wartime status which revealed divergent views within the Colonial Office: some adopted a traditional laissez-fair attitude, while others wanted a more interventionist approach. Although no intervention in the groundnut trade took place, the sentiment was symptomatic of a more focused concern in London as a result of the war effort, and economic stringencies at home and in the Empire.

In addition to the closure of the French market, the German market was inevitably closed, which also affected food imports. As Figures 4.5 and 5.4 demonstrate, from 1901 onwards Germany (in particular Hamburg) had gradually become an important source of rice, and immediately before the war it was the primary supplier. The upshot was rice imports were rapidly reduced and by December 1914 the Bathurst merchants had introduced a form of rationing to

---

[19] Hatton, P.S. 1966, "The Gambia, The Colonial Office and the Opening Months of the First World War" *Journal of Afr. Hist.*, vol. 7 (1): 123–131.
[20] CO 87/198, J.A.H. to Fiddes, min no. 42732, 2nd Nov. 1914.
[21] CO 87/198, min no. 47943.1914. See also Hatton, 1966. op. cit.
[22] Hatton, 1966, op. cit.

cope with the shortages.[23] As we have noted above it was lucky the food shortages caused by the 1913 drought had been dealt with, and were followed by the bumper food harvests of 1914–15. However, export and import trading was at a standstill, and the Colonial Office expressed the view that the Gambian Government would have to "live off its fat"![24]

Because of the smallness of The Gambia, neither the Governor nor the Colonial Office expected active military involvement of the Colony, yet some 351 men of the Gambian Company of the West Africa Frontier Force were sent to join the expedition to Cameroon, which was a small contribution to the 30,000 West African troops used by the British.[25] In November, a scare occurred in Bathurst when it was thought it was under attack from a German cruiser which turned out to be a British ship.[26] This caused some argument about what should happen if The Gambia were attacked, and a split occurred between The Chief Magistrate of The Gambia van der Meulen, and Governor Cameron. The former thought action by Gambians would be foolish and ineffective, but the latter supported resistance. This was referred to the Foreign Office, where the response mirrored the differing opinions between juniors and seniors. The former had little sympathy with van der Meulen, while Harcourt the Colonial Secretary and others took a more cautious (and racist) view; they were not convinced of the necessity of native peoples showing the same levels of bravery and patriotism as Europeans. The recruitment of Africans into the war also posed other problems; Lugard for example worried about Africans killing white men and being given instruction in the use of weapons, as well as seeing white men "budge when they had stood fast".[27]

Once early alarms had subsided, the buying of groundnuts recommenced in January 1915, and by May 1915 it became apparent that it was a bumper harvest and exports had reached a record 96,152 tons. Alas, the price of 3d per bushel was widespread, except for a freak period when it rose to 1s 3d.[28] In parts of South Bank there

---

[23] CO 87/198, Cameron, to SS, 18th Dec. 1914.
[24] Hatton, 1966, op. cit.
[25] Crowder, 1968, op. cit.
[26] Hatton, 1966, op. cit.
[27] Crowder, 1968, op. cit.
[28] Blue Book, 1915.

were no traders in evidence, and because of the low nut prices, at times as low as 9d per bushel, it became difficult to collect the rice and seed debt contracted due to the drought of 1913. Hopkinson, the South Bank Commissioner reported difficulties early in 1915 in collecting taxes and farm rents, as well as managing to collect only £537 out of £2,233 of the rice debt. And, once again, people were temporarily supplementing their diet and that of their cattle with seeds and leaves.[29] In MacCarthy Island the Commissioner noted one of the best nut crops ever, but prices opened at 1s 0d per bushel and then fell as low as 3d. Some farmers did not bother to take groundnuts from the stacks to thresh them, preferring to keep them for seed.[30]

Fortunately the good foodstuff harvest of 1915 was a lucky break for the Administration, as at least the people now had food, although they lacked a cash income from their groundnuts to pay their debts. Less fortunate was a fall in government revenue from £124,995 in 1913 to £85,421 in 1914, against an expenditure of £120,921. (Fig. 5.1), a situation affected by the government's arrangement in early 1914 to pay for imported rice and seed nuts on delivery, instead of after the sale of the groundnut crop.[31] Added to this liability, in 1914 the British government persuaded The Gambia to contribute to the war effort through a donation of £10,000 to the Prince of Wales National Defence Fund. Later this small colony gave another £10,000 to the King George Fund for sailors, and a further £10,000 was donated to buy an aeroplane.[32] These expenditures and shortfalls of revenue blocked planned spending in 1915 on new roads, better sanitation and a survey of the river Gambia.

After the initial shock of the War the French resumed buying in January 1915, but this occurred just after the entry of a new British firm, Palmines Ltd. who were a subsidiary of Maypole Dairies, a British chain of grocers. Much to the delight of the Board of Trade and the Gambian Administration, Palmines signed a contract in 1915 with Bibby's of Liverpool to supply 30,000 tons of groundnuts,[33]

[29] RHL Micro Afr. 485, Annual Report, South Bank Province, 1914–15.
[30] RHL Micro Afr. 485, Annual Report, MacCarthy Island Province, 1914–15.
[31] Blue Books, 1913, 1914, 1915.
[32] Macmillan, A., 1920, *Red Book of West Africa: Historical, Descriptive, Commercial and Industrial Facts, Figures and Resources*. London.
[33] CO 87/200, Gwynn to SS. 26th May 1915.

while a big incentive for British firms in The Gambia was the establishment of new groundnut crushing factories, such as the one at
Erith in Kent set up in January 1915.[34] Therefore, the trade was
rescued by a newfound demand in Britain, which had been vigor-
ously pushed by the government. Groundnut production and prices
strengthened as the war progressed and, whereas in 1914 Britain
had taken 5% by weight of Gambian nuts and France 85%, by 1915
the respective figures were 38% and 51%. By 1919 British firms
dominated the groundnut trade: Palmines was the most substantial
business and had absorbed Arnold Eugster, The African Association
had absorbed the Société Commercial de Sénégambie, and the
Bathurst Trading Company was taken-over by Lord Leverhulme.
(Fig. 5.5) One American firm appeared, Grace Brothers, which was
a reflection of the increased trade between The Gambia and the
United States, especially in rice.

British firms' interest in groundnuts was assisted in 1916 by the
publication of a circular by the Technical Information Bureau in
England on 'New Markets for British Indian and Colonial Groundnuts
and their Products'.[35] This was followed by a monograph on Oil
Seed and Feeding cakes issued by the Imperial Institute, published
by John Murray, which had a wide circulation.[36] These initiatives
were part of the War effort and of changing attitudes to the role of
government. When Lloyd George became Minister of Munitions in
May 1915, he assumed almost dictatorial control: the civilian population in general had to accept more disciplined centralized direction than hitherto, while the state evolved new forms of control and
planning.[37] On the other hand the French were not best pleased by
these developments, and the Consul General of France in The
Gambia, (also the head of Maurel et Prom's Bathurst branch) protested
to the Colonial Secretary about the entry of Palmines into the trade
and how on their entry in February 1914 they forced up the price
to 1s 3d per bushel, albeit for a limited period.[38] The British were
not impressed, and dismissed the complaint as commercial jealousy.

---

[34] CO 87/200, minute no. 57376, Conf., 23rd Nov. 1915.
[35] CO 87/203, Campbell, Report on Blue Book for 1915.
[36] Ibid.
[37] Thomson, 1981, op. cit.
[38] CO 87/200, minute no. 57376. Conf. 23rd Nov. 1915.

Fig. 5.5: *Principal importers and exporters in the Colony of The Gambia, 1914 and 1920*

| *1914* | |
|---|---|
| Bathurst Trading Company | London |
| Barthes et Lesurier | Bordeaux |
| CFAO | Marseille |
| Commerciale de Sénégambie | Dakar |
| Arnold Eugster | USA |
| Maurel Frères | Bordeaux |
| Maurel et Prom | Bordeaux |
| Vezia and Co. | |
| | |
| *1920* | |
| Bathurst Trading Company | London |
| Barthes et Lesurier | Bordeaux |
| CFAO | Marseille |
| Maurel Frères | Bordeaux |
| Maurel et Prom | Bordeaux |
| African and Eastern Trading Co. Ltd. | Liverpool |
| Palmines | London |
| Grace Bros. | London |
| Horton, Jones and Co. | London |

*Notes*: Horton, Jones and Co., took over A.B. Horsely and Anton Blain of Banjul.
Grace Bros. was largely American
Palmines had absorbed Arnold Eugster
Bathurst Trading Co. was taken over in 1917 by Lever Bros.
*Sources*: CO 87/209 Cameron to SS, 21st May 1919; GNA/253, 1920, Foodstuffs in Upper River Province; MacMillan, A. 1920, *Red Book of West Africa, Historical and Descriptive, Commercial and Industrial Facts, compiled and edited,* London.

*Groundnut producer prices and rice imports, 1913–1920*

The export duty levied on the record groundnut tonnage of 96,152 tons in 1915 slightly boosted the government's finances, and reversed the previous year's excess of expenditure over revenue, but as we have noted producer prices were extremely poor. The 1915 producer price averaged only £4 3s 0d per ton compared with £10 0s 0d in 1914. (Fig. 5.1). The drop in price initially curtailed planting at the end of 1915, and only at the last moment did the merchants forecast better prices, but this came too late to affect the 1915–16 trade season. Predictably, the groundnut crop was only half of that for 1915, but the price doubled to an average of £10 18s 0d. And between 1916 and 1920 producers received consistently higher prices than hitherto, climbing from £10 18s 0d per ton in 1916 to a remarkable postwar high of £27 0s 0d in 1920. (Fig. 5.1) These were the highest groundnut prices recorded since 1857, which had ended a period beginning in 1836 when prices averaged £12 0s 0d per ton. But the Administration was aware that these prices far from giving farmers opportunities to invest in cattle and to buy more imported goods, were offset by the need to buy imported rice to supplement local food production and feed Strange Farmers.[39] While rice imports had been associated with the groundnut trade since 1857, the acceleration of imports in the 20th century was remarkable, but of particular concern was the huge price increases during and after the war. (Fig. 5.4) For example, rice imports were high in 1913 and 1914 (after the drought), when the price was about 10s 0d per cwt. From 1916–18, imports were lower, but the price was nearly £2 0s 0d per cwt. And, the price of rice soared even higher after the 1918–19 floods and drought, which we discuss later. It was at this time the United States entered the Gambian rice trade, when it became a food supplier to the West African colonies as a result of the shortage of foodstuffs and shipping in Europe. (Fig. 5.4)

At the beginning of the war the Governor and the Commissioners had exhorted farmers to grow more food as part of the war effort, and as a precaution against a shortage of imports which in fact did not materialize. Producers apparently grew a lot of foodstuffs in 1915, not simply due to exhortation but as a partial response to the poor groundnut prices of 1914 which shifted them back into grain farming.[40] Officials felt that growing more foodstuffs should have allowed Gambians to benefit from rising groundnut prices after 1916, yet it was acknowledged that their ability to purchase more imported goods was offset by wartime inflation. As Sproston noted, whereas the rate per ton for groundnuts was the same in 1916 and 1917, the cost of all goods increased, in some instances as much as 50% on pre-War prices.[41] And in particular imported rice was subject to these inflationary pressures. McCallum, the Commissioner for MacCarthy Island noted in his 1917–18 report, "that before the war local rice was 1d per Wills cigarette tin, but now it was fetching 2d, which he deplored

[39] CO 87/209, Gueritz, Ag. Rec. General to CS, 16th May 1919.
[40] CO 87/209, Jackson to Cameron, 21st May 1919.
[41] CO 87/206, Sproston to Cameron, 3rd July 1917.

as he believed the costs of production were no greater and that this
was merely mimicking Bathurst, where the price is high and rice
was being sold at 6d per pound".[42] Part of his concern appears to
have been that local rice prices might affect the petty traders coming up the river each season, who relied on locally bought rice for
their food during the rains. Thus rising groundnut prices appear to
have been illusory for Gambian producers, and it was at the very
end of the War that price controls on food were implemented, when
each Commissioner had the power to control prices in his own
Province.

Early in 1917 a Proclamation was issued prescribing the maxi-
mum retail prices for food: rice was fixed at £3 0 0d per 224 lbs,
or 2d per Wills cigarette tin, and 4d per lb for less than 12 lbs. But
the upward trend of imported rice costs saw the retail price raised
on three occasions in 1917 alone; to £3 7s 6d, £4 0s 0d and finally
£4 12s 6d per 224 lb (5d per lb).[43] To what extent the controls
were observed is not known, although the Trade Report for 1918
declared they were a success.[44] Food scarcity was also commented
on by the Commissioner for Kombo and Foni in 1917, when he
pointed out that the price of imported rice had doubled since the
outbreak of war, and in Kiang West many people took goats and
cattle into Foni to sell them in order to buy food.[45] Also, the feeding of Bathurst was becoming a problem, and in 1918 some relief
was given to the town's populace when the government decided to
distribute rice to its employees.[46] At first rice was given out on
demand, then there were suspicions about an over-demand and illegal trading, so lists of officers and their families were prepared and
rice was given out on a monthly basis.

The Blue Book for 1917 reported that imported foodstuffs were
expensive and scarce, but went on to observe that wages and prices
for nuts had risen. This view certainly was not shared by one
Commissioner, McCallum, who pointed out that although the prices
of groundnuts had improved producers had seen nothing like the

---

[42] RHL Micro Afr. 485, Annual Report, MacCarthy Island Province, 1917–18.
[43] Proc. No. 10 of 1917, Revised No. 16 of 1917 and Revised No. 21 of 1917.
[44] The Gambia: Trade Report 1918. Govt. Printer, Bathurst.
[45] CO 87/206, T.C. Kombo and Fogni to Cameron, 26th July 1917.
[46] GNA 3/30, Sale of Rice by Government.

increases in the price that groundnuts fetched in Europe.[47] McCallum stated in his 1917–18 Report that he had exhorted people "to grow more foodstuffs and nuts as part of the War effort, yet some encouragement is needed: every year they get approximately 2s 3d to 2s 9d, but the price has risen at home so should not planters as well as merchants get the benefit?" McCallum went on to suggest prices should be under government control, and then the Strange Farmers would flock in. He also noted the unfairness of payments by scale weight rather than the bushel: farmers couldn't read the payment slips, bags were thrown on the scale, deductions were made for bags, as well as for sand whether there was any or not.[48]

As on previous occasions arguments developed within the Administration about the fairness of the prices producers received compared with the amount groundnuts fetched in Europe. In 1918, Gwyn The Receiver General also drew attention to the poor f.o.b. prices in The Gambia: nuts were sold f.o.b. at £11 15s 0d per ton, while in Europe even when costs of transport were taken into account they fetched in bulk £32 per ton.[49] (Fig. 5.1) Gwyn and McCallum were arguing that firstly, high groundnut f.o.b. prices during the War did not increase the producer's purchasing power as they were offset by rising costs of imported rice and trade goods, and secondly, f.o.b. prices were not high when judged against European prices for groundnuts. The Acting Governor and other Commissioners were not impressed and took a more conservative view, rejecting any move towards price controls and government intervention. Also, contrary to Gwyn and McCallum the other Commissioners thought native planters were doing remarkably well, in support of which they cited the increased numbers of Strange Farmers coming into the country, although conveniently forgetting the exodus from Senegal was connected with military conscription. Notwithstanding these arguments among administrators, there was no resistance from the producers for example in the form of *tong*, largely because producers had only limited information about European markets.[50]

[47] Blue Book, 1917.
[48] 39 RHL Micro Afr. 485, Annual Report Upper River Province, 1917–18. See also CO 87/207, McCallum to CS, 18th July 1918.
[49] CO 87/207, Gwyn to CS, 6th June 1918.
[50] CO 87/209, Heaton to SS, 21st May 1919.

The price of groundnuts was taken up by the Ministry of Food and the Secretary of State for the Colonies, who wished to have details of prices paid in West Africa for produce together with stocks held by the firms, the costs incurred transporting nuts to the port, and freight costs to Europe relative to the price received there.[51] The Travelling Commissioners were also asked to supply prices paid to farmers in December 1917. The context of this request was the possibility of the Ministry of Food, or possibly an Anglo-French Oils and Oilseed Executive being empowered to buy groundnuts in West Africa. The demand for this information was consonant with increased government activity in the sphere of food purchases, and rationing at home as a result of the War, but it cut little ice in Bathurst where the merchants and the Chamber of Commerce refused to supply the information. The Governor while taking note of the quoted £32 0s 0d per ton paid in Britain pointed out the only way to get the information was to search the companies' books, and he had no such powers.[52] Thus the resistance of the merchants once more greatly outdistanced that of the producers and the wishes of the government.

In 1918–1919 Bathurst was asked to examine information from Dakar about food supplies, which is interesting not so much for any outcome, but because it shows the differing views among the Travelling Commissioners. In 1917 the British Consul General in Dakar sent the Secretary of State a copy of a paper on food supplies for France prepared by the Governor General of French West Africa, which in turn was sent to Bathurst for comment.[53] Part of French War policy was the utilization of its West African possessions not only as a source of soldiers, but also of foodstuffs. Dakar proposed an arbitrary requisitioning of all agricultural produce at fixed prices either directly from producers, or through the commercial houses. A suggestion was made that requisitioning should be organized through a Comité Commercial de l'Afrique Occidentale, to which French and British houses had agreed to belong. The difficulty with this plan was that shipping was in short supply, and could only be chartered on license, so the State in effect would have to become a freight

---

[51] GNA 2/259, Prices of groundnuts.
[52] Ibid.
[53] GNA 3/31, Conf. File on foodstuffs and the development of their cultivation in West Africa.

agent. What the French really wanted was access to British mercantile tonnage.

The report was circulated among the Commissioners under the heading of 'Improved Food Production in The Gambia'. The response of the Commissioners was unanimous in declaring the export of food to be impossible, which was not surprising: however the report encapsulated their divergent views on food production which were summarized and sent to London.[54] Hopkinson of the South Bank believed there was some room for improved production, but the problem was the low population of The Gambia and incomers should be encouraged. The Commissioner for MacCarthy Island believed that people should work harder and grow Indian corn (maize), sweet potatoes and cotton. But as he noted, "at the moment there was not enough surplus rice to supply Bathurst, and this is the immediate problem". And, dismissively added "all people feel hungry towards the end of the rains before the first corn harvest." The Commissioner of Kombo while being concerned about rainfall variability was insistent that self-sufficiency had been achieved, as the government had not distributed rice since 1914, but he seemed unaware of the huge purchases by natives from the merchants and the very good rice crop of 1915. But Pryce of North Bank succinctly remarked, "how can we export food when we have to import rice?" And, he continued, "all food has to be grown between July and November, and an increase in foodstuffs means a smaller area under groundnuts". This indeed had become a central problem for the Gambian Administration and its people, together with levels of indebtedness and environmental disturbance.

An examination of the statistics on rice imports and Strange Farmers provides an interesting gloss on these arguments, which was not directly referred to in the reports. The Blue Books show that in 1915–1918 rice imports were low, no doubt due to high prices and limited availability, but it was precisely at this point that the number of Strange Farmers surged, with an exceptional influx of some 32,000 in 1915. (Fig. 5.6) Therefore in these circumstance how was the food supply managed in order to feed the numbers? Were some Commissioners correct in thinking greater efforts could produce more food with less reliance on imports, although there was a strong

---

[54] GNA 3/31, Conf. Governor to SS 4th Feb. 1918.

Fig. 5.6: *Estimated number of Strange Farmers in The Gambia, 1904–1934*

| | |
|---|---|
| 1904 | 4657 |
| 1905 | 6402 |
| 1906 | 4600 |
| 1907 | 4772 |
| 1908 | 4571 |
| 1909 | 6982 |
| 1910 | 6598 |
| 1911 | 5292 |
| 1912 | 6527 |
| 1913 | 9938 |
| 1914 | 14912 |
| 1915 | 32220 |
| 1916 | 9390 |
| 1917 | 20727 |
| 1918 | 20509 |
| 1919 | 24440 |
| 1920 | 24150 |
| 1921 | 22058 |
| 1922 | 20018 |
| 1923 | 14824 |
| 1924 | 14116 |
| 1925 | 14192 |
| 1926 | 13392 |
| 1927 | 17237 |
| 1928 | 206640 |
| 1929 | 18874 |
| 1930 | 16592 |
| 1931 | 9763 |
| 1932 | 16513 |
| 1933 | 14537 |
| 1934 | 8332 |

*Sources*: Blue Books and K.W. Blackburne, 1943.

suspicion that a good deal of the rice imported had been traded over the border As we shall show, the most likely explanation is that the 32,000 Strange farmers were something of an anomaly: the number was artificially inflated by the war, as men from French territory temporarily avoided conscription, and they probably had access to food supplies stored over the border. Certainly, rice was expensive and more food had been planted, and belts were tightened. After the war rice imports increased once again as a result of environmental disturbance, and there can be little doubt that drought and floods required rice distribution to maintain the groundnut trade, especially if Strange Farmers were to continue as a significant element in the labour force. And the link between migrant workers and food consumption was now a recurrent issue in the Administration's discussions, as it became aware of the increasing number of Strange Farmers.

### Strange Farmers and groundnuts in the early 20th century

From 1903 to 1912 the Administration's reports show the number of Strange Farmers varying between 4,000 and 6,000, but after 1912 reporting became more systematic, which allows a closer look at whether they significantly affected the size of the groundnut crop. Clearly in terms of numbers 1913 was an important year as there was a dramatic increase that accelerated during and after the war. (Fig. 5.6) In 1916 the Governor reported that an estimated 56,000 people were employed in agriculture, and that between 1912 and 1916 the addition of an average of 12,500 itinerant planters each year (in fact the correct figure was 14,604) had considerably influenced output.[55] Furthermore, Gwyn in 1915–6 pointed out that of a total 9,135 farmers in Upper River, nearly 5,000 were Strange Farmers who grew the bulk of the crop in what had become the major producing area of The Gambia.[56] The Strange Farmer presence in this region underlines why the government was concerned about the lack of foodstuffs. Gwyn's comments led him to speculate that the population of The Gambia was insufficient to meet its needs, by which he meant it was incapable of sustaining the present levels of groundnut exports.[57] In March 1915 the influx of migrants peaked at 32,300, a number not exceeded in the whole colonial period, and the presence of so many migrants coincided with a record output of 96,152 tons. (Figs. 5.1; 5.6)

There seems little doubt that the correlation between groundnut exports and the number of Strange Farmers was a positive one, as show by the graph in Figure 5.7. But what were the effects of migrants and the increased levels of production on land use in the Gambia? Did higher production levels proceed from an intensification

---

[55] CO 87/206, Jackson to Cameron, 13th Aug. 1917.
[56] CO 87/206, Gwyn in Cameron to SS, 9th April 1917.
[57] Ibid.

Fig. 5.7: *Gambian groundnut exports (tons) and Strange Farmers, 1912–1923*

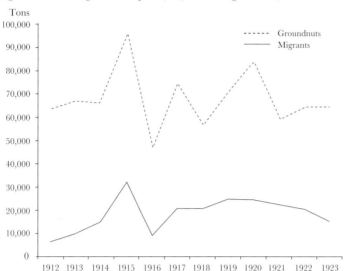

*Source*: Blue Books and Agricultural Department Reports.

of existing farmland, or the extension of farming into hitherto unused
or areas of long fallow? The answer is probably that both occurred.
Gambian villages were surrounded by intensively cultivated farms
growing foodstuffs and groundnuts that relied on dunging, whereas
outer areas of long fallowed bush were often given to Strange Farmers
for their groundnut farms The Blue Book of 1916 speaks of land
which until recently has been idle being brought into cultivation by
Strange Farmers, although "there is still a lot of uncultivated land,
the country being so sparsely populated".[58] In 1917 Gwyn was writing of Strange Farmers extending the cultivated area in Upper River,[59]
while Leese confirmed that Strange Farmers were actively opening-
up land on the South Bank.[60] Leese was also at some pains to point
out that they were not inevitably attracted by an abundance of
foodstuffs, which were scarce now in a onetime area of surplus.[61]
The situation as it developed in The Gambia is interesting in the
light of debates about rising population levels and agrarian change;

---

[58]  Blue Book, 1916.
[59]  CO 87/205, Gwyn to Cameron, 9th April 1917.
[60]  CO 87/211, Leese to CS, 28th June 1920.
[61]  Ibid.

for example, as conceptualized by Boserup.[62] The argument is that population increases is a positive factor in agrarian change, leading ro more intensive forms of cultivation. It would seem that in The Gambia both the expansion and intensification of Gambian agriculture were taking place simultaneously, and were principally a product of a large seasonal increase of population rather than a permanent one, the effects of which were tempered by the importing of substantial amounts of rice.

There were four factors promoting an accelerated influx of Strange Farmers during the early 20th century. The first was the erosion of domestic slavery we discussed in the last chapter. Second, a change between 1908 and 1910 in the host-migrant contract: the old system of 4–5 days labour was reduced to 2 days, but it is not clear whether this proceeded from the wishes of hosts, the migrants, or the Administration, nor whether it was universal throughout the country.[63] Third, higher export duties were imposed on groundnuts in Senegal in 1914 which probably boosted The Gambia's attractiveness to migrant farmers.[64] Fourth conscription for military service by the French was important, and this contributed to the huge total of migrants recorded in 1915. It should also be noted that this influx also occurred in the aftermath of the 1913 drought, which as we noted earlier was severe in the middle and upper Senegal valley. Conscription was part of French policy in Senegal, and, for example in January 1913 the Commissioner for MacCarthy Island noted hundreds of French Africans coming into the Province, and that there were reports of the French demanding District Heads to supply 10% of the population as soldiers.[65] Conscription increased during the 1914–18 War, although according to the North Bank Commissioner conscription was suspended in border districts, as the French realized just how porous it was.[66] The North Bank Commissioner's Diary for January–March 1917 records his response to fugitives from conscription; in Kerewan 70 had been handed back to the French, while a town near the border erected without

[62] Boserup, E., 1965, *The Conditions of Agricultural Growth*. London: Allen and Unwin.
[63] Annual Reports, The Gambia, 1908, 1909 and 1910.
[64] CO 87/206, Jackson to Cameron, 31st Aug. 1917. Also CO 87/205 Gwyn to Cameron, 9th April 1917.
[65] RHL Micro Afr. 485, Annual Report MacCarthy Island Division, 1913–14.
[66] RHL Micro Afr. 485, Annual Report, North Bank, 1913–14.

permission had been pulled-down.[67] News of swarms of French
Africans coming into MacCarthy Island in 1916 was declared incor-
rect by the Commissioner, although he did warn the Chiefs against
taking-in absconders.[68]

On the South Bank large numbers were crossing the border, mostly
Turankos, and as Hopkinson opined "the Government would like
them to stay, but has to support the Allied cause"[69] with the result
that in 1917 a 'show of force' was mounted on yards with Turankos
who were sent back over the border.[70] This action was the outcome
of an Ordinance no. 40 of 1916 proscribing the acceptance of desert-
ers and it led to some debate about stopping the influx of French
conscripts, with Hopkinson asserting that the best method was for
the British to introduce conscription in The Gambia.[71] Quite clearly
while the British attempted to stem the influx of migrants from
Senegal, it must have been almost impossible to distinguish between
absconders and genuine Strange Farmers, which rendered the British
exercise a token effort. One other practice by the Senegalese authorities contributed to the stream of Strange Farmers, the use of forced
labour on the Dakar-Tambacounda railway to which we referred in
the last Chapter. The Annual Report of 1910–11 for MacCarthy
Island reported an enormous number of Strange Farmers and settlers were coming into the Province because of the forced levées of
workers who were required to perform heavy work on the railway,
although Manchuelle believed the 'pull' of good prices was more
important.[72] But if the government welcomed the presence of Strange
Farmers as contributors to larger groundnut tonnages, it was accompanied by anxiety about the amount of food they consumed, not
least in times of environmental crisis. The issue of Strange Farmers
and food supply again came to the fore with a resurgence of rice
importing after the floods and droughts of 1918–19, which followed

---

[67] RHL Micro Afr. 485, Commissioners' Diaries, North Bank Province, Jan.–Mar.
1917.
[68] RHL Micro Afr. 485, MacCarthy Island Annual Report, 1915–16.
[69] RHL Micro Afr. 485, Annual Report South Bank Province, 1915–16.
[70] RHL Micro Afr. 485, Annual Report South Bank Province, 1917–18.
[71] Ibid.
[72] RHL, Micro Afr. 485, MacCarthy Island Annual Report, 1910–1911. See also,
Manchuelle, *Willing Migrants: Soninke Labor Diasporas, 1848–1960*. Athens: Ohio Univ.
Press.

two other disasters, the cattle epidemic of 1917 and influenza pandemic of 1918.

*Pestilence, floods and droughts, 1917–1920*

The War years in The Gambia had been marked by relatively favourable climatic conditions and the groundnut trade had prospered, with only a temporary blip in 1918 when exports dropped to 56,490 tons. This might have been due to fewer groundnuts being brought in from Senegal, but it was also associated with the West African Cattle Epidemic, which hit the Gambia in 1917–1918 and the consequent loss of manure. The epidemic saw the death of large numbers of animals, and Hopkinson, The South Bank Commissioner gave the best account of the disaster. His extended Annual Report for 1917–18 notes that:

> although the War was the epoch making event of the past four years, and while it was difficult to write of the petty happenings in a little Province in a little Colony, nevertheless an event which is to our people epoch making is the cattle disease of 1917–18, and the resulting loss (in common with the rest of West Africa) of the greater part of the horned livestock. In South Bank, the epizootic first appeared in June. . . . and swept rapidly westwards, till by August the whole province except Central Kiang was infected, and cattle were dead or dying. By Christmas it had also overtaken Kiang. Some attempts were made to isolate herds, but by March (1918) not a herd, nor a beast had escaped.[73]

Hopkinson hoped the survivors would be immune and there the matter would rest. He quoted at some length the work of M. Aldige of the French West African Zoological Service, who believed the disease seemed to have been some kind of bovine pneumonia which could exist in apparently healthy animals.[74] Aldige also reported the serious outbreak of rinderpest, an intestinal disorder that according to Hopkinson affected cattle on the North Bank. Thus two quite different kinds of cattle disease were experienced. Aldige hoped for immunization programmes, quarantine posts at borders, and controlled movements of cattle. But as Hopkinson observed, nothing

---

[73] RHL Micro Afr. 485, Annual Report South Bank Province, 1917–18.
[74] Ibid.

could be done because of the war, and anyhow The Gambia had
so few resources it would have to wait for a lead from the French.

In his report of 1918–1919 Hopkinson reported no further outbreaks, but went on to express a concern echoed by other Commissioners, that it would be some time before cattle herds were rebuilt
and there would be a serious loss of manure on farms. As cultivation had intensified, so farmers had become dependent on dunging
by Fula herds brought down from the Futa Jallon to the river in
the dry season.[75] Unfortunately cattle being brought into the Gambia
after 1918 were subject to French custom and tariff regulations, and
although cattle could 'drift' into The Gambia there were risks of the
herds being caught crossing the border, and herders could lose not
only cattle but all their possessions.[76] Hopkinson noted the Gambian
cattle which survived the epidemic had grown fat, as there was
less competition for the grass, but manure was lacking especially in
the clearings around towns which were more or less permanently
cultivated.

Without much prompting from the Commissioner local farmers
had responded to a dearth of manure by cutting new bush farms,
and despite the possible long term effects of this practice, the groundnut trade took priority encouraged by high producer prices and government exhortation. Hopkinson agreed the cutting of trees was not
good, but crops must come first; in addition he seized upon Napier
Shaw's 'sunspot report', which Hopkinson took as meaning the theory that trees were connected with rainfall had now been ques-
tioned.[77] Thus there was a selective reading of the evidence to bolster
the case for expanding agriculture. He rather cynically noted that it
was what the French were doing to the vegetation that would really
affect The Gambia; it was too small to be of consequence as a climatic agent.

Hopkinson also was at pains to eradicate what he termed "noxious animals", that is those which attacked farmers' crops.[78] He opined
that "unless a great many of the beasts get killed off, the present
loss due to this must increase". He went on to point to the abandonment of swamp farms because of baboons by day, and wart hogs

[75] RHL Micro Afr. 485, Annual Report South Bank Province, 1918–19.
[76] Ibid.
[77] Ibid.
[78] RHL Micro Afr. 485, Annual Provincial Reports for The Gambia, 1917–1920.

by night. The war had seriously limited the distribution of powder for cap rifles when there were also anxieties about issuing natives with guns, but Hopkinson argued the new technology of warfare would render cap guns innocuous. In 1917 a bounty was offered for noxious beasts, and in 1918 Hopkinson issued chiefs with a limited number of shotguns.[79] The results were impressive, and Hopkinson took some pride in the strike-rate compared with the number of cartridges issued. This onslaught contributed to the reduction of Gambia's wildlife to the present pitiful levels, and the extinction of lion and leopard. And whatever the agreed wisdom on forest clearing may have been at this time, it appears the Commissioners were always likely to prioritize groundnut and food production.

No sooner had the cattle epidemic subsided than September of 1918 was marked by an influenza epidemic which was in part of the pandemic affecting Europe, Africa and Asia.[80] This proved to be the worst outbreak of infectious disease in World history; 20 million died, twice the number killed on military service during the 1914–18 War. In Africa there were between one-and-a-half and two million deaths, and although influenza virus had occurred before, the strain (then believed to be a re-combination of swine and human influenza) was previously unknown. The infection spread to The Gambia from Sierra Leone from the SS Prah, which arrived from Freetown with three dead on board,and despite surveillance of the ship the disease was spread up-river by a launch. The authorities were unprepared, only having limited medical staff and no accurate records were kept. Some 31 deaths were recorded in Georgetown and 19 in Kuntaur, while in Bathurst 317 deaths were recorded due to influenza, which gave a total mortality rate of 3.9%.[81] Mortality was much higher among Europeans, 7.3%, although this particular statistic may have been skewed by better recording. Compared with other parts of West Africa Gambian mortality was high: 2.6% for the total population of The Gold Coast, 3% percent Nigeria and 3.75% in Senegal.

For two weeks all trade was stopped, and although deaths were limited in the Provinces as it was a milder type of 'flu, the Medical

---

[79] Ibid.
[80] Patterson, K.D., 1983, 'The Influenza Epidemic of 1918–19 in the Gold Coast', *Journal of African History*, 24, 485–502.
[81] Ibid.

Officer noted that "natives became emaciated wrecks unable to work".[82] The epidemic stopped at the end of September, but as the North Bank Commissioner observed it prevented weeding of farms especially in Lower and Upper Niumi, and he estimated that out of a population of 4,000 some 300 died.[83] In the South Bank out of a population of some 30,000, reported deaths numbered 1,337 giving a mortality rate of 4.4%, while In the Kombos and Fonis influenza was widespread and severe in some towns, with all the inhabitants laid-up.[84] Furthermore, it occurred when women should have been setting out rice plants and therefore some rice was lost.

The impact of the 1918 pandemic on agriculture was less on groundnuts and more on millet and rice production, as the weeding of early millet and the preparation of local rice plots was delayed. Groundnuts were less affected, as the influx of relatively fit young Strange Farmers sustained the labour force. However 1918 also was notable for very heavy rains and floods, especially in Upper River where there were severe food shortages. Worse was to follow when the heavy rainfall in 1918 was followed by low rainfall in 1919, together with outbreaks of blight and infestations of caterpillars. The outcome was the resumption of rice distribution by the government; in 1919 rice imports suddenly increased and then rocketed in 1920. (Fig. 5.4) The full impact of this particular food shortage was initially obscured because it immediately followed good groundnut harvests and rising producer prices. While there was a certain amount of foreboding, the government and traders encouraged producers to 'buy their way out' of food shortages caused by the bad weather, in the hope of continued high groundnut prices. This was a hope which subsequently proved forlorn, and one with catastrophic consequences.

A letter from Sproston, the Upper River Commissioner dated January 15th 1919 to the Governor, spoke of "starvation", while meetings with the chiefs of all districts indicated conditions were universally bad.[85] Sorghums and rice were reported to have failed as

---

[82] CO 87/208, Ag. Governor to SS: encl. report by Ag. Senior Medical Officer, 8th Nov. 1918.
[83] RHL Micro Afr. 485, Annual Report North Bank Province, 1918–19.
[84] RHL Micro Afr. 485, Annual Reports for the South Bank Province and Kombo and Fognis, 1918–19.
[85] GNA 2/2253, Foodstuffs in Upper River Province, Sproston to Governor, 15th Jan. 1919.

heavy rains had killed-off the rice, while blight had affected the other two crops. His diary for December 1918 also records the loss of the sorghums *basso* and *kinto* grown near to the river due to excessive flooding.[86] Sproston believed this to be the worst year for foodstuffs in his eight years as Commissioner, and warned that rice and seed distribution both for local farmers and Strange Farmers would be needed to avert a famine and a failure of the groundnut crop. The food crisis in Upper River was (and still is) a timely reminder that floods and pests can be just as disastrous as drought, while in general sharp alternations of wet and dry periods can trigger outbreaks of pestilence. The rainfall for 1918 was 54.03 inches (1350.75 mm), compared with 37.68 inches (942 mm) the previous year, and was the highest rainfall since 1909. Rainfall was heavy along the whole of the river, but in the constricted upper reaches it appears it rapidly overflowed, and backed-up into the smaller tributary valleys, thus destroying the rice fields.

An adequate supply of food supply during 1919 was of particular concern in Upper River because this Province had gradually emerged as the principal area of groundnut cultivation. The food crisis provoked a number of reports and investigations as the government decided how to deal with the situation. The redistribution of rice was reluctantly agreed to, but since it had not distributed since 1914 new arrangements had to be made quickly. Cameron the Governor, in a letter to the Secretary of State asked whether supplies from USA via the British Trade Department were forthcoming, while he pointed out that cheaper rice was available in England, therefore would the Crown Agents send a quote.[88] This quote was eventually received and was £32 11s 0d per ton including all charges landed at Bathurst.[89] Meanwhile the Colonial Secretary was warning Sproston that although he had taken 324 tons in 1914 after the drought, the price since then had doubled, so did he really want the same amount?[90] A minute on the papers noted that the price of rice had increased by 217% since 1914 in The Gambia, although cheap

---

[86] RHL Micro Afr. 485, Upper River province, Commissoners' Diaries, Dec. 1918.

[87] RHL Micro Afr. 485, Annual Report North Bank Province, 1918–1919.

[88] GNA 3/353, *File on Foodstuffs in Upper River Province*, Cameron to SS, 17th Jan. 1919.

[89] Ibid. Telegram, SS to Governor, 25th Mar. 1919.

[90] Ibid. CS to Sproston, memo no. 18.

rice was still available in Liverpool.[91] Sproston's reply was unequivocal in asking for 9,000 bags, and if possible as many as 12,000–14,000 bags.[92] By April 1919 the Colonial Secretary had turned to the Bathurst Chamber of Commerce for immediate help and asked for tenders to supply 400 tons of rice to Upper River Province, to be landed at places named by the government.[93] The government asked for two price quotations; the price payable on delivery in Bathurst ,and price after next year's groundnut harvest had been sold. Palmines won the tender and offered rice by quoting respectively £34 and £36 per ton.[94] The first price was accepted, so the Administration crucially took the decision to pay in advance as it believed it would collect the rice debt the next year after the 1920 groundnut season.

Despite a request from Sproston for 485 tons, Upper River was sent 400 tons of rice and people were charged £3 12s 0d per cwt bag, which amounted to £36 per ton, a £2 per ton surcharge.[95] Thus the government's intervention and direct purchase arrangements secured rice for consumers at 7.7d per lb. This translated into the distribution of £14,396 8s 0d of rice, to which was added the cost of seed nut distribution. But the distribution of rice in Upper River had triggered demands from MacCarthy Island and South Bank. Crop failures were reported in five districts of the former, and they were allowed 90 tons, with a token 10 tons for South Bank.[96] Thus in 1919–20 the government reluctantly became further involved in the distribution of rice, and in addition to taxes the Commissioners once again had to collect rice debts. The Governor in a letter to the Secretary of State explained the old system of distribution, whereby merchants delivered rice to places appointed by the government, and then waited until after the groundnut harvest for repayment with an understanding that the government was a guarantor. But as the Governor observed, "the current problem is the price of rice and the ability of people to pay for it. Therefore the government had to buy rice on arrival in Bathurst to secure the best price, and then collect the debt itself."[97]

[91] Ibid. Minute no. 6.
[92] Ibid. Sproston to CS, 23rd March 1919.
[93] Ibid. Col Sec to Hon. Sec. Chamber of Commerce, Bathurst, 9th April 1919.
[94] Ibid. Col Sec to Palmines 18th April 1919.
[95] Ibid. Memo Col Sec to Sproston, 1st May 1919.
[96] Ibid. Rice Account, 1919.
[97] Ibid. Governor to SS, 29th March 1919.

The floods of 1918 caused widespread food scarcity, but worse was to follow in the wet season of 1919. The rainfall of 1919 was only 39 inches (1065 mm), rather better than 1917, but as we have observed in Chapter Three in terms of 'effectiveness' it is a matter of timing. According to the North Bank Commissioner the rains came to an early and sudden halt, the swamps dried out very quickly and affected the late maturing rice, while by December the rice fields were "burnt up" around Kerewan and Suara.[98] If this was not bad enough, millet was eaten down three times in succession by a plague of caterpillars. Reports from MacCarthy Island and South Bank also expressed concern about the level of failure both of rice and corn crops, and as in North Bank noted that corn, especially *basso* failed because of blight.[99] The impending shortage of food prior to the rains of 1920, and the implications for further rice imports were apparent to the Administration by late 1919.

The immediate response to the crisis was the institution of an inquiry into food shortages in the Protectorate carried out by Captain Greig, the Commissioner of Police.[100] Based on his visits together with a report from the Travelling Commissioners, Greig estimated that there had been a general failure of up to 50% of the rice crop in 1919, and 20% of corn. Detailed figures supplied by Hopkinson for South Bank and MacCarthy Island indicated that food failure showed considerable variation among the districts within these provinces, and he was quite certain of where the need was greatest,[101] whereas Greig admitted he was unsure of how much rice would be needed as quantitative information was lacking on the total crops grown in normal years. However Greig accepted the Chamber of Commerce's estimate of 2,000 tons as being of the right order.

Greig's report is interesting as it again underlines the importance of the Strange Farmers, and that the Administration and the chiefs in the Protectorate took the contribution of migrant farmers very seriously. Greig makes it clear that he believes the people could probably survive with some difficulty, but the success of next year's

---

[98] RHL Micro Afr. 485, Annual Report North Bank Province, 1919–1920.

[99] RHL Micro Afr. 485, Annual reports for South Bank Province and MacCarthy Island, 1919–20.

[100] GNA 2/362, *Report on failure of rice and coos crops*, by C. Greig, 10th April 1920.

[101] GNA 2/332, *Crops in the South Bank Province*, 30th Dec. 1919 to 22nd March 1920.

groundnut crop depended on Strange Farmers. And as one chief opined, "if I can't get rice, then there is no point in the government sending me seed nuts, as 50% of the groundnut crop is grown by Strange Farmers."[102] Greig cited Sproston the Upper River Commissioner who believed that Strange Farmers grew 70–75% of the crop, and that two-thirds of the country's groundnuts came from Upper River. The latter may have been special pleading for his Province, but it does seem to suggest that by the early 20th century the focus of groundnut cultivation had shifted from the historic core of North Bank towards Upper River. Greig estimated that 12% of Upper River's population comprised Strange Farmers, and 7.7% in South Bank. But he rightly points out that these were young active males, and therefore represented a very important segment of the adult male population who were primarily responsible for the groundnut crop. To what extent the local price of rice was also increased by the demand generated by Strange Farmers is not overtly explored in the Administration's reports, although clearly the feeding of migrants was a significant element in the sales of rice along the river.

Greig's report ends with a series of calculations illustrating the Administration's optimism about groundnut prices, which was used to justify the issue of large quantities of rice.[103] Greig's basic premise was that there would be no problem with repayments as long as the price for groundnuts remained at the current levels. The 1919–20 crop of 84,000 tons had sold for £1,680,000, which represented an astonishing 5s 0d per bushel. On this basis Greig argued that the necessary 2,000 tons of rice at £160,000 could be paid for by 10% of the producers' takings; if the nut prices fell by half, then the native could still afford 20% of the takings. Greig's calculations seem to have ignored any questions about the geographical and social distribution of earnings from groundnut farming, or the money owed by farmers on the 1918 distribution together with their taxes, and importantly that host farmers had to provide food for Strange Farmers. Yet curiously he ends by dwelling on the huge amount of debt currently outstanding in the Provinces, which he estimated to be £1.0 million compared with the £1.5 million raised from the sale of groundnuts. He also noted that the agent of one old established firm

---

[102] Greig, op. cit. 1920.
[103] Ibid.

told him that in the past 5 months they had given out £100,000 of shop goods.

One further outcome of Grieg's report deserves mention before we move to the credit crisis of 1921, and that is the comment of M.T. Dawe the Inspector of Forests and Agriculture for West Africa. Grieg's report of April 1920 was passed on for comment to Dawe, who responded in February 1921 with a note on "the unstable and unsatisfactory conditions underlying the principal industry and export trade of The Gambia". By March 1921 Dawe had submitted a full report of the 'Agricultural Conditions and Needs of The Gambia.'[104] He declared that "the link between groundnuts, Strange Farmers, food supply and unreliable rainfall is entrenched", and suggested the encouragement of rice, cassava and maize, especially cassava as it was resistant to drought and pest.[105] But significantly he added that dry season irrigated rice was needed, which would mean enough food and a surplus for export. And, it might lessen the area devoted to millet, and so allow more land for groundnuts. He recommended the appointment of two irrigation officers to survey possible sites, although a minute shows that the Administration had considered this course of action a year earlier.[106] Therefore it appears the failure of food crops during the period 1918–1920 had revived the interest in irrigation first debated in 1900, but now quite specifically the irrigation agenda had shifted to rice. Rice farming in the dry season would 'cut the Gordian knot': it would allow an adequate local food supply, substantially reduce food on credit, while actually increasing the amount of groundnuts grown and exported. But this optimistic scenario ran into immediate trouble, as contrary to Grieg's expectations of continued high groundnut prices, in 1920 they plummeted, and by 1921 the economy was plunged into disarray. (Fig. 5.1)

### The credit crisis of 1921

In 1920 the government and the merchants were optimistic about the economic future of The Gambia, which was based on their belief

---

[104] GNA 2/362, *Report on the failure of rice and coos crops*, Comment by M.T. Dawe, 3rd February 1921.
[105] Ibid.
[106] Ibid. Minute no. 2, 24th Feb. 1920.

that groundnuts would continue to sell for around £22 per ton f.o.b. At these prices the merchants would be able to press farmers for the repayment of debts incurred in previous years, and reports from the Commissioners for MacCarthy Island and Upper River agreed with Leese in Kombo and Foni, that about 6s out of the 9s per bushel received by producers were being used to pay-off accumulated debts.[107] To the merchants this seemed a vindication of their policy of large advances to farmers, and in this mood of optimism they made even larger advances against the 1920–1921 groundnut crop. Imports of rice in 1920 rose to an all time high of 157,811 cwts, which exceeded the exceptional amounts imported after the 1913 drought (Fig. 5.4). Estimates made by the Travelling Commissioners suggested that credit was given out to farmers to the extent of over £80,000 in Foni and Kombo Districts,[108] over £190,000 in MacCarthy Island,[109] and over £300,000 in Upper River.[110] In addition the government had already distributed rice principally in the aftermath of the epidemics, floods and drought of 1918 and 1919, and during these years producers had taken £87,000 of seed nuts and rice. The government and the merchants continued to believe that high groundnut prices would continue, and as for the weather, they appeared ready to chance that it would remain favourable.

Despite assurances from the traders in 1920 that groundnut prices would be maintained, the following year the price in Europe fell sharply and the Gambian price dropped from £22 0s 0d to £8 0s 0d per ton f.o.b. (Fig. 5.1) It soon became clear the post-war boom had ended, a boom generated by a very sharp rise in prices as a result of the pent-up demand released after the war, and facilitated by the removal of wartime controls and the release of shipping. The buoyant post-war market for oilseeds had led to a big speculation in these commodities, but by 1920 it became apparent that post-war Europe was importing only 52% of the 1913 levels, and of particular importance for the groundnut trade was the decline in margarine production. After 1910 margarine production had been

---

[107] CO 87/213, Leese to CS, 20th Jan. 1921.
[108] CO 87/211, Leese to CS, 20th July 1920.
[109] CO 87/211, McCallum to CS, 11th Aug. 1920.
[110] CO 87/211, Sproston to CS, 18th July 1920.

accelerated, especially in Holland and England which had imported considerable quantities of groundnuts. But the release of stocks of butter held during the War shifted English consumption back to cheap butter, and price-cutting started among oil seed processors. Many merchants had been caught out both as importers and exporters, as well as the considerable time lags in forward buying. It was at this point the Niger Company got out from the oilseeds trade and sold their business to Lever Brothers, whose capacity for soap making as well as food producing spread their risks.[111]

In The Gambia the seriousness of the situation was such that Armitage, the new Governor, went on tour in January of 1921 and his party included Captain Greig and M.T. Dawe. The Report of the Governor's tour and associated correspondence indicates the severity of the situation, while also showing the predictable attitude of the Administration to the producers on the one hand, and the merchants on the other. The reports, diaries and correspondence of the Commissioners in 1921 indicate outbreaks of violence, evidence of malfeasance and corruption, and what may be termed 'social banditry'. Armitage reacted with the patrician disdain of the Administrator who on the one hand was beset by simple natives, and on the other, by avaricious ungentlemanly traders. His Report of 1921 regretted the period of "fictitious well-being" and he treated the assembled chiefs rather as errant children, and "preached the folly of putting all their eggs in one basket".[112] Armitage went on to opine that, "the present state of affairs has been brought about to a certain extent by themselves, and they have ruined the good name of Gambian nuts by adulterating them with foreign matter, therefore they are un-saleable in the home market in competition with those from other sources". The adulteration to which Armitage referred was the old practice of using sand to increase the weight of nuts; a form of resistance exercised by relatively powerless producers faced with the sudden fall in prices and huge debts, largely brought about by misinformation. In fact by late January buying was temporarily suspended, as producers were refusing to sell nuts. As for the traders, Armitage reserved his sterner strictures for the Europeans heading

---

[111] Shenton, R.W., 1986, *The Development of Capitalism in Northern Nigeria*, London: James Currey.
[112] GNA 3/52, *Governor's Tour in the Protectorate*, 11th–25th Jan. 1921.

the firms, in the belief that they as Europeans had the greater responsibility. He noted in a letter to the Secretary of State that:

> Natives have spent and spent assured that high prices would continue.
> Native agents of the mercantile firms gave unlimited credit at shame-
> ful and extortionate prices. Rice was sold on credit at 2s 3d per pound
> in Upper River, when the firms' maximum invoice price was 10d per
> pound. . . . European agents have shown criminal neglect in allowing
> native agents to do this, and I have told them so.[113]

The Upper River Commissioner confirmed the inflated prices of
goods in 1920, with rice being advanced at up to £25 per bag, but
he also made plain that in addition credit was given out to sub-
traders and the Head's of towns in the form of cash.[114] In response
to producers complaints about their inability to repay their debts at
high interest rates, Armitage secured an agreement that the firms
would accept the 1920 invoice price of goods, but the chiefs remained
unimpressed and asserted a need for more time for repayment.[115]

The outcome of the Governor's tour and a subsequent Travelling
Commissioners Conference was an agreement to collect not more
than half the government's rice and seed debt, which now amounted
to £88,579: the remainder was to be carried over into 1922–3.[116]
The meeting also decided that rice and seed nuts were to be issued
to farmers only in cases of dire necessity during the 1921 rains, while
Armitage became particularly attached to the notion of stopping the
supply of seed nuts altogether. After discussions with the Secretary
of State and the Commissioners, seed nut distribution was allowed,
largely because it was feared any abandonment would inhibit the
influx of Strange Farmers.[117]

The diaries of the Upper River and North Bank Commissioners
for 1921 illuminate some of the problems the crisis created at the
local level, as well as providing additional information on social disruption. The collection of the government debt was given priority
over traders' debts, which amounted to three or four times the
amount owed the government: in Fatoto in Upper River every trading company was owed money. Wannell, the Commissioner of Upper

---

[113] Ibid.
[114] GNA 59/3, Commissioner's Diary, Upper River Province, May–Dec. 1921.
[115] CO 87/213, 28th March 1921.
[116] GNA 56/1, Travelling Commissioners Conference, Jan. 1921.
[117] Ibid.

River thought that if the amount of credit given out was correct, then if all nuts sold at 2s 6d per bushel after paying the government debt, hut taxes and farm rents, "the natives might manage to pay 25% of the traders debts". But producers were unable or reluctant to pay even half the government debt, which was the amount targeted by the Governor. In the town of the head Chief of Wuli district, the Commissioner managed to collect just £80 0s 0d of a debt of £816 0s 0d.[119] While often sympathetic to producers, Wannell's notes show that to some extent he took the official line that the producers had brought it upon themselves, conveniently forgetting that the Administration had been just as keen as any other group to climb aboard the postwar boom. However, it is clear that rice distribution was rigged, and that chiefs and members of Native Tribunals allocated to themselves far more rice than they needed. In Fulladu East the average received per yard was one and a half bags, while the chief and his relatives had 100 bags.[120] It appears that local officials were once again selling-on rice into Senegal.

Not surprisingly the debt crisis increased the number of robberies and fires, especially as stocktaking approached. Another response was for producers to move temporarily into French territory: Hopkinson estimated that in the North Bank during 1921–22 some 10% of the population had decamped across the border. Meanwhile corruption increased, exemplified by a police sergeant and his men who were discovered collecting the debts of the traders "for a consideration".[121] In Upper River there was evidence of strong-arm tactics and thuggery. Momadu Faal an agent for Maurel et Prom in Fatoto was owed £6,000, so he resorted to using his labourers to fetch headmen who owed him money and forcibly detaining them until their friends paid-off the debt.[122] More serious complaints were made that after Faal had asserted that his store had been robbed, he demanded workers be subject to trial by ordeal. In another incident an agent of Palmines was found to be imprisoning debtors.[123] Whenever possible

---

[118] GNA 59/3, Commissioner's Diary 1921, Upper River Province.
[119] Ibid.
[120] Ibid.
[121] RHL Micro Afr. 485, Annual Report 1921–22 and GNA 3/43, Feb. 4th 1922.
[122] RHL Micro Afr. 485, Upper River Province Commissoner's Diary 1921.
[123] Ibid.

the authorities acted to stamp out these practices, but one must
assume many went unreported.

At this time another insidious practice that proliferated was the
use of 'coaxers'. Coaxers were those who went out on the road
searching for donkey men who they 'coaxed' into their employers
compound, where they were detained until they sold their groundnuts. Detainment could amount to physical force or threat, in the
which case it amounted to assault. On the other hand food was used
as an inducement, which as one Commissioner was moved to remark
was like "putting a horse-trough outside hay suppliers in London".[124]
Sometimes coaxers were employed by traders, alternatively they were
individuals working for a commission. Another ploy was for an agent
to pay an influential man in a village a fixed sum if he would persuade his neighbours to take groundnuts to a particular firm. It also
appears coaxers were used to 'black' certain firms and direct trade
away from them. The Commissioners and Governor agreed they
were a nuisance, but legislation was difficult to enforce.[125]

The debt crisis had severe implications for food supply throughout 1921, as it led to the suspension of credit by the merchants and
rice advances by the government. Once again people were driven
back to the old standbys of leaves and wild fruits and nuts, which
were combined with fishing and fish drying. Wannell, the Upper
River Commissioner kept a particularly detailed diary for 1921 possibly because he was new and was expected to trek through his new
area.[126] His notes show the considerable differences in food supply
among different parts of Upper River, as well as among the yards
of any one settlement. This was probably due to a combination of
the varied ecology of farms and social differentiation; for example
we have noted above that chiefs, their families and clients appro-
priated larger shares of the government distribution. Wannell also
comments on the relatively good food supplies in Fula yards, compared with the Mandingo.[127] Probably this was a reflection of the
different economies operated by the two: the former were principally upland farmers who reared cattle, which were 'tradeable entitlements' in times of shortage, compared with the latter who were

[124] GNA 56/1, Travelling Commissoners Conference, June 1922.
[125] Ibid.
[126] RHL Micro Afr. 485, Upper River Province, Commissioner's Diary 1921.
[127] Ibid.

much more heavily involved in groundnut production with limited room for manoeuvre. Alternatively, poor food supplies could in some measure be explained by food being hidden either in the village, or across the border. Then as now, food distribution to alleviate severe food shortages was beset by difficulties.

Wannell also alluded to a major pre-occupation of his fellow Commissioners at this time, that of the problems surrounding the currency.[128] In 1921 the Maria Theresa dollar was prohibited, and the new alloy and paper currency was introduced prior to de-monetization (discussed below). The new currency was bitterly resented by the people, and formed another element in the debt crisis as it developed during 1921. When the paper notes were introduced there was widespread uncertainly about their value, and for a brief period locals and Strange Farmers actively sought payment in French paper dollars or silver. As Hopkinson noted, the silver dollar was popular because it was widely used for 'brideprice' in French territory, and in the absence of banks it could be buried in people's yards.[129] Dislike of the new British alloy and paper currency led to a lot of fast spending, which, coupled with the devaluation of the French dollar was exploited by merchants and traders making quick profits, with one trader reputedly making £2,000 in a few months.[130] The currency situation became serious, and was itself a product of The Gambia's unusual geography, the history of the groundnut trade, the Strange Farmers, a highly mobile population and the effects of the 1914–18 War. In 1922 the currency issue had to be squarely faced, which led to "de-monitization" and another crippling blow for The Gambia.

### De-monetization

The timing and nature of the monetary crisis of 1920–1922 was peculiar to The Gambia, but it also reflected the changes taking place within the world monetary system from the 1870s onwards. After 1870 the international price of silver dropped as the world supply was increased, while at the same time the gold standard was

---

[128] Ibid.
[129] RHL Micro Afr. 485, North Bank Province, Annual Report, 1921–22.
[130] GNA 3/43, Cameron to SS, 29th April 1920.

being adopted throughout Europe.[131] The real value of the silver dollar by 1879 was reduced to 3s 7d, whereas in The Gambia it was still being exchanged at the old rate of 3s 10 ½d established in 1843. The silver five-franc coin (the dollar) was made legal tender in The Gambia in that year as a means of assisting the groundnut trade, and an exchange rate was established at 25.67 francs to the £1 0s 0d. The falling value of silver prompted the suggestion in 1880 that the Gambia should de-monetize the franc as quickly as possible, a suggestion which was put into practice in Nigeria.[132] In 1880, five-franc pieces comprised some 85% of the specie in circulation in The Gambia, which made devaluation a formidable problem. Devaluation was rejected as the government argued the people—and especially the Strange Farmers liked and had confidence in the silver coins.[133] Thus the five franc coin continued as legal tender at the 1843 rate (largely in deference to the Strange Farmers), which continued into the 20th century despite the establishment of the West African Currency Board in 1912–13, as well as another call for Gambian de-monetization in 1916.[134]

The warnings about an overvalued currency went unheeded in 1880 and 1916 because of The Gambia's geographical position *vis-à-vis* French territory, the dependence on Strange Farmers, and the willingness of the French to maintain a rate at francs 25 to the £1 0s 0d assisted by the rapid circulation of the silver dollar. The 1914–1918 War was used as an excuse to delay de-monetization, but after 1920, depressed trading conditions and the crumbling of the French economy eventually precipitated a monetary crisis. However, in 1920 the government hoped that the introduction of the new alloy and paper coins would drive out the silver dollar and so solve the problem. Unfortunately this did not materialize, and by February 1921 the strength of the franc in the international money market had collapsed leading to its de-valuation. As the Governor ruefully noted, a collapse had occurred "from 25.67 to 50 francs to the

---

[131] Nussbaum, *A History of the Dollar*. New York, p. 134. See also: A.G. Hopkins "The currency revolution in Southwest Nigeria in the late 19th century". *Journal of the Historical Society of Nigeria*, 3 (3) 1966, p. 478.
[132] Annual Report, The Gambia, 1880.
[133] Ibid.
[134] CO 87/214, J.J. minute no. S7257, 16th Nov. 1921.

£1 0s 0d".[135] Therefore, a five-franc coin was worth only 1s 11d, except of course in The Gambia where it was still legal tender at 3s 10 ½d, and for the purposes of the groundnut trade generally exchanged at 4s 0d. This signaled the beginning of the monetary crisis as the two Bathurst banks, the Bank of British West Africa and the Colonial Bank refused to accept the five franc piece for transfers abroad, except at the world rate of 1s. 11d. This precipitated a great demand for postal money orders, especially from kola and Syrian traders using dollars to send remittances to Freetown in Sierra Leone.[136]

In April 1921, the government banned the importation of coins when the Bathurst Treasury estimated there were 1,500,000 five franc pieces in circulation worth £300,000 calculated at 4s 0d, the prevailing rate in the Gambian groundnut trade.[137] Overvaluation continued, but sensing a likely adjustment speculation became widespread: by June reports showed five franc coins were being smuggled-in, and changed for British coins which were then taken back to Dakar to buy more five franc pieces! Silver was being offered to holders of notes at the rate of 5 × 5 franc pieces to the £1 0s 0d, which could be resold in Dakar at the rate of 50 francs.[138] Thus the number of coins in circulation by June had grown to an estimated 2,000,000 (£500,000).

In the same month June 1921, five franc pieces flowed into Bathurst in payment of taxes and into deposit accounts in the two banks. Governor Armitage had to admit that de-monetization was inevitable, and the Treasury in London approved de-monetization in July 1921, but on "a day to be proclaimed by the Governor".[139] Armitage was reluctant to proceed immediately, and argued that if de-monetization took place at once as the merchants and the British Treasury wanted, then the government would bear the loss and the merchants gain at the expense of both government and people.[140] The Governor was aware that the banks were replete with dollars after the end of

---

[135] GNA 2/441, 1921.
[136] GNA 3/56, Conf. Ag. Receiver General, 19th Nov. 1921.
[137] Colonial Office List, 1923 p. 201.
[138] CO 87/214, Workman to SS, 20th June 1921.
[139] CO 87/214, CO minute no. 43462, 30th Aug. 1921.
[140] GNA 3/56, De-monetization of the 5 franc piece. Minute on Governors meeting with Chamber of Commerce, 15th Nov. 1921.

the previous trade season, while the merchants were steadily accu-
mulating dollars in the expectation of their redemption by the
government at the old rate. And, Armitage had to assure the banks
that the government would accept all the five franc pieces. The concentration of silver dollars in the banks and the hands of the merchants exacerbated the government's problem; however Armitage
managed to get the merchants to agree to withdraw silver dollars
from the banks for use in the 1921–22 trading season.[141]

Armitage's main concern was to de-monetize at the end of the
1921–22 trade season, not at the beginning, because then dollars
would be widely dispersed. A key element in his thinking was the
possibility of dumping the coins on unsuspecting Strange Farmers
who after selling their groundnuts at the end of the trade season
would take them back into French Territory.[142] This was contrary
to advice given by the Treasury, and was premised on the belief
that the merchants would honour their promise to withdraw francs
from the banks to finance the trade season, and that the strangers
would not get wind of what was happening. Armitage's plan was
seen as very risky, and the Treasury's reservations were outlined in
a dispatch, of 12th September 1921, together with a review of the
situation.[143] Ultimately Armitage shifted his ground, especially as
Gwyn and Workman pointed out that in addition to the immediate
risks, it was wrong to assume Strange Farmers took the money home:
on the contrary they spent the money on trade goods in The
Gambia.[144] Furthermore, the Bathurst Chamber of Commerce were
pressing for rapid de-monetization, and in a letter of November 16th
estimated that the banks' receipt of dollars was increasing at the rate
of £5,000 per month.[145] Thus, at the end of December 1921, Armitage
invoked the Order in Council of August 3rd 1921 and proclaimed
that de-monetization would take place between the 17th and 31st
January 1922.

The de-monetization issue was surrounded by a number of conflicts
among the interested parties. First, there were the shared interests
of the British Government, Treasury and West African Currency

[141] CO 87/214, Conf D. 12th July 1921.
[142] CO 87/215, JF in min. no. 39542, 30th Aug. 1921.
[143] GNA 3/56, De-monetization of the 5 franc piece. SS to Governor Gambia
12th Sept. 1921.
[144] CO 87/ 214, Minute no. 57257 in Conf. D, 20th Nov. 1921.
[145] GNA 3/56, Telegram Governor to SS, 16th Nov. 1921.

Board. Second, there were those of the Governor and his administrators who were often opposed to the Treasury, as well as being at odds with each other. Third, the merchants, traders, banks and the Bathurst Chamber of Commerce inevitably formed another largely opportunistic bloc. The minutes attached to the various papers at this time are worth noting for the insights they give into these several interest groups. Finn, the Assistant Colonial Secretary of The Gambia clearly believed the government was not to blame as it was the fault of the traders: he also noted it was odd that the important dispatch of September 12th 1921 about the timing of devaluation from the Treasury should arrive when the Governor was en route for England and had to be dealt with by the Acting Governor, Gwyn.[146] The implication was that the Treasury was 'bouncing' The Gambia into a preferred line of action, although they had stated they would not directly interfere. Finn also expressed the view that if all silver dollars were not brought in, then, those remaining would be only worth 2s 0d, and that it was likely (and it proved to be so) the merchants would buy them at 2s 0d, and pay natives for produce as if old rate of 4s 0d obtained, so dumping them on producers.[147]

Adams, the Acting Receiver General, took a different view and felt aggrieved that the Receiver General had not been consulted about formulating the de-monetization policy. Furthermore he asserted that the over valuation of the currency had been identified in a Report by the Receiver General in 1917, and that the government was advised to act, but they resisted. Adams' minutes also point out the impracticability of dumping dollars on Strange Farmers, as negligible amounts of coin left the country this was because as Adams rightly noted the credit system of advances demanded debts be repaid after the harvest. And, given that Senegalese merchants came into The Gambia at the end of the trade season to buy goods, then at the end of the season there were *more*, not less dollars in circulation given that the merchants had received so many over their counters.[148]

This particular episode demonstrates the levels of acrimony and recrimination that could develop within the European ranks of administrators and traders, as well as disagreements between London and

---

[146] GNA 3/56, *De-monetization of the five franc piece*, minute no. 1. B.A. Finn.
[147] GNA 3/56, Minute no. 7 Adams, Ag. Receiver General.
[148] Ibid.

colonial governments. Such disagreements reflect the debates about
the often-ignored levels of conflict *within* the European colonial communities, compared with the prominence often given to conflicts
*between* Europeans and those they ruled.[149] It also supports our previous contention that the Gambian government was able to do little to alter the structure of the local economy so dependent on
groundnuts. The government could scarcely be seen as an instrument that willingly supported the merchant interest, and in truth
neither government nor producers in the final analysis could do much
against the power of the trading houses and merchant capital. And,
in this instance the Gambian government also was marred by internal wrangling, and given no support by the Treasury in London.

The direct costs of de-monetization were principally born by the
Gambian government and a special warrant was issued to cover the
loss of £189,890 6s 0d, which represented the difference between
redemption of silver coins at the prevailing rate of 1s 11d and the
old rate, together with other costs including the boxing and han-
dling of the dollars.[150] A loan was advanced by the West African
Currency Board, which Armitage unsuccessfully tried to negotiate
interest free, and the government had to pay a rate of 4% from the
date of each repayment. Also, there were further arguments with
Elder Dempster Lines about the freight rates to transport the dollars back to England. But there were also indirect costs of de-monetization, and it would appear that Gambian producers lost out to
the merchants and the government: the merchants made substantial
profits from the ignorance of producers, while Gambians were denied
the benefits of development initiatives cancelled by a government
strapped for revenue.

During the period set aside for the redemption of dollars, receiving stations were set-up across the Protectorate under the control
of the Commissioners, where dollars were replaced by alloy coins,
much disliked and mistrusted by the people. The reports from the
Commissioners indicated a variable response to the de-monetization
process. In Upper River less dollars were taken-in than forecast;

---

[149] Cooper, F. and A. Stoler, 1989, 'Tensions of Empire: Colonial Control and
Visions of Rule', *American Ethnologist*, vol. 16 (4), 609–631.
[150] Annual Report, 1922. Also GNA 2/496, Final report on de-monetization. SS
to Governor, 2nd Jan. 1922.

some 90,000, most of which came from traders.[151] Apparently producers believed the whole process was a ploy by the government to see how much money they actually had, and such fears allowed trickery to prosper. For example, one unscrupulous agent of the African and Eastern Company was taking in dollars from producers by assuring them in so doing they could avoid official knowledge of their assets as he would pass the dollars off as the Company's.[152] In MacCarthy Island Province, again less dollars were received than anticipated, and there were rumours spread by unscrupulous traders that if farmers waited, the dollar would be worth 4s 6d after January 31st.[153] Presumably the traders were planning to take payment in dollars after the 31st, when they were no longer legal tender in The Gambia, and would only accept them at a hugely discounted rate, after which they would redeem them over the border. In the Kombos and Fonis,[154] as well as South Bank, redemption proceeded satisfactorily, but in North Bank about half the dollars came from traders, and many people held back as they disliked alloy and didn't want the government or their relatives to know how much money they had.[155] Some people just waited too long, and the deadline was passed. In a dispatch to the Secretary of State, the Governor opined that the people of the Protectorate were reluctant to part with silver because of the enormous sums they owed to the Government for rice and seeds, and unpaid credits to the Trading Companies.[156] The people believed de-monetization was a government stratagem to recover these debts, rather than it being necessary that dollars were exchanged for British currency.

The currency crisis of 1921–22 was a horrendous episode in the economic life of The Gambia and it left its people confused and cheated; a government faced with a huge financial outlay, as well as signs of internal divisions about how the crisis was handled. As for the merchants, they suffered least and many traders opportunistically benefited from de-monetization. As for the British Government, it saw the episode as a necessary move to establish a common

---

[151] CO 87/216, Wannell to Armitage, 7th June 1922.
[152] GNA 2/496, Report on De-monetization, Commissioner Upper River Province.
[153] Ibid. Commissioner MacCarthy Island.
[154] CO 87/216, Leese to CS 20th Jan. 1922.
[155] CO 87/216, Hopkinson, July 1922.
[156] GNA 2/496, Gov. to SS, 14th April 1922.

currency throughout West Africa, yet it also was a flagrant example of a lack of responsibility for the welfare of a colonial area.[157]
Arguably, the Treasury failed in 1880 and 1916 to insist that a reluctant Administration de-monetize, and when the crisis occurred in
1921 Armitage was still allowed to set a date himself, thus ensuring
a considerable delay. Both the government and the merchants believed
the costs should have been born by the Treasury, but their pleas
fell on deaf ears.[158]

For the year 1922 gross expenditure exceeded gross revenue by
well over £200,000, while the 1921 reserve fund of £286,396 had
shrunk to only £99,687 by the end of 1922.[159] (Fig. 5.1) The de-
monetization disaster led to economy drives and curtailed development projects, which required the shelving of plans for the supply
of electricity to Bathurst, the drainage of part of Half-Die swamp
and improvements to Bathurst harbour. And it was not until 1935
that any significant attempt was made to provide medical and health
services in the Protectorate. Education also suffered; the government
decided it could not spend £2,000 on education, yet the de-monetization debacle had cost almost £200,000.

Despite the government's dismay over the episode and its impact
on producers, it did not prevent their thoughts turning to increasing taxation as a remedy for the Gambia's financial losses. The necessity for a budget surplus remained paramount and inhibited any
development initiatives.[160] The government initially looked at Strange
Farmer rents and the inconsistencies about their definition: as the
Acting Receiver General made clear, the rents were not actually law
but a result of the British formalizing a custom.[161] Difficulties emerged
with altering existing legislation so a new bill was canvassed which
would double Strange Farmer rents: a long argument also took place
about squeezing more revenue form the population in general, and
whether huts, yards, land rents, and Strange Farmers were the appropriate categories.[162] In the end the matter was deferred, and while

---

[157] Gailey, H.A. 1964, *A History of The Gambia*, London: Routledge, Kegan Paul
p. 168.
[158] Ibid.
[159] Blue Book 1921, 1922.
[160] Gailey op. cit.
[161] GNA 2/505, Hut Tax in the Protectorate, 1922.
[162] Ibid.

the government wanted to raise more revenue, it was particularly cautious about the issue of Strange Farmer rents.

*Summary*

After the ending of the Merchant Combine groundnut production increased, only to be temporarily halted by the outbreak of the war. However, by 1915 trade recovered and despite fluctuations in output groundnut tonnages averaged 60,000 per annum from 1913 to 1923. Rising production levels were attained by the use of more migrants from French territories, which also helped to extend the groundnut growing areas. The war triggered a number of changes: rising prices stimulated production during and after the hostilities, although producers benefited only marginally as they were counterbalanced by the high cost of imported food. The war substantially altered patterns of trade as British firms replaced French as the principal buyers of groundnuts, while rice imports came from the United States.

The war also intersected with a cluster of environmental disturbances such as drought, floods and outbreaks of pestilence. After the 1913 drought rice imports soared, dropped and rose again to record highs after the floods and drought of 1918–1919. After this second environmental disaster producers ignored the setback and bought their way out of trouble, encouraged by a steep increase in groundnut prices, as well as being encouraged by government and traders who made large advances of rice, seeds and goods on credit. And, the government was relatively unconcerned about the possible environmental dangers of clearing of more bush in order to expand groundnut cultivation. Optimism was unbounded and extended credit was floated on the back of high groundnut prices.

By 1920 the crash in commodity prices had precipitated a severe credit crisis centred on the repayment of the rice and seed debt. The situation was compounded by the de-monetization of the inflated silver coinage, so long the backbone of the groundnut trade that had remained in place in deference to the interest of Strange Farmers. De-monetization was an immediate product of the post war situation in Europe, as well as a long period of masterly inactivity vis-à-vis the artificial rates of exchange which obtained between sterling and the silver French franc. The whole of this period from

1913–1922 exposed the weaknesses in the government when dealing with crises, as well as the merchants and traders who at times
provoked outbreaks of violence from producers who increasingly felt
confused and cheated. Thereafter, economic development was inhibited, and principally took the form of the setting-up of an Agricultural
Department, together with experiments in irrigated and mixed farming. It is to these new agricultural initiatives that we finally turn, as
they attempted to improve the groundnut trade and solve the problem of food importing.

CHAPTER SIX

TOWARDS AN AGRICULTURAL POLICY, 1923–1933

Attempts to diversify the Gambian economy before the 1914–18 War had largely failed, while the collapse of the post-war boom and the de-monetization debacle had radically reduced the chances of serious economic development. But in the face of deteriorating economic conditions something had to be done, so the Administration began to turn its attention to the development of a coherent agri-cultural policy. A number of options were canvassed and discussed, some of which were espoused with confidence, others were approached with a degree of ambivalence, while most rested on limiting the impact of factors beyond the control of The Gambia. Not surpris-ingly the firmest commitment was rooted in past responses to moments of crisis, namely the need to increase the supply of groundnuts, but now supported by a number of initiatives to regulate the quality of produce in order to compete in an increasingly hostile world market. The foundation of this policy of improvement lay in the establish-ment of an Agricultural Department to supervise the quantity and quality of groundnuts produced, as well as promoting 'scientific man-agement' assisted by outside experts and advisors. As it turned out, many of the Department's initiatives came to nothing due to financial constraints, but they were 'markers' for future development path-ways constructed after the Second World War.

If the increased production of groundnuts was a readily agreed objective, there was less agreement how to achieve it. In the short run, the easiest option was the well-tried one of more Strange Farmers backed-up by food imports when necessary, but after 1922 this option became particularly contentious. The Administration realized that *ad hoc* arrangements from one season to another were no longer sufficient: it was now necessary to try and achieve a formulated agricultural policy. And, it was at this point that there was a revived interest in dry season irrigation, which had briefly appeared on the agenda some 20 years earlier. By the late 1920s a combination of irrigation and mixed farming was seen as a panacea for food shortages, and represented a scientific response to the vagaries of the Gambian climate, and the perceived shortcomings of local farming practices. However, any substantial developments were hindered by the downturn in trade in the late 1920s, as well as disputes among administrators and agricultural experts. We begin by reviewing the groundnut trade from 1923 to 1933 in the context of the depression of the world commodity trade.

*The Gambian groundnut economy and the world trade depression, 1923–34*

The inter-war trade depression had general as well as specific consequences for colonial economies, especially those dominated by primary exports. The conventional view is that Africa suffered badly in the inter-war years because of specialization in primary commodities, which were particularly affected by the dramatic decline in the volume and value of the world commodity trade. This led to a fall in money incomes, the tightening of local credit and the pressure to pay increasingly heavy taxes as other government revenues decreased. Alternatively, the revisionist literature posits a modified version of events, which suggests the depression was not wholly damaging to colonial economies.[1] For example, it has been suggested that the trade depression was a stimulus for industry in primary exporting countries, that there was increased resistance to money lenders and the state, that there was a return to subsistence farming, and that real incomes were maintained because of a fall in the costs of imported manufactured goods, especially as the colonial market place was penetrated by cheap Japanese textiles.

It has also been argued that the inter-war trade depression needs some periodization as it was not a single event, nor was its impact uniform across colonial states, and it varied according to different types of export commodities.[2] After the 1914–18 War there was a boom in most, but not all commodities, which came to a halt in 1921 when falling prices marked the first period of depressed trade during the inter-war years. However, this was not the crucial break, it merely represented a sharp contraction in demand. A second period stretching from 1921 to 1930 witnessed a return to price

---

[1] Brown I., 1989, *The Economies of Africa and Asia in the Inter-War Depression*. London: Routledge. 1–7.
[2] Ibid.

stability in the commodity markets, but this was halted by a steep fall in prices from 1931 to the mid-1930s, which heralded a third phase of severe contraction in world trade, especially for agricultural produce. In Africa and Asia this was exacerbated by overproduction, and a shift in market preferences by the metropoles. A brief revival of trade occurred, only to falter in 1937 in the run-up to the Second World War.

The three periods of change in trading conditions are consonant with The Gambia's experience, and some elements of the revisionist scenario apply, such as increased resistance to the state and price stability in the mid-1920s. Clearly 1921 signaled an important break in the economic fortunes of the groundnut trade: prices dropped from record highs of 8s 0d–9s 0d per bushel in 1920, to 2s 0d in 1921. Government credit was suspended, and the merchants engaged intermittently in price-fixing through what was known as 'participation', although the French and independent traders would not always 'participate'.[3] On the other hand, the costs of imported rice were reduced as the price stabilized. Nonetheless, rice was an important issue and formed the focus of resistance to the state, as a struggle developed between producers and government over the repayment of the 1919–20 rice and seed debts. Producer resistance to the merchants was less effective, and in the 1922–23 season price fixing was resumed and continued until the 1926–27 season. Prices were held at around 2s 0d to 2s 6d per bushel despite improvements in quality, and it would appear the merchants were making some attempt to recover their disastrous losses on the credit they extended in 1920.

Producers attempted to resist the resurgence of a Merchant Combine and lower prices by implementing a *tong* in Upper River, but a more effective strategy—at least near the border—was taking groundnuts into Senegal where according to the North Bank Commissioner in 1923–24 prices were twice those offered in The Gambia.[4] On the South Bank farmers told Acting Commissioner Doke that they had their own remedy for intransigent merchants: in order to frighten the traders they would grow just enough nuts to afford cloth and clothing which they would buy over the border, and devote more

---

[3] GNA 3/52, Governor's Tour of The Protectorate, January 1921.
[4] RHL Micro Afr. 485, The Gambia. Annual Report for the North Bank, 1923–4, and Annual Report for Upper River Province, 1924–25.

time to food crops.[5] Not surprisingly Doke reported that he had
stamped on this suggestion immediately, fearing it might spread. He
further commented on the lack of trust producers had in the traders,
who at times were guilty of fixing local exchange rates, while local
traders would mark-up prices when the agent was not in the district. Fortunately the rains of 1925 were exceptional, the grain harvest
was good and food imports were reduced in 1926.

While elements of the revisionist view are applicable to The Gambia,
for example resistance to the state through delaying debt repayments,
as well as a reduction in the costs of imported rice, there can be
no suggestion of economic compensation through industrialization,
while even attempts to diversify agriculture had failed. Nor was a
return to subsistence agriculture a viable long-term option given the
commitment to groundnut production, which was dependent on
migrant labour and imported foodstuffs. Certainly the issue of more
homegrown food and migrants was hotly debated, but there was no
material shift in policy towards self-sufficiency. What did happen was
that groundnut production was generally maintained at high levels
from 1923 to 1933, and only dropped below 60,000 tons on three
occasions, despite low groundnut prices. (Figs. 6.1, 6.2) However, producers experienced some relief from 1923–1929 when groundnut prices
were steady, and the cost of rice was reduced in real terms. Arguably,
central to the producer calculus was the amount of groundnuts grown
and the price received, compared with the amount of imported rice
they needed and its price, especially when it was essential to feed
Strange Farmers. Therefore the terms of trade between groundnuts
and rice were of some significance, and can be used to illuminate
the periodization of the inter-war trade depression outlined above.

The price indices in Figure 6.3 show the price of exported groundnuts and imported rice from 1911 to 1933, and while they usefully
demonstrate general trends, it is important to note the following qualifications. The groundnut price is an average for the buying season
and masks the quite wide variations in prices received by producers,
while the price of imported rice does not take account of the frequent
huge mark-up by traders. In facts the effects of both positive and

---

[5] GNA 2/519, extract of conf. 1031 T.W. Doke, Ag. Commissioner South Bank,
May 1926.

Fig. 6.1: *Gambian groundnut exports by tonnage and value together with government finances, 1923–1933*

| Year | Tons | £ value | Price f.o.b. | UK Price c.i.f. | £ Revenue | £ Expenditure |
|------|------|---------|--------------|-----------------|-----------|---------------|
| 1923 | 64178 | 864885 | 13.47 | 23.1 | 229688 | 161126 |
| 1924 | 60622 | 86925 | 14.21 | 22.5 | 208613 | 168112 |
| 1925 | 48700 | 693097 | 14.23 | | 189086 | 194690 |
| 1926 | 61072 | 862578 | 14.12 | | 214181 | 168112 |
| 1927 | 69240 | 967941 | 13.97 | | 252419 | 168812 |
| 1928 | 76772 | 1222253 | 15.91 | | 255385 | 175037 |
| 1929 | 58090 | 785576 | 13.52 | | 214266 | 184921 |
| 1930 | 74761 | 867634 | 11.60 | | 216739 | 188577 |
| 1931 | 66811 | 506125 | 7.50 | | 184825 | 197642 |
| 1932 | 37351 | 391659 | 10.70 | | 203368 | 180716 |
| 1933 | 67370 | 500766 | 7.40 | | 225606 | 167701 |

*Source*: Blue Books

Fig. 6.2: *Gambian groundnut exports (tons), 1923–1933*

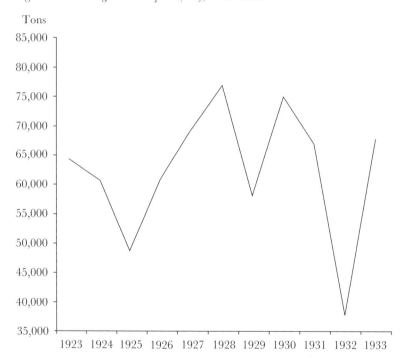

*Source*: Blue Books

Fig. 6.3: *Price indices for Gambian groundnuts (f.o.b.) and imported rice (c.i.f.) 1911–1933 (1911 = 100)*

| Groundnuts | | Rice |
| --- | --- | --- |
| 1911 | 100 | 100 |
| 1912 | 86 | 126 |
| 1913 | 101 | 116 |
| 1914 | 107 | 104 |
| 1915 | 46 | 128 |
| 1916 | 120 | 189 |
| 1917 | 128 | 268 |
| 1918 | 155 | 397 |
| 1919 | 179 | 367 |
| 1920 | 303 | 425 |
| 1921 | 116 | 193 |
| 1922 | 132 | 172 |
| 1923 | 148 | 155 |
| 1924 | 156 | 172 |
| 1925 | 156 | 157 |
| 1926 | 156 | 159 |
| 1927 | 153 | 159 |
| 1928 | 175 | 138 |
| 1929 | 148 | 138 |
| 1930 | 127 | 129 |
| 1931 | 83 | 95 |
| 1932 | 115 | 97 |
| 1933 | 62 | 72 |

*Source*: Blue Books

negative shifts in the terms of trade are to some extent masked by the large debts which producers carried over several seasons.

Despite the limitations, the indices illustrate the three distinct phases in the trade depression. First, it is important to remember that the dramatic fall of groundnut prices in 1921 were from historically high levels, which were matched by very high prices for imported rice. As we have shown in the last chapter rice sold at record prices during and after the war which offset high groundnut prices, and it is apparent the terms of trade were by no means as good as the export prices might suggest. Indeed, Martin has shown for West Africa as a whole the decline in terms of trade of the inter-war period were already apparent during the war.[6] In The Gambia the impact of the terms of trade would also vary among farmers and depend on the

---

[6] Martin, S.M., 1989, 'The Long Depression: West African Export Producers and the World Economy, 1914–45' In I. Brown, 1989, op. cit. 74–95.

amounts of imported rice they needed for themselves and their families. Secondly, It would seem as Martin has suggested, trade contracted rather than collapsed in 1921, and in The Gambia after the demonetization crisis of 1922 prices stabilized when there was an equitable balance in the net barter terms of trade which actually improved slightly in favour of producers during 1927–29. The prices f.o.b. received by producers were as good as, and in some years better than the period 1916–18 which had the disadvantage of high rice prices. Of particular importance was the cancellation of the government rice and seed debt after 1925 (see below). Statistics for Ghana and Nigeria show that prices of imported goods fell by 40%, while UK wholesale prices fell 20%, and the gap between British and West African prices narrowed.[7] With respect to The Gambia, the c.i.f. price in UK for groundnuts was only twice the price offered f.o.b. in The Gambia, whereas two to three times had been common before and during the War. (Fig. 6.1)

Compared with palm produce and cocoa, this was a relatively buoyant period for groundnuts, largely because alternative uses for palm produce were difficult to find (in the United States coconut oil from the Philippines became a strong competitor), while cocoa had an inelastic supply function. By comparison, groundnuts had a wider spread of uses, such as oils, soap and cattle feed. An exceptional output in The Gambia was achieved in 1928 when 76,772 tons of groundnuts exported, which were valued at over £1,000,000. Although the Administration was sensitive to the role of Strange Farmers in The Gambian economy, it did not prevent them increasing Strange Farmer rents on the back of this bumper crop, when the levy was increased from 4s 0d to 6s 0d. The co-operation of local chiefs in the collection of these fees and taxes was ensured by the Protectorate Amendment Ordinance of 1929, which allowed Commissioners the option of remunerating chiefs by up to one half of the taxes they collected. This was another step in the incorporation of local officials and rulers into the service of the Administration, which contributed to cheaper and easier government.

The exceptional output of 1928 was possibly inflated as a result of the yellow fever epidemic in Bathurst, and the reaction of the French authorities that imposed a 'cordon sanitaire' around the

---

[7] Ibid.

Gambian enclave. According to Hopkinson's reports from the North Bank, the French border guards were vigilant, and as he put it, "the French have us bottled-up".[8] The result was a stop on border trading, so there was no 'leakage' of groundnuts into Senegal. But there appear to be more important reasons for the bumper crop, namely the presence of so many Strange Farmers. The number in The Gambia had risen sharply in 1927, probably due to the 1926 droughts, which made food scarce the following year in Senegal and elsewhere. Rice distribution by the Gambian government in 1927 made it an attractive migrant location: once in The Gambia, the 1928 cordon sanitaire meant that many may have remained for the 1928 season leading to the second highest number on record. (Fig. 5.6) The 1928 output of groundnuts was exceptional, assisted by Strange Farmers and the closed borders, but generally exports remained at good levels, as well as Strange farmer numbers, until 1932. Yet by 1927 there were already signs that the fall in prices was becoming so severe that offsetting them by increased production was becoming very difficult.

Groundnut farmers managed to offset declining prices by keeping up production levels in difficult circumstances, as a means of supporting themselves, paying their debts and supporting the colonial state. In The Gambia exports of 60–70,000 tons of groundnuts were maintained throughout the late 1920s, which sustained the net income terms of trade for producers, as well as customs revenue for the government. Matters decidedly worsened when the end of the relatively stable period ended in 1931: groundnut prices fell drastically from £15 9s 0d per ton in 1928 to £7 5s 0d, and at these levels the relatively good net barter terms of trade were of decreasing value to a majority of producers. In general the crisis in merchant capital deepened in the late 1920s, which posed severe problems for primary export producing countries, especially colonial states heavily dependent on export and import revenues. In The Gambia production was maintained by means of government exhortation and intervention, and the necessity for household reproduction and debt

---

[8] RHL Micro Afr. 485, Annual Report for the North Bank, 1928.

repayments in a difficult situation. And, as in Northern Nigeria the government additionally resorted to increased taxation to bolster its revenues and stimulate production.[9]

By 1931 there was an unmistakable collapse and not just a contraction of the market, shown by a significant deterioration of both prices and output that reflected the extent of the trade depression in Europe. Groundnut prices slumped to levels below those which obtained 22 years earlier in 1912, and the number of Strange Farmers almost halved. (Fig. 6.4) The Upper River Annual Report for 1929–30 noted that groundnut prices were abysmal; opening at 1s 0d which at the beginning of December had fallen to 9d, and by the end of December 4½d per bushel.[10] The Report for the North Bank for 1931 reported opening prices of 7½d per bushel and at smaller wharves 4½d;[11] at times the price dipped as low as 3d per bushel.[12] The result was that the chiefs imposed a *tong* in every district which was not lifted until February 7th 1931, when the government agreed to suspend the collection of the rice and seed debt until the next year.[13] Producers were clearly unhappy with their situation, but the violence experienced in 1922–23 was not repeated, possibly because of the government's retreat on the rice debt.

The fact that the prices of imported goods had also fallen after 1931 was of little consequence, other than to produce a very low level equilibrium. Faced with prices below 1s 9d per bushel, and the continued demand for taxes and food expenditures, Gambian producers were facing the worst of circumstances. As one colonial official observed, whatever the situation rice and seeds cannot be advanced when nut prices have fallen below 2s 0d per bushel, otherwise the chances of repayment will be nil.[14] It was estimated at the beginning of December 1930 that at 9d per bushel for groundnuts, producers would have to sell four bags to pay back one bag of seeds borrowed,

---

[9] Shenton, R.W., 1986, *The Development of Capitalism in Northern Nigeria.* London: James Currey.
[10] RHL Micro Afr. 485, Annual Report for the Upper River Province, 1929–30.
[11] RHL Micro Afr. 485, Annual Report fro the North Bank Province, 1931.
[12] GNA 59/4, Annual Report for Upper River Division, 1930–31.
[13] Ibid.
[14] CO 87/232/1, Agricultural Department Report, 1930–1931.

while low prices exerted a serious pressure on Strange Farmers who had to repay seed nuts at 3s 0d per bushel and tax at 6s 0d.[15] Worse was to follow in 1931; government expenditure exceeded revenue for the first time since 1925 so taxation was increased, despite the difficulties facing producers. (Fig. 6.1) The Protectorate Amendment Ordinance of 1932 replaced the old 1913 tax schedule, and increased the yard tax of up to four huts from 4s 0d to 5s 0d, with additional huts at 1s 6d, while Strange Farmer rents were increased from 6s 0d to 8s 0d.

In Upper River producers responded to low prices by extracting groundnut oil at a rate of four imperial pints per bushel, which sold at 3d to 4d per pint compared to 1s 0d per litre of imported cotton seed oil sold by the merchants.[16] Groundnut cake could also be kept for up to 12 months and mixed with leaves and made into soup, while a local type of soap was made from groundnut oil: thus producers turned to the principal export as a means of supplying food and raw materials. It is also recorded that producers had turned to new methods of adulterating the crop as a response to low prices. The Governor in 1929 commented on reports that that small nut-sized pieces of rubble were being introduced into loads of groundnuts which escaped the rotary screens, and in some instances as much as 1lb 3oz of foreign matter was found in one imperial bushel.[17] Reports also noted that Mandinka were trading sheep and goats with the Jola in return for corn and rice, which suggests the historic role of the South bank as an area of food surpluses had not entirely disappeared.[18]

While production levels were maintained at around 60,000 tons, despite falling prices in a highly competitive market, there was one particular irony for producers: that all of this took place as the quality of Gambian groundnuts had steadily improved. The Agricultural Report of 1927–28 states that Gambian nuts inspected at Marseilles and Bordeaux showed a high yield of oil and low levels of fatty acid, which made them superior to Senegalese groundnuts.[19] Groundnut prices briefly recovered from the abysmal levels of 1930 and in 1932

[15] GNA 59/4, Annual Report Upper River Division, 1930.
[16] Ibid.
[17] CO 87/229/6, Comments by the Governor on the Report of the Director of Agriculture, year ending March 31st 1929.
[18] CO 87/236/11, Provincial Reports, South Bank, 1931.
[19] CO 87/227/15, Annual Agricultural report, 1927–28.

producers were offered 2s 0d per bushel, but the price dropped again in 1933. (Fig. 6.1) At such low prices producers could not afford rice on credit, repay their debts and pay higher taxes. So in 1932 the merchants once again suspended credit, while in the previous year price controls were introduced to try and stabilize the rice price at 1½d per pound.[20] One particular effect of these low groundnut prices and reduced trade levels could be seen in their impact on African traders, who had bought second-hand lorries from the European firms. The lorries were old and they became costly to run and maintain at a time when farmers could not pay the carriage charges.[21] One final blow was the poor rainfall of 1931 when the rainfall total was both low, 30.95 inches (773.75 mm), and badly distributed: most of it fell in the early part of the growing season which led to extensive planting followed by prolonged drought.[22] There was also blight on sorghum, and locusts were widespread. The result was sorghum, rice and groundnuts were very poor and only millet produced relatively good yields. (Fig. 5.3) Once more, The Gambian producers found themselves on the treadmill of low groundnut prices, poor rains, and debt.

The period of trade depression and the challenges facing producers brings us back to the vent for surplus theory and the mechanics of the export trade. It may be true as Myint asserts that the cash crop economy took off with no technical innovation, but at times producers operating labour intensive faming systems were hard pressed by a set of economic and environmental uncertainties, which meant real hardship for many farmers. The maintenance of production levels in he face of falling prices required extra labour time and possibly land, as well as time spent complying with the adulteration of produce measures, discussed below. And, when the product improved, there was little or no reward in prices paid. Perhaps the crucial element was the number of migrant workers, whose numbers although falling, were still attracted to The Gambia, where they were relatively better off. Alternatively, radical analyses argue that sustained production at this time was secured by merchant capital and the state, who were squeezing producers and extracting absolute surplus

---

[20] CO 89/18, Sessional Papers, Agricultural Report, 1932–33.
[21] CO 87/236/11, Provincial Reports, The Gambia, 1931.
[22] CO 87/232, Annual Agricultural Report, 1931–32.

value from them in the absence of any technical innovation. Whatever explanation one may prefer, our analysis has frequently shown it was the uncertainty of conditions from one year to the next that bore heavily on Gambian farmers.

*The Agricultural Department*

The response of the government to the vicissitudes of the ground-nut industry and the deterioration of world trade was to set up an agricultural service. The Gambian Agricultural Department began in 1924 (Nigeria started one in 1916) and was prompted by rec-ommendation made by M.T. Dawe in his report on The Agricultural and Forest Products of The Gambia in 1921.[23] Dawe, as we observed in the last chapter had been invited to The Gambia to examine the state of the groundnut economy, after the crash in prices in 1920: as a result attempts were made to improve the quality of ground-nuts prior to the setting-up of the Department. The trading season was prescribed for the first time in 1922–23, and lasted from December 1st to April 30th in an attempt to stop groundnuts being pulled too early.[24] Also in 1923 the Travelling Commissioners had their status changed to permanent Commissioners as they had to spend the rains in their provinces, whereas hitherto they had returned to Bathurst.[25] This measure was designed to improve the surveillance and control over the rural population.

A more important step was the introduction of the Adulteration of Produce Ordinance of 1920 and its Amendment in 1922; mea-sures promoted by the long established ploy of merchants lobbying the Secretary of State through the Liverpool Chamber of Commerce.[26] This was a particular instance of the government being pushed by London to accommodate the interests of the merchants. Inspectors were appointed with the power to stop and check groundnuts for foreign matter, and in 1922 clean nuts were designated as those with only 2% foreign matter, a substantial change from the 12% formerly

---

[23] CO 87/215, M.T. Dawe, Agricultural Conditions and Needs of The Gambia, 16th Mar 1921.
[24] RHL Micro Afr. 485, Annual Report for the North Bank, 1922–23.
[25] GNA 56/1, Travelling Commisioners' Conference 1923.
[26] Adulteration of Produce Ordinances, 1920 and 1922. See also Brooks, 1924 op. cit.

allowed. Under the new Amendment of 1922 nuts had to be cleaned before they were offered for sale, which proved problematic at the end of the season, when there was more foreign matter as the bottom of the groundnut heaps were reached.

The introduction of quality control was a result of the declining market for oilseeds and the success of new suppliers—in the case of groundnuts it was India—and the need for any one producing region to acquire as large a share as possible of the reduced market. Competition was increased not only among different European empires, but also among their constituent territories, where colony was set against colony.[27] The introduction of quality control was also shaped by new attitudes in Europe towards the legitimization of state intervention through the control of foodstuffs, first in terms of a protector of purity, and second as a purveyor of welfare.[28] The concern about the adulteration of produce in Europe had surfaced in the mid-19th century, while concerns over standardization of measures, units of currency, pure water and better sanitation were part of the need to regulate a burgeoning capitalist society. The state became increasingly a protector of purity through scientific devices, rather than older moral or religious adjurations. The impetus for state intervention was accelerated during the 1914–18 War, when new government departments were created, and the state became the guarantor of basic levels of welfare, albeit temporally during hostilities. In the colonies purity became an idiom in the politics of production, and the share of world markets among countries was fought out over standards of purity. However, it was purity for the foreign, not the domestic consumer which was instituted in the colonies.

Metropolitan interventions, gathered pace after the War, largely born out of financial crises both within the metropoles and the colonies. During the trade depression, merchant capital needed some restructuring, which became linked with the transposition of new administrative structures and expertise to the colonies from the metropoles. There was a convergence of interest of business and government in certain spheres, especially in the export of staple commodities such

[27] Shenton, 1986 op. cit.
[28] Guyer, J.I., 1991, *British Colonial and Post-Colonial food Regulation with Reference to Nigeria: An Essay in Formal Sector Anthropology*, Working papers in African Studies, No. 158, African Studies Center, Boston University.

as groundnuts, which included quality control as well as the possibility of an improved agriculture through the appliance of science. The 1914–18 War, together with changing curricula in British Universities accelerated developments within the applied sciences, and the Empire became an important field of experimentation. In 1922, Lugard in 'The Dual Mandate in Tropical Africa' was urging the use of new technical advances to improve agriculture and industry in the Empire, but not outside the control of the Governors and those administrators who had experience in the field.[29] In this context Lugard spoke of the "tyranny of the expert", something which was to prove contentious in the 1920s and 30s, well before its re-appearance as an issue in the 1970s and 1980s.

In The Gambia, the implementation of the adulteration measures proved to be a messy business, causing confusion, resentment and resistance among producers, especially so given the fall in prices and price-fixing by the merchants. The manipulations by the state in the interests of the market, colonial revenues and ultimately foreign consumers at times made the people and the state open adversaries, despite the government having some sympathy with the producers. The Travelling Commissioners Conference considered the adulteration issue in 1922, and Hopkinson on the North Bank wanted nuts inspected at the ocean shipping points, while Ogden of the Chamber of Commerce favoured inspection at the local wharves.[30] The argument rested on whether the burden of inspections should fall on the buyers or the producers, and the consequent 'costs'. The government sided with the producers on the grounds that when they had tried to deliver clean nuts the prices offered them had been no better. The Conference decided that the appointment of a Director of Agriculture next season (1923–24) would in effect deal with the problem, together with hiring more inspectors.

The meeting also recorded the entry of a new voice in support of the producers, that of Edward Francis Small, the Gambian delegate to the West African National Congress. Small had written to the Secretary of State referring to the Ordinance of 1922 as a "brutal one and the natives are groaning under its application".[31] The

---

[29] Lugard, F.D., 1926, *The Dual Mandate in Tropical Africa.* London.
[30] GNA 56/1, Travelling Commissioners' Conference, 1922.
[31] Ibid.

Congress was founded in 1920 by J.E. Casely Hayford, a Gold Coast barrister, and Small's part in it was roundly denounced by the Commissioners and Governor, as it represented "unwarranted interference". They dismissed it as of no consequence, as "the up-country natives would have little idea of what it was about".[32] However, Small persisted and attempted to form a farmers' co-operative union, to challenge the monopoly of the traders.[33] The issue of inspection rumbled on and a compromise was reached when it was decided to inspect producers' groundnuts at buying stations within prescribed areas, as well as at the loading ports, but not the ocean-going ships.

The adulteration issue was further addressed under the new Department of Agriculture in 1924, when a new Adulteration of Produce Order stated no groundnuts could be bought, or stored until they had been through a rotary screen approved by the Director of Agriculture.[34] But this measure further increased levels of disenchantment among producers, whose sentiments were voiced by Hopkinson, now Commissioner for the North Bank. In 1925 Hopkinson pointed out that the new arrangements introduced in 1923–24 meant that in order to comply with the screening requirements, farmers had to take their produce to approved buying stations to which they had limited access.[35] The abandonment of farm-side buying meant longer journeys and increased costs for producers. Farmers were also disgruntled because of low prices: hitherto they had been told they were due to the amount of dirt in the nuts; now they had cleaned them they were still given low prices fixed by the merchants. They argued that even if prices had remained the same, they would be receiving less than in previous years. Hopkinson also noted that screening was discouraging Strange Farmers as there were no similar requirements in French territory: reports also showed Gambians (as ever voting with their feet), were taking their groundnuts into French territory to avoid screening.

---

[32] Travelling Commissioners' Conference, 1922 op. cit. 24 Adulteration of Produce Ordinance, 1924.

[33] See D. Perfect, 1991, 'The Political Career of Edward Francis Small', in *The Gambia Studies in Society and Politics*, ed. A. Hughes, Birmingham University African Studies series, 3.

[34] No. 6, 1924, Adulteration of Produce Ordinance.

[35] RHL Micro Afr. 485, The Gambia, Annual Report for the North Bank Province, 1925.

While aware of the position of the producers, the government
viewed the introduction of standardization and quality control not
only in the interest of the merchants, but as necessary for The
Gambia's viability as an exporter of groundnuts, and beneficial to
the country's fiscal position. Certainly the difference between Rufisque
and Gambian groundnuts narrowed dramatically as a result of quality controls: the difference dropped from 30s 0d per ton to 5s 0d,
and then 2s 6d per ton between 1923 and 1925.[36] But there was
limited, or no improvement in producers' incomes, as they were at
the mercy of the markets and merchants. The move towards improved
quality imposed new constraints on producers: it increased the control over them by the merchants and government. Control of groundnut quality also opened up new social spaces, which were contested
by producers, merchants and the government.

Europeans were not only exercising greater economic control over
production, but also generally advancing new concepts of con-
formity and standardization. Colonialism was as much a clash of
cultural perceptions of what constituted time, work and material
production, as it was about political and economic formations. It
was also part of the process of advancing concepts of the material
world rooted in experimental science, inherent in both liberal and
radical discourse—what Bourdieu has called *orthodoxy*, as opposed to
social systems and practices rooted in *doxa*. Bourdieu refers to *doxa*
as representing practices where collective time assigns acts at particular moments of the day and season, where the natural and social
order is taken for granted and is self-evident and unquestioned, other
than at moment of crisis.[37] It might also be said tp that Gambian
farmers *experienced* reality, whereas Europeans, and increasingly their
appointed scientific experts *measured* it. Thus European concepts of
work were shifting 'patchy' circular time into linear continuous time,
and simple reproduction into indefinite accumulation. Therefore the
setting-up of Agricultural Departments was as much a cultural, as
an economic event which in The Gambia continued to sharpen the
impact of the groundnut trade on rural people, a process which had
begun in the 1850s when specialization and production for the international market gathered pace.

---

[36] Annual Report 1925.
[37] Bourdieu, P., 1977, *Outline of a Theory of Practice*. Cambridge: CUP.

The Agricultural Department was responsible for a number of innovations, as well as focusing the government's attention on the major issues of the groundnut trade and The Gambia's agricultural future. An Agricultural Department was presented as an attempt to assist producers, who apart from occasional seed issues had in Armitage's words "cultivated . . . without a particle of European intervention".[38] In the Annual Report for 1924 the Governor outlined this new initiative to assist the efforts of farmers by demonstrations, field trials, organization of seed storage, regular crop inspection, pest control and up-to-date harvesting methods.[39] The first Director of Agriculture was Archibald Brooks, who prior to his appointment in 1924 had already written a report which dwelt on the vulnerability of a 'one-crop economy'. Apart from emphasizing the need for quality control, he expressed the need "to teach the native the proper methods of tillage", yet he also asserted that the Department would proceed with caution, and there would be no sudden upheaval of existing groundnut farming methods.[40]

Brook's arrival was greeted with a good deal of enthusiasm, although he realized that the success of the Department in a very great measure depended on the relations between producers and the Agricultural Officers.[41] Brooks held meetings along both banks of the river between February and April 1923 in order to explain the aim of the department. The response from the farmers was impressive: in Kombo District alone 2,382 farmers attended the meeting.[42] The North Bank Annual Report for 1923 describes the Director's visit to examine growing crops just before the main harvest as an innovation, which in the word of the Commissioner, was "more than any of our former Agricultural experts have done, with their flying visits in the dead dry season".[43] This Report also records that the people expressed their hope that the 'learned farmer' could grow a race of *Basso* that will grow west of Upper Baddibu, which might suggest that the farmers had priorities other than improved groundnut crops. And, despite Brook's declared aim of proceeding cautiously with agrarian change,

---

[38] Annual Report, 1924.
[39] Ibid.
[40] CO 87/219 Brooks to CS, 7th July 1923, Report on the Agricultural Problems and Requirements of The Gambia.
[41] Ibid.
[42] Ibid.
[43] GNA 2/60, Annual Report for the North Bank Province, 1922–23.

the North Bank Report for 1923 does record that he embraced the orthodoxy of the 'colonial forestry school' over the question of rotational fallowing. Brooks tried to persuade the North Bank farmers against grass burning, and instead adopt green manure and mulching techniques.[44] In 1924 he also undertook a 430 mile tour of the Protectorate, where he observed that the groundnut disease *cercospora personata* was pandemic and began work for its eradication.

The Agricultural Department at its inception accepted responsibility for ensuring the inspection of groundnuts and by 1925 the Executive Council agreed to spending £1,500 on 12 groundnut seed stores for the next trading season.[45] Farmers were required to reserve not less than half their seed requirements, and could use their own stores or the government's. Some 1,000 bags of seed were purchased from the merchants, and farmers were able to exchange their own seed for improved varieties if they wished to do so. Under the new arrangement seed nuts would be available every year on credit. The 12 seed stores were also to be the centres for experimental groundnut seed farms, which would serve as agricultural training centres.[46] The experimental farms ran trials of 7 strains of groundnuts and used artificial fertilizers, but by 1926 it appeared fertilizers only worked over limited periods. In addition a new problem appeared, that of white ants attacking the crops.[47]

The experimental farms did not meet with unqualified acceptance, and once again Hopkinson was the most articulate on this score. Hopkinson, writing of the experimental farm at Kerewan believed it had not much to show, and that "growing nuts against the Mandingoes will be no easy job".[48] He described how he had once set-up an experimental plot which had failed, and didn't even cover the food he had given the boys who worked it during the rains. Another instance he cited was of a trader in Jowara who tried farming, but he also failed despite on three occasions calling 100 people to clear and weed the farm. The end result was that his harvest produced less than he had paid for the seeds. Hopkinson's report concludes with an appreciation of the abilities and virtues of the Gambian farmer:

[44] Ibid.
[45] GNA 3/90/11A, Conf. Correspondence. Policy of the Government with Regard to Agriculture, 10th May 1925.
[46] Ibid., Min. 17, Brooks to Workman, 23rd Oct. 1926.
[47] CO 87/226/14, Annual Report, 1926.
[48] GNA 2/60, Annual Report for the North Bank Province, 1926–27.

The longer I stay here and the more I see, the more I am convinced that the groundnut is a one man crop, one that responds to what can be called individual treatment, and is largely dependent for its success on inherited knowledge of each particular patch of ground and its needs. To European ideas the irregular farming, here deep, there shallow sometimes with, sometimes across the slope, looks untidy, and is often attributed to slackness or the like, but I really believe that the very irregularity is based on a vast amount of traditional knowledge of the soil and its cultural requirements, which has been accumulated by the growers and their forbears and that it is this traditional lore which makes the difference between a good and bad result. It is most certainly not the mere haphazard performance so often imagined.[49]

Brooks, may have been keen to push the experimental farms, but his report of 1927–28 shows that by this time he had no illusions about his ability suddenly to change Gambian agriculture, and that he like Hopkinson believed either from a sense of prudence or financial necessity, it was necessary to consider carefully what local farmers were doing. Brooks seems to have tempered the earlier advice he gave to North Bank farmers, and while he still paid lip service to criticisms that had been leveled against shifting cultivation, in 1928 he declared that the Department's policy was one "of an open mind and that methods developed elsewhere should be tested in the context of Gambian conditions".[50] He noted that shifting cultivation produced some 60–70,000 tons of groundnuts per annum, and that while economists may well point to the defects of this cultivation system, it must be continued until a practicable and profitable alternative could be found. Experiments with crop rotations and permanent farming would continue, but so far it had been found that groundnuts could not be grown continuously on the same piece of land, even if fertilizer applications were increased. In Brook's view humus was the crux of replenishing fertility, and as rainfall was spread over a short period then sufficiently large quantities of vegetable matter would not decay on the surface. Furthermore, deep ploughing was out of the question as thin soils and light textures caused drifting, and ploughs could not get sufficient purchase. In his view a green manure crop every three years might be the answer. Brooks' 'leit-motif' for the Department had now become 'investigation before demonstration'.

[49] Ibid.
[50] CO 87/227/15, Agricultural Department Report, 1928.

These observations would seem to pre-figure a principle thrust of writing in the 1980s about African agriculture that appeared under a variety of headings such as 'ethno-science' and 'indigenous technology', which advocated a necessary integration of local farmers' knowledge into attempts to transform agriculture.[51] But there had been others before Hopkinson and Brooks, who had made similar pleas that the 'African farmer knows best'. One notable observer was E.D. Morel, a journalist much preoccupied with the matter of African labour, especially the use of indentured and slave labour. His book on *Nigeria its People and its Problems* published in 1911, express similar views to those of Hopkinson.[52] When Morel visited Sokoto he wrote "the soil may look incapable of sustaining crops, but every year blossoms like the rose . . . this means and needs inherited lore and sustained and strenuous labour". Morel may have been genuinely impressed by what he saw, although it should be remembered he was a lobbyist on behalf of the merchant interest in Liverpool, who were happy to see a prosperous peasantry with the companies collecting produce and retailing manufactured goods rather than the emergence of a plantation system backed by industrial capital. On the other hand, it may be that these writers represented a shift in the attitudes towards African peoples, along the lines of the ideas of Mary Kingsley, who in 1919 was promoting a belief in cultural diversity, and the integrity of non-European systems.[53]

What does seem evident is that the likes of Hopkinson, Brooks and Morel were relatively lone voices, whose notions were over ridden by the 'scientific experts', supported by London. The belief in the scientific exploitation of the Empire was advocated by the Imperial War Conferences of 1917–1918 and the Colonial Conference of 1927: all expressed concern about the decline of the British economy faced by foreign competition underpinned by new technology.[54] It is important to appreciate that there was a wide spectrum of ideas, institutions, ideologies and technical possibilities in existence, from which there was a selective application at any one particular point

[51] See for example, P. Richards, 1985, *Indigenous Agricultural Revolution*. London: Heineman.
[52] Morel, E.D. 1911, *Nigeria its' People and its Problems*. London: Smith Elder.
[53] Rich, P.B., 1990, *Race and Empire in British Politics*. Second edition, ch. 2. Cambridge: CUP.
[54] Correlli Barnett, 1972, *The Collapse of British Power*. London: Methuen.

in time. As Guyer had argued, the colonial world was complex, and metropolitan systems were not set down in their entirety in any one colony; ideational, institutional and technical elements were selectively transposed.[55] The question is what were the principles of transposition? At one level there were guiding principles such as contemporary parallelism, where colonial governmental structures duplicated those of the current metropolitan world; on the other hand there was evolutionary parallelism where colonial practices were drawn from earlier phases of development in the metropole. Finally, there was complementarity, where an administration's policies reflected a functional division of labour between the colony and the metropole.

All three methods were used during the 20th century as part of the development of bureaucratic rubrics and the technical capacity building, which were central to establishing legitimacy, as well as the efficacy of colonial regimes. It is also important to realize that there were also transfers of institutions, practices and technologies among the colonies, as well as between them and the metropoles. In the case of The Gambia, the question of improved quality of produce can be couched more in terms of complementarity, at least as far as the higher levels of government and the metropolitan merchant interest were concerned. African producers were the complement, a part of the international division of labour. On the other hand the lower levels of administration were more interested in evolutionary models, and had some faith in farmers' abilities to the meet the standards required by European markets, especially if prices were sufficiently good.

### The Strange Farmer debate

The inception of the Agricultural Department coincided with a period of financial difficulties. The collapse of groundnut prices in 1921 saw a return to price-fixing by the merchants; the government was concerned about the rice and seed debt which remained unpaid; the distribution of rice had once again been suspended; and opinion within the Administration was divided as to whether the farmers could pay-off their debts, or indeed should be asked to do so. Furthermore, food and seed nut distribution in the minds of some officers was inseparable from the issue of Strange Farmers and the downward

---

[55] Guyer, J. 1991, op. cit.

trend in their numbers. In 1919 and 1920, the boom years had been underpinned by as many as 24,000 Strange Farmers, but after 1920 the numbers showed a downward trend, although from admittedly high levels, and by 1925 had fallen to 13,392 which was still considerably better than pre-war. (Fig 5.6)

The Commissioners and Brooks were circulated in March 1925 to find out their views on Strange Farmers, and included was a memo from Armitage the Governor who believed that the source of the problem was that they were treated badly by chiefs and headmen.[56] The Governor felt they were treated like slaves and were called upon to act as carriers as required, whereas Strange Farmers needed every encouragement and should not be used on either public works or roads. Moreover, Armitage believed that the hosts of Strange Farmers should not impose levies to assist with the payment of seed nut and rice debts, and any breach of this instruction should be dealt with severely. The responses from the Commissioners indicate either Armitage's misunderstanding of the essentials of the Strange Farmer contract, or that he preferred the 'mistreatment' explanation as it negated arguments about the incentive of rice and seed distribution.

All the Commissioners refuted the Governor's assertion, but Hopkinson's comments encapsulate the general view. His response begins with the rather acid comment that if they were treated so badly why did so many return; and he continued that they undertook a share of the compound's tasks because this was expected of all the resident young men, including acting as carriers for the Commissioners.[57] And, part of the lodging and feeding contract between host and strangers rested on shared work. Hopkinson agreed the Strange Farmers didn't get enough encouragement, but this was the fault of the merchants and the government. For example, they didn't like the new paper currency while the low prices paid for nuts was a significant factor in reducing numbers. In fact, as we have shown, production was being sustained despite the low prices while the number of strange farmers was substantial; and the terms of trade were improving, but the government's mind seemed permanently fixed on the brief period of 1919–21 when the boom was at its height. Hopkinson believed the distribution of rice was important, and the

---

[56] GNA 2/519, CS to all Commissioners on subject of Strange Farmers and their replies, March 12th 1925.
[57] Ibid.

current indebtedness should not be judged in isolation, but against the effects of "the biggest war in history and the biggest slump in prices on record." Hopkinson continued, "that if rice distribution is to work properly, then it required co-operation between the government and the merchants".

Despite the prolonged discussion on rice, officials make no mention of the large amounts of rice which were being imported throughout the 1920s, once again from France and Germany. (Fig. 5.4) This would appear to be paradoxical given a fall in migrant numbers and their potential food requirements, while such large rice imports can only be partially explained by environmental hazards, for example during 1926–27. The explanation probably lies in accelerated border trading into Senegal to meet the demand created by the further extension of the Dakar-Bamako railway; it had already been shown in 1910 that the railway could have a substantial effect on the flow of Strange Farmers into The Gambia. Brooks cited an article in *West Africa* reprinted from *Depeche Coloniale*, which reported a decline in the number of Strange Farmers entering The Gambia as a result of the completion of the Niger-Kayes-Thiès railway, whereas in 1910–11 the part-finished line had facilitated migrants moving into Upper River.[58] In 1926 Hopkinson described the current situation as "the railway rush": farmers were being attracted to the railway as good groundnut prices were paid along the line, while food (probably brought in via The Gambia) was cheap and the prices of imported trade goods lower than elsewhere. Border trading was the problem, and from its inception Bathurst had provided an entrepôt for a wide hinterland, which was extended eastwards as the railway reached Bamako.

The fall in the number of strangers in The Gambia also had a knock-on effect as it reduced the dry season labour force needed along the river, especially at the wharves: railway work had now become preferable to wharf work. Hopkinson's account also introduced for the first time another dimension of the migratory system, by observing that the relatives of some Strange Farmers joined them after the harvest, when they all went to work loading cutters and ocean going ships as a source of further income.[60] In the same

---

[58] GNA 2/519, Extract from *Dépêche Coloniale* cited in *West Africa*, March 24th 1924.
[59] CO 87/226/5, Provincial Reports for The Gambia, 1926.
[60] Ibid.

account Hopkinson also noted the impact of the lorries which had appeared in the early 1920s and the enhanced mobility this gave to seasonal migrants, as the lorries carried passengers and became the means of redistributing the labour force, especially young Gambians as they too joined the Stranger Farmer migrations.[61]

But Hopkinson was also aware that the *rate* of in-migration was a complex issue and not just a function of groundnut prices, or rice issues, but also the relative exchange rates of French francs against the new British currency after de-monetization.[62] One fact which did emerge as a result of discussions about Strange Farmers was that there had occurred a significant shift towards young Gambians leaving home and finding employment as migrant farmers. A report from the Commissioner of Kombo and Foni in 1926 indicated that some 73% of Strange Farmers were Gambians, 18% came from French territories and 9% from Portuguese Guinea.[63] Brooks Annual Agricultural Report for 1926–27 estimated that in total 50% of migrant farmers were Gambians.[64] These figures should be treated with some caution, especially as figures collected by the authors for the 1950s and 1960s show that the Kombos had a disproportionately high number of Gambian 'strangers', because they liked to farm close-by Bathurst, to which they conveniently moved for dry season work. On the other hand, Upper River, the main area of groundnut production had very few Gambian Strange Farmers.

The Strange Farmer estimates for the mid-1920s may be approximate, but in general the reports show an awareness of an internal seasonal redistribution of young Gambians. As to why this shift occurred it is only possible to speculate. Possibly the declining numbers of Francophone migrants opened-up niches for young Gambians, while the inability of heads of households to provide bridewealth for their sons gave an impetus for them to find their own resources. It has been suggested that in Northern Nigeria in the 1920s similar forces were at work in the cotton and groundnut areas: increased British monetization combined with indebtedness undermined family structures, and the ability of heads of households to meet their

---

[61] Ibid.
[62] Ibid.
[63] GNA 2/519, Screening of Nuts and Strange Farmers, 2nd May 1926.
[64] CO 87/226/16, Agricultural Department Report, 1926–27.

traditional commitments.[65] Also the Strange Farmer contract provided food during the wet season at a time of food shortage, which must have held some attraction for poorer families when faced with indifferent harvests, or the need to purchase food. On the other hand wet season migration meant a reduction in the household labour supply, but poorer families may at best have had to make a trade-off, as they were frequently between a 'rock and a hard place'. However, it has been suggested that the seasonal loss of labour was the means whereby poorer households were increasingly ratcheted downwards in times of economic and environmental stress.[66]

### The rice and seed debt

By 1922 the government was struggling to collect the rice and seed debt of 1919–20: a process exacerbated by de-monetization in 1922, as well as a period of price-fixing and the regulation of produce orders. It was discussed at length at the Travelling Commissioners' Conference in 1923, when the proposition was floated that the 1920 debt should be remitted.[67] It was reported that some chiefs were in fact holding back repayments, in the expectation of the debt being cancelled, therefore it was necessary to come to some agreement on what should happen about repayments and the future distribution of seed nuts and food. Hopkinson from the North Bank believed there should be a remittance as some farmers neither would not, nor could not pay their debts, and as an aside he observed the government debt was nothing compared with that owed the traders. Leese, the Commissioner for Kombo, thought the debt was difficult to collect and increasingly time wasting, and that if pushed the farmers would leave the Province and move into French and Portuguese territory. Some measure of the burden of debt collection can be gained from the Upper River Annual Report for 1922–23, when £7,269 1s 3d was paid off leaving a balance of £20,759 10s 4d.[68] Wannell the Commissioner believed farmers shouldn't be let-off, as

---

[65] Shenton, R.W. and L. Lenihan, 1981, "Capital and Class; Peasant Differentiation in Northern Nigeria", *Journal of Peasant Studies* IX (1), 47–70.
[66] Ibid.
[67] GNA 56/1, Travelling Commissioners' Conference, 1923.
[68] GNA 59/4, Annual Reports for Upper River Divisions, 1923–32: Report for 1922–23.

they had taken more rice than they needed and traded it across the border, which was a persistent problem, now exacerbated by the railway work near Tambacounda.

As the government's intervention in the rice market had been at prices only a little above the cost price, compared with the large mark-up made by the merchants, it created the conditions for hoarding and border trading by better-off farmers. Wannell thought 80–90% of the debt could be repaid, although he admitted Strange Farmers had decamped without repaying their debts. However, by 1923–24 after another £4,561 19s 5d had been paid-off, Wannell had to admit that the limit had been nearly reached, and that if producers were pressed further "people will go across the border".[69] On the other hand he had not given out any seed or rice in 1923, and opined nor should any ever be given out again. He supported this position by noting that the Fulas didn't require food distribution, and that the Mandingoes and Serahuli were idle and treated their Strange Farmers like slaves. This was another voice raised to decry the treatment of Strange Farmers in The Gambia as an explanation of their declining numbers, although Wannell like one of his predecessors seemed to have forgotten that Fula farming systems included a considerable reliance on cattle and less on groundnuts that other groups. But Wannell did note the disincentive of sharp practice by traders, when they manipulated the exchange rate of the French 5 franc note by buying groundnuts at one rate and selling goods at another.

The rice and seed debt repayment debate rumbled on, and in April 1925 the Colonial Secretary sent a Confidential Memo to all Commissioners and the Director of Agriculture, asking for their considered opinions on the policy to be adopted regarding the supply of seed nuts and rice, and what the government line should be on Strange Farmers.[70] This represents the first occasion when the Administration collectively tried to confront the issue which was at the nub of the groundnut industry, and so attempt to formulate some kind of policy. The Director of Agriculture made the point that a policy was necessary; something had to be laid down and known to replace

---

[69] Ibid., 1923–24.
[70] GNA 3/90, Conf. Correspondence, File on Policy of Government with regard to Agriculture. CS to all Commissioners encl. memo from Director of Agriculture, 11th April 1925, and Commissioners' replies.

the existing confusion evidenced by recent Travelling Commissioners' meetings.[71] Brooks believed that the Gambian population of some 200,000 (with an average density of 51 per square mile) was largely dependent on imported food, a result of the natives being told for 20 years to grow groundnuts at the expense of food. This was a policy that delivered them into the hands of the merchants who paid what they liked for produce and charged what they liked for food. Food self-sufficiency should be the objective and it was necessary that people should work harder to achieve self-sufficiency.[72]

Such sentiments about the efforts of local farmers echoed the 'lazy native' hypothesis, which in part reflected an ignorance of the irregular tempo of African farming to which we referred in Chapter Three, as well as European middle class attitudes that were also applied to their own working class back home. The Colonial Secretary replied to Brooks' concerns by stating that the government was considering three questions; how to increase local food supply; how to maintain the groundnut crop; and finally how to further develop the colony's trade.[73] He noted that it was difficult to convert a narrow enclave from an entrepôt into a self-sufficient unit, and that opinions differed as to the proportion of imports and exports passing over the borders. This was an overt recognition of the function of Bathurst, and the problems created by the border.

The responses from the Commissioners were varied. The Acting South Bank Commissioner Brooks, thought it necessary to attract migrants and therefore a minimum of seed and rice should be distributed to cover inevitable shortfalls, but that chiefs and headmen should guarantee its repayment. In his Annual Report he wrote of the efforts made by farmers to increase the acreage under groundnuts, and while some believed Gambians to be lazy, in his opinion they were not, "as men, women and children worked with a will, both early and late."[74] Macklin, the Commissioner for MacCarthy Island took the rather quixotic view that what he would do would depend on what the others did.[75] The Kombo Commissioner believed Strange Farmers were attracted by food and seed issues, and that

---

[71] Ibid.
[72] Ibid.
[73] Ibid.
[74] RHL Micro Afr. 485, Annual Report for the South Bank Province, 1925.
[75] Conf 3/90, Agricultural Policy, 1925, op. cit.

he would apply for them as necessary. He went on to express the
view that the populace didn't grow food because they knew the government would provide; yet people worked hard, and were not indo-
lent as often supposed. In his opinion the failure to produce enough
was due to disease, light rains, or an unfavourable distribution of
rain, together with the outbreaks of caterpillars.[76]

Streeter the Acting Commissioner for Upper River had already
made known his views on rice distribution in correspondence prior
to the Colonial Secretary's circular of April 1925. Streeter believed
that it was poor nut prices in The Gambia that sent Strange Farmers
into Senegal, not the food supply.[77] Streeter re-iterated his prede-
cessor's opinion that once rice was issued, it was traded across the
border into Senegal, while if government issues were re-started the
producers would automatically assume their debts were written-off.
Streeter believed only famine or burned towns warranted rice distribution, thus teaching the natives self-reliance. He noted there were
some shortages of food in Wuli and Kantora, but the natives were
managing by eating *duto* and fruit, and certainly they were not starving (malnutrition seems not to have entered into the equation). Streeter
further reported offering a Wuli chief 100 bags of rice, which were
refused as not being worth the effort. Whether Streeter's hard line
stance was that of a relatively new official seeking the approbation
of the Governor, or his concern that Upper River was the biggest
debtor cannot be ascertained, but it certainly met with Armitage's
approval and his minute on the paper reads, "I applaud his decision".[78] Hopkinson in the North Bank was quite clear that the question was either to attract Strange farmers by issuing rice, or do
without them: a mixture of both would spoil the other.[79] It is also
evident from his response that he believed the Governor was against
a pro-Strange farmer policy, which used rice as the means of ensuring a sufficient influx of migrants.

The Commissioners' and the Governor's comments reveal the level
of disagreement among the officials at this time, and the continued
'hand-wringing' about food and migrant workers. A minute by the

---

[76] Ibid.
[77] GNA 3/81, Conf. Proposed Rice distribution. Streeter to CS, 3rd July and
Aug. 1st 1924.
[78] Ibid. Armitage, 3rd Aug. 1924.
[79] GNA3/90, Conf. Agricultural policy, 1925.

Receiver General perhaps summed up the arguments succinctly when he wrote "Is the population of The Gambia too small, or is its' population too lazy?"[80] The arguments among the Administration to some extent reflected the degree of autonomy they enjoyed. Within the larger parameters devised in the metropoles, the Governor, and then each Commissioner depending on their seniority exercised considerable control over the administration of a colony and its constituent provinces and divisions. Small points mattered enormously to individual careers (vide Streeter), as well as a commitment to different policies and ideologies. As Guyer has opined, the contours of administration were created by blueprints from above, occasional volcanic eruptions from below, but also by small scale judicious constructions by local administrators, who inhabited the micro-ecology of regulations.[81]

In The Gambia food distribution policy was not one based on concerns for local diet or calorific intake, that is the state was not seeking to parallel the metropole where it had become a purveyor of welfare, it was more concerned with food as a policy instrument to support the groundnut trade through ensuring a sufficient influx of Strange Farmers. For the general populace, food distribution was a dole in times of trouble usually triggered by a deficiency in rainfall, or after a disastrous harvest, but for some such as chiefs and petty traders it could be an opportunity to engage in accumulation through border trading.

In the end the Administration had to write-off the rice and seed debts as they were faced by an array of attendant problems: difficulties of collection; fixed producer prices; producer resistance and the fragile border which allowed people to decamp, at least temporally into French territory. They also were worried about the colony's ability to attract Strange Farmers, and reluctantly felt they must make some positive gesture in their favour. In July of 1925 the Secretary of State for the Colonies agreed to a proposal from the Executive Council to write-off the rice and seed debt, and at a stroke £32,564 of debts were cancelled.[82] Brooks in his report for 1925, believed that this would mark the end of "subsidized laziness', which was the

---

[80] GNA 2/519, Memo. 13A, Screening of Nuts and Strange Farmers, Receiver General, 2nd May 1926.

[81] Guyer, J., 1991 op. cit.

[82] CO 87/226, Annual Report, 1925.

real cause of food shortages: he also took heart from the record corn crop of 1925 which rather strangely he believed to be unconnected with the rainfall of that year—an excellent 53.56 inches which he wrongly reported as being the same as other years.[83] After all the inquiry and debate, the government did not come to any firm policy decision on the wider issues surrounding food supply, but all agreed that French encirclement and the railway extension menaced the Gambia's economic position. Thus in 1925 the official 'bottom line' was the unenviable geographical position of the country, an argument which became commonplace as the years progressed. One outcome of these deliberations to which we referred earlier was the new scheme for groundnut storage, and while this was a useful advance for the groundnut trade, the question of food supply and migrant labour remained largely unresolved.[84]

Food policy throughout the colonies was a rather delicate sensor that picked-up a wide spectrum of ideas, values, practices, and institutional arrangements, as well as pragmatic policies. The smallest of implementational details can be linked to the greatest of moral and political symbols. As The Gambian case shows, there were often few guiding principles and the Administration's actions were justified by situational logic. Perhaps as Guyer suggests, the reason lies in the moral dilemma of a laissez-faire economic philosophy, where the ramifications of allowing markets to deliver the goods are not always politically tolerable.[85] In the case of The Gambia, given the dependence on groundnuts, migrant labour and a variable climate, they were also frequently impossible. The conclusion which can be drawn from the discussions about rice distribution and Strange Farmers is a re-iteration of the fact that by the 1920s The Gambia was a migrant-driven economy, where an active male labour force of some 50,000 could be inflated by as much as a third or a half by some 14,000–20,000 Strange Farmers. Furthermore, the migrant labour force was supported by food imports. The colonial state had created in The Gambia a precarious economic and social edifice that was becoming increasingly difficult to balance and control.

---

[83] CO 87/226, Agricultural Department Report, 1925.
[84] GNA 3/90, Agricultural Policy op. cit.
[85] Guyer, J., 1991, op. cit.

## The resumption of rice distribution

Notwithstanding the avowed resistance to rice issues by some of the Commissioners, the Director of Agriculture and the Governor, an about turn occurred in 1927 which restored food distribution, and once again it was the climate that proved to be the trigger. In 1927 and 1928 record imports of rice occurred, 158,772 and 228,797cwts respectively: the first to offset the poor rainfall of 1926 and the failure of rice, the second to offset the failure of corn due to flooding from heavy late rains in 1927, as well as support for the mini-boom in groundnut exports and the large number of Strange Farmers. (Figs. 5.4, 5.6, 6.1) The poor and erratic rainfall of 1926 was widely reported across West Africa, and has been recorded in oral histories collected in Senegal, Niger and Nigeria.[86] In Senegambia and further east it was distinguished as not being as severe as the 1913–14 famine, when food availability in some areas was so restricted it could not be purchased. What did distinguish the 1926 drought in Senegambia, was that it was unexpected, as it was not preceded by a run of very poor years. Gambian Provincial reports, and those of the Director of Agriculture show that it was the irregular distribution of rainfall which was the chief problem: from June to September in 1926 there were 5 periods of more than 6 consecutive days of no rain.[87] Groundnuts were twice sown and germinated and spoilt by dry spells, while in September there was a 16 day spell of dry weather which caused early ripening and a lightweight crop.

In the case of rice the lack of rain in the growing period was highly detrimental, and some areas were abandoned. On the South Bank thousands of acres of rice failed to mature because of dry periods in September, and transplanted rice was abandoned as the polders were so parched. It was at this point that the Director of Agriculture observed that there would be a need to issue rice "if there were to be sufficient food for our own people and Strange Farmers".[88] However, the corn crop including *basso* was good, which again underlines how crucial it was for farmers to continue with a diversified crop regime. This particular drought was relatively well recorded, and illustrates that despite a generally poor harvest there was considerable

---

[86] See M.J. Mortimore 1989, *Adapting to Drought*. Cambridge: CUP. ch. 2.
[87] CO 87/227/15, Agricultural Department Report, 1927–28.
[88] Ibid.

variation in yields among crops, as well as spatially within the country. The rains during the following wet season of 1927 were particularly good, some 77.05 inches (1937.5 mm) being recorded at Cape St. Mary, and excessive rains at harvest time spoilt some groundnuts and corn was badly affected. But of more concern was the outbreak of pleuro-pneumonia among cattle herds with the resulting loss of some 16,000–18,000 animals.[89]

The sudden climatic perturbation of 1926–27 undercut any attempts to resist rice distribution, as the food supply underpinned the economy so heavily dependent on groundnuts. As Brooks remarked, there are few alternative commercial crops without using irrigation, although the Agricultural Department had begun trials with sesame seed. The exploration of the irrigation option was a few years off, but in the meantime government rice issues were resumed and rather than being a temporary relief the amounts distributed actually increased.[90] In fact from 1927 to 1930 as we noted above, there was a mini-boom in groundnut exports which was facilitated by an influx of Strange Farmers, rice imports, merchant and government credit, as well as generally stable terms of trade. (Figs. 6.1; 5.4; 6.3). Unlike the previous environmental disruptions of 1913, and 1918–19 that triggered rice distribution, the late 1920s were characterized by relatively stable groundnut and rice prices. In 1927 in Upper River 1400 bags of rice were issued by the government on credit primarily to meet the demands of Strange Farmers, whose numbers had marginally increased, which in Brooks view was a result of the Agricultural Department's seed nut storage and distribution scheme, an explanation which gave credence and legitimacy to his department's innovation.[91] In the following year 1928, 5,690 bags of seed nuts were issued in Upper River at 18s 0d per bag of four bushels, and repayment was collected along with the Yard Tax.[92] In the same year the government distribution of rice rose to 3,869 bags at 34s 0d per bag, on which an advance of 8s 0d was collected: the mark up of 2s 0d per bag was placed in an emergency fund for the Provinces. However, if the 8s 0d advance was not paid by recipients, they were charged an extra 2s 0d per bag.

---

[89] CO 87/227/15, Agricultural Department Report, 1927–28.
[90] Ibid.
[91] GNA 59/4, Annual Reports for Upper River, 1927.
[92] Ibid., Annual Report, 1928.

The new system was much more efficient and tightly controlled than in previous years, and it appears that in association with the adverse weather in Senegambia to have had an impact on Strange Farmer numbers, which increased from 17,237 in 1927 to 20,640 in 1928. The 1927–28 groundnut crop was excellent, and as in all good years rather than any one factor being responsible, it was a convergence of the principal elements on which a good harvest depended: a well distributed rainfall, an increased number of migrants combined with seed and rice issues. Prices were modest and producers had received little benefit from an improvement in the quality of groundnuts, but as we noted earlier there had been an adjustment in the price of imported goods that made the net barter terms of trade relatively good, while net income terms of producers were sustained by increased production. The generally stable situation at this time encouraged the government in 1929 to increase the amount of seed nuts issued to 6,456 bags, with issues of rice amounting to 5,200 bags.[93]

By now it was plain the old system of credit was restored, albeit under a stricter regime. The North Bank Annual Reports suggest that Hopkinson's concerns about co-operation with the merchants over seed and rice issues had to some extent been met.[94] He reported that after the rice crop failed in 1926 3,000 bags of imported rice were issued at a cost of £5,228, of which £2,445 was paid in advance and the rest before December. All the rice was supplied by one firm, Maurel et Frères and delivered by their cutters to places specified and then taken by local traders who distributed the rice to the chiefs. The firms were paid in advance, and according to Hopkinson the system worked well. Over all the total amount of rice imported into The Gambia had risen from 4,612 tons (£72,270) in 1926, to 7,939 tons (£124,457) in 1927.[95] (Fig. 5.4)

Rice and seed distribution occurred throughout the country and the groundnut trade was stabilized with strict supervision of the repayment of debts. In 1928 there was a setback in the form of another outbreak of cattle disease, and between 16,000–18,000 cattle were lost, of which 3,523 fatalities occurred in the South Bank district of Fulladu Central. Brooks noted this had a considerable

[93] CO 87/227, Agricultural Department Report 1929.
[94] GNA 2/60, Annual Report for the North Bank, 1926–27.
[95] Blue Book, 1926.

impact on corn production, which was especially disappointing as this district exported corn across the river to Sandu.[96] This is one of the few references which suggest that the old south bank-north bank trade in foodstuffs, which was so strong prior to 1857 had continued, albeit in a much reduced form. In general, the food situation and groundnut production had stabilized in the late 1920s, but this was sonn to end, when in 1930 the depression in trade became really severe.

Meanwhile, the merchants also distributed of rice on credit and it was reported that more 'Syrians' were setting-up as traders, who were making large advances of rice and trade goods. Earlier in 1912 there had been discussion among administrators whether Syrian immigration should be limited, ostensibly on the grounds of insufficient housing in the Protectorate, and that they were a health risk. They were deemed susceptible to yellow fever, as well as "living in unsanitary conditions among the natives".[97] Syrian was a general term used to include Lebanese from Beirut; Levantines either from the North African littoral or from Asia Minor and the Greek Islands; Spaniards from the Canaries; and Moroccans. The real issue was that they were posing a challenge to established trading companies, and the Administration was unable to neatly categorize them as Europeans or Africans. The Syrians and Lebanese appeared in West Africa at the end of the 19th century at a time when small European firms were disappearing and consolidation was taking place. They were small traders who were enterprising low cost operators, who lived among Africans and were prepared to settle in remoter areas. The MacCarthy Island Report for 1912–13 indicates they were located in Kuntaur, Kaur and MacCarthy Island, where they were operating some 30 trading establishments.[98] In 1928 the Upper River Commissioner reported some 35 Syrians who gave out credit on a large scale: he identified them as the chief culprits in making large advances at usurious rates, especially rice during the hungry season and when the rains were inadequate.[99] By the 1920s the Syrians had efficiently occupied a niche between the large merchant houses and

[96] CO 87/227/15, Agricultural Department Report, 1927–1928.
[97] GNA 2/172, Immigration of Syrians. Minutes between the Governor, Colonial Secretary, Hopkinson and the Senior Medical Officer, 13th Feb. 1912.
[98] RHL Micro Afr. 485, Annual Report for MacCarthy Island Division, 1912–13.
[99] GNA 59/4, Upper River Province Annual Report, 1928. See also, GNA 77/6, Historical Notes on the History of Upper River Province, c. 1933.

the smaller African traders, and were especially important as lorry operators. Although their numbers were small, they occupied an increasingly important role in The Gambia and elsewhere in West Africa, while providing the government with a ready target when they felt the trading community was behaving badly.

### The irrigation and mixed farming schemes: enter the experts

From 1928 onwards the Agricultural Department had to address more than groundnut quality control and extension work: it was required to confront the recurrent problem of food importing and associated indebtedness compounded by an unreliable climate. Initially, the preferred option was to provide more rice through dry season irrigation, and the possibility of extending flood land rice cultivation during the wet season. The attempts to improve agriculture are interesting as they encapsulate the tensions, careerism, and personal grudges lodged in the interstices of colonial administration, while the new band of advisors from London also created new contested spaces. Notwithstanding, the wealth of expertise, the irrigation plans were clouded by uncertainty as to the most appropriate method: whether it was to be upland or lowland, or a combination of both along side mixed farming projects, the latter being seen as an alternative means of improving agricultural performance. On the larger stage, there were the fiscal constraints imposed by government (local and metropolitan), and a deteriorating economic climate. The irrigation scheme was one of the first in West Africa, and although it faltered, it became the lynchpin of large-scale Gambian development planning after the Second World War, while many of the arguments were to be repeated elsewhere in West Africa. The proposed irrigation scheme and the changing fortunes of the Agricultural Department became metaphors for the deterioration of the Gambian economy, while the scientific arguments of the experts hinted at the new idioms that were to shape development thinking after World War Two.

The irrigation and mixed farming schemes occasioned the retrieval of past reports, as well as being preceded in 1928 by a soil survey in the hope it would contribute to a better agriculture. The conclusions were that generally soils were light and sandy and low in humus content except for the riverine soils, although in the lower river they were saline: much better were those in the middle and upper river developed on fresh water grasslands. Hill, the Director of the Royal Botanical Gardens at Kew, observed that while some useful preparatory work had been done in The Gambia, the whole question of tropical soils needed to be addressed in a much wider context. Tropical soils in his opinion were being considered in the light of the knowledge of temperate climates (a view re-discovered in the 1970s), and there was a danger of soils being considered by soil chemists alone, rather than jointly with botanists as vegetation was an important element.[100] Such a comment suggests that already there was a certain compartmentalization of expertise in the analysis of tropical environments, something which became prevalent in the years which followed.

In the same year 1928, Denham the new Governor of The Gambia made a request to the Colonial Office in London for reports from other colonies where irrigation on riverine tracts had been tried using simple lifting devices. Hemming, the Secretary of the Committee for Civil Research sent details of devices such as the sakia, Archimedes screw, shaduf and talbut, while the Secretary of State forwarded references on India and Egypt.[101] London also sent copies of Parker's Second Irrigation Report written in 1903, which apparently was unavailable in The Gambia. This report advocated that the dry season irrigation of rice could replace millet, therefore giving farmers more time to produce groundnuts.[102] Meanwhile, Denham in sending his thanks belatedly notes that he had now found and read Dawe's 1921 'Report on The Agricultural Needs of The Gambia', and noted the recommendation for dry season rice irrigation, together with the use of Egyptian wheel buckets.[103] By 1929 Dawe's report had become central to the irrigation issue, as he also believed that in addition to solving the problem of food imports and the declining fortunes of the groundnut trade, irrigated farmland would attract population towards the Gambian enclave.[104] In 1929 Denham decided to take up Dawe's recommendation that The Gambia needed an irrigation officer conversant with Sudan or Egypt, but that any large

---

[100] CO 87/229/6, A. Hill, Director Royal Botanic Gardens, Kew to USS, 5th Nov. 1929.
[101] CO 87/228/5, Irrigation file on The Gambia.
[102] CO 87/228/5, Denham to Hemming, 26th April 1929.
[103] CO 87/228/5, Parker's Second Irrigation Report on The Gambia 23rd Nov. 1903.
[104] Dawe, M.T., 1921, op. cit.

scale scheme was out of the question. Apart from the costs Denham believed the Gambian population was insufficient to develop such schemes, and therefore he suggested to the Secretary of State that the modest sum of £1,000 might be allocated for irrigation experiments in the 1930 estimates.[105]

The renewal of interest in irrigation as part of a plan to improve The Gambia's economy was furthered in 1928–29 by the visit of F.A. Stockdale, the Agricultural Advisor to the Colonial Office. His visit also marked a shift to alternative solutions. Stockdale had a distinguished career: a First in the Natural Science tripos at Cambridge, a job as a mycologist and then a post in the West Indies and Dutch Guyana, as well as being Director of Agriculture in Mauritius and Ceylon.[106] Stockdale, in essence was a member of the new class of professional scientists, unlike Brooks the Gambian Director of Agriculture who entered the Royal Botanical Gardens at Kew and later became Officer in Charge of an agricultural school in Dominica.[107] Stockdale's Report on the Agricultural Department was highly critical of the area devoted to economic trials of crops, and he complained that the methods employed to conduct field trials were inadequate.[108] Furthermore, he began to push the idea of the need for up river experimental stations near Georgetown that would combine dry upland and wetland farms within one experimental area. His real concern was for accurate data on which extension proposals could be based, while he was also alert to the possibilities of intercropping foodstuffs using crop relays. As for wet season rice cultivation, he believed this could not be extended because of labour constraints, and the only means of increasing local production was through dry season irrigation using cheap water lifts, together with diversification by adding vegetable crops and cotton. Finally, Stockdale wanted the Agricultural Department to test cattle ploughs of the Indian and Egyptian type, which was consonant with his overriding interest in mixed farming.

---

[105] CO 87/228/5, Denham to SS, Oct. 10th 1929.
[106] Colonial Office List, 1931.
[107] Ibid.
[108] CO 87/228/5, Report by F.A. Stockdale on the Agricultural Department, 5th Dec. 1929.

After Stockdale had returned to England a series of discussions indicate the various responses to his suggestions, as well as those made earlier by Denham. One dispatch from the Secretary of State to Denham is based on Stockdale's subsequent comments, which emphasized that while he thought cheap lifting device were a possibility, they should only be introduced in association with cattle for dunging the irrigated areas; also Georgetown must experiment with cattle as well as irrigation and crops.[109] Moreover, the Department should find out whether men would co-operate in rice production, which traditionally was considered a 'women's' crop. Stockdale doubted men's co-operation and therefore again emphasized it should be upland irrigation on mixed farming plots with cattle.[110] Therefore, the Governor's (and Brooks's) idea of sending irrigation officers to Sudan and Egypt would be of little use, and, more usefully Pirie the Assistant Agricultural Officer should be sent to northern Ceylon where he would find a great variety of local devices, as well as irrigation using oil-engines. There is a hint here that the transposition of repertoires of expertise and associated policies from one colony to another clearly included argument about which was most appropriate and most suited to the area in question, a stance which was not always conspicuous after World War Two. Stockdale re-iterated the need for information from controlled experiments, and that it would be unwise to change the farming system without them. An approving note by Flood the Colonial Secretary reads, 'the native must not be driven', and that even with help from the Colonial Development Fund, large scale schemes were unwise.[111] Any help from the Colonial Development Fund created in 1929 was in fact likely to be minimal, since a mere £1,000,000 was allocated annually for all colonies, comprising some 66 million people.

Stockdale's comments about the gendered division of labour were to prove prophetic, as the rice schemes started after 1947 frequently failed from a lack of understanding of the social disruption new technologies might cause.[112] As to his commitment to experimental farms, they represented the virtues of applied science and the transfer of

[109] CO 87/228/5, SS to Denton, 28th March 1930.
[110] Ibid.
[111] Ibid. Note (undated) by J.E.W. Flood.
[112] See for example, J. Dey, 1980, *Women and Rice in The Gambia: the impact of irrigated rice on the farming system*. PhD thesis University of Reading.

new technologies which would increase groundnut and food production to prop-up the colony's revenues at a time of financial crisis. Meanwhile, the mixed farming idea was being touted elsewhere, especially Northern Nigeria, where it was introduced in 1928 in the hope that semi-mechanization would reduce costs of cotton production and enhance its competitiveness in world markets.[113]

Brooks' comments on Stockdale in 1930 were to the effect that it was not the methods of change which were the problem, but generally getting more farmers to adopt rice farming, although he conceded that the most powerful factor might yet be necessity, as the groundnut industry showed every sign of overproduction.[114] However, Stockdale's ideas were taken seriously by the new Governor, Palmer, who had come from Northern Nigeria to replace Denham. Palmer reported to the Secretary of State that a station at Georgetown was being established, the Wuli seed farm was to be used for general farming investigations, while Brooks was looking for a site to combine upland and lowland farming experiments but, "that he is having difficulty finding suitable sites compatible with costs".[115] It was in Stockdale's minute on this dispatch where he expressed the opinion that Brooks was not up to the job: "He has insufficient scientific knowledge and his field methodology is poor.[116] This vignette of the new versus the old style agricultural expert was to be further developed in subsequent exchanges.

In 1930 another visiting expert also pronounced on the means of improving agriculture in The Gambia, this time it was H.C. Sampson from Kew.[117] Sampson's comments are broadly in agreement with Stockdale, and underline the burgeoning belief in the value of mixed farming and cattle ploughing in the savanna environments of Africa. While acknowledging the development of permanent cultivation around the older villages in The Gambia, his chief concern was the lack of pulses grown and insufficient mixed-cropping, unlike Madras where groundnut acreages had been substantially increased as part of a mixed farming strategy. Sampson believed local strains of bulrush millet 'tillered' too strongly, and were unsuited to mixed cropping, but he seems to have been unaware of the number of times local

---

[113] Shenton, 1986, op. cit.
[114] CO 87/236/14, Irrigation Minutes Brooks, 3rd April 1930.
[115] CO 87/230/1, Palmer to SS, 9th Oct. 1930.
[116] CO 87/230/1, minute Palmer to SS, 9th Oct. 1930.
[117] CO 89/230/6, Suggested Means for the Improvement of Agriculture H.C. Sampson, Feb. 28th 1930.

millets had saved Gambian farmers in times of drought, or poorly distributed rainfall. And, while he approved of the range of local rice varieties, he felt they must be sorted out and grown in pure stands. On the subject of irrigation he believed this would diversify cropping, while ox-ploughing would spread the benefits of dunging, as at present cattle herds were too concentrated. Finally he suggested an agricultural officer should be sent to visit Northern Nigeria and the Tamil area of Ceylon, but Pirie in fact had already been sent to to Ceylon and Madras early in 1931.[118]

Another twist to the irrigation saga was added by Palmer, the Governor, who was anxious that Stockdale and Pirie returning from Madras should meet in England, to discuss the irrigation scheme.[119] Palmer seems to have seized upon the difficulty of introducing irrigated rice, as men would not easily be involved, while he also seem to have developed the idea that the real problem was not the Protectorate, but Bathurst whose inhabitants could no longer live indirectly off the groundnut trade, and relied exclusively on imported food.[120] Palmer, by April 1931 appeared distinctly lukewarm about a full blown irrigation project, while a report of the meeting of Pirie with Stockdale in London showed they were committed to cattle ploughing and simple lifting devices for irrigated farming, with experiments concentrated at two sites at Georgetown and Basse. However, irrigation at Basse proved to be difficult, as the lift from the river was too great during the dry season.[121] In response to Palmer's doubts they agreed the gender problem would take time to resolve, as for Bathurst they believed that "the more you help the primary producer, the more you help Bathurst."

Brooks eventually sent a copy of Pirie's 1931 report on his Madras visit to the Colonial Secretary and to Stockdale, and he was at some pains to stress that economic conditions in The Gambia had changed since Stockdale's 1929 visit due to the trade depression, a view which he repeated in his Annual Report for 1930–31.[122] By 1931 groundnut prices had collapsed, and Brooks could see no option but retrench-

---

[118] Ibid.
[119] CO 87/236/14, Irrigation Minutes Palmer to SS 20th April 1931.
[120] Ibid.
[121] CO 87/233/4, Irrigation and other Agricultural Improvements, 1931.
[122] CO 87/233/4, Brooks to Acting. CS, 28th May 1931.

ment, a view held by most colonial officials faced with depressed trade and the close connection between public revenue and customs receipts. Retrenchment was the orthodox policy of the time (also adopted in Europe), together with increased taxes and duties, which as we noted earlier were implemented in 1931. Brooks argued that the situation in The Gambia had become sufficiently grave as to merit an Agricultural Retrenchment Committee being formed to consider how to cut expenditure. Therefore while extension work was needed, it was a bad time to embark upon additional expenditure. In particular he was finding it difficult and costly to set-up the two linked upland and wetland farms near Georgetown, which he estimates would cost £1,820 in the first year and £684 in the second; if two stations at Georgetown were necessary, then the one from Wuli should be transferred there.

However, Brooks' 1930–31 Departmental report did indicate that Stockdale's recommendations about field trials had been adopted, and were proceeding on the Rothamstead pattern which were amenable to statistical evaluation.[123] But by July of 1931 retrenchment of the Department was brought forward and the gist of local discussions was that Palmer and Brooks now believed that the irrigation schemes would be useless, too expensive, and therefore should be abandoned.[124] Real improvements in Gambian food production Palmer argued would be brought about by economic necessity. On the other hand there would be no harm in encouraging farmers to use the shaduf as this would be at no cost to the government, and it would prove whether the farmers were willing to try irrigated dry season farming.[125] Palmer stated the necessity of making savings by cutting the staff of the Department of Agriculture, and as the irrigation scheme was to be abandoned then Pirie as the irrigation expert should be the one to go.[126]

The result of this dispatch was a riposte from Stockdale, which illustrates the cleavage that had developed between the London-backed scientific advisor and the Governor and his Agricultural

---

[123] CO 87/232/1, Annual Agricultural Report, 1930–31.
[124] CO 87/233/18, Department of Agriculture, Expenditure and Retrenchment, Palmer 6th July 1931.
[125] Ibid.
[126] Ibid.

Director; a reminder of Lugard's view of 'tyrannical experts'. And, it became a personalized encounter in which Brooks' qualifications (already denigrated on a previous occasion) and his personality became the vehicle for the dispute. A minute by Stockdale described Brooks as one who "wobbles with every breath of wind from whatever the quarter".[127] In Stockdale's view, The Gambia deserved assistance through mixed-farming and small scale irrigation schemes, and as for retrenchment, what The Gambia needed was "retrenchment for the pretty ornamental gardens at Cape St Mary . . . . . and a change from the Kew trained botanic garden outlook to an economic minded agricultural department".[128] Stockdale was also vehement that Pirie had to stay: "Mr. Pirie is a Scot and a sound agriculturalist", while the minute also noted that "Brooks, will be 50 this year"![129] By August of 1931 the Governor had accepted that ploughing was essential on the basis of experimental trials, and also that well and creek irrigation work should be investigated on an experimental basis. The staffing dilemma was solved by sending Hayes another assistant officer to Uganda, although this still annoyed Brooks who wanted Pirie to go, although he agreed to reduce the horticultural work at Cape St Mary.

A year later in 1932, Palmer writing to London summed up the irrigation debate vis a vis the various advisors and his own Agricultural Department, and the steps he had taken.[130] He proposed that the cheapest immediate approach to the irrigation question would be the use of shadufs by individual farmers, who would be encouraged in their use and given advice on shaduf irrigated farming. Other methods, for example pump irrigation in the Sudan were inappropriate as Gambians had no history of irrigation, and could not maintain the machines (again this proved prophetic). On the other hand shadufs could be made using local materials and farmers would not need supervision once the idea had been grasped: many had seen shadufs as pilgrims on the *haj* and importantly shaduf irrigation was easily subsidized. Brooks agreed to send his assistant Sparrow to MacCarthy Island to look for suitable farmers, while Palmer agreed to a £30 subsidy at a rate of £1 0s 0d per half acre, or per shaduf.[131]

---

[127] CO 87/233/18, Department of Agriculture, Expenditure and Retrenchment, Stockdale, 30th July, 1931.
[128] Ibid.
[129] CO 87/233/18, Memo. Governor's meeting with Stockdale, July 13th 1931.
[130] CO 87/236/14, Governor to S.S. conf. 9th Sept. 1932.
[131] CO 87/236/14, Brooks to Governor, September 2nd 1932.

Meanwhile, a notice in the Gazette of November 1932 announced that shadufs would be on view at Cape St. Mary and Georgetown: farmers would be paid £1 0s 0d for erecting a shaduf and raising an adequate amount of food crops from January to May. Finally, a prize of £5 0s 0d would be paid to the best irrigated farm in each Province.[132]

In addition, the Governor approved the use of light ploughs as advocated by Dawe in 1921, which were part of the push towards mixed farming as a means of improving the competitiveness of Gambian groundnuts. To this end, in 1932 the use of ploughs was being encouraged by their demonstration and sale by Maurel Freres at Bathurst and along the river. Thus financial incentives of the smallest kind, and the salesmanship of the firms had largely replaced the experimental approach using scientific methods and government investment. So rather than launching new forms of irrigation, the Administration had fallen back on the long established forms of indigenous irrigation, which were found in other parts of the West African savannas, although they were not primarily used for dry season cereal cultivation.

But the Governor undertook an important initiative to re-locate the Agricultural Department and its Director near Georgetown at Yoro Beri Kunda, where a greater degree of supervision could be exerted over the seed storage schemes, and where there might be a resolution of "the fruitless discussion of what and what cannot be done by simple irrigation".[133] Brooks retired at the end of 1932 when the Department's staff of five European officers and eighteen Africans was quickly retrenched. The retrenchment of the Department started with the transfer of Hayes back to Uganda, together with the loss of three African staff, while Brook's post was left unfilled and the Department was put on a care and maintenance basis, which lasted until 1942.[134]

After Brooks retired, Hall as Senior Agricultural Superintendent ran the department, and he undertook its re-organization that entailed considerable disruption to the irrigation experiments. In 1932 and

[132] CO 87/236/14, Gazette 35, 15th Nov. 1932.
[133] CO 87/236/14, Governor to SS, 9th September, 1932.
[134] Blackburne, K.W., *Development and Welfare of The Gambia*, Colonial Office June 1943, pp. 5–6. CO 89/18, Sessional Papers, Agricultural Department Report, 1932–33.

1933 the Agricultural Officers and the Commissioners toured the Protectorate urging farmers to grown more food, to retain sufficient groundnut seeds, and to close-plant groundnuts to reduce the risk of rosette disease.[135] This propaganda drive was in partly a result of the low prices of groundnuts and the poor groundnut harvest of 1932, following the low rainfall of 1931. Meanwhile irrigation experiments were started at Basse and Georgetown in late 1932, but so late that it was not until the dry season of 1933–34 a successful trial of crops was achieved. At Basse, at a cost of £10, bunded beds and a single shaduf were laid out near a stream close by the market to irrigate one quarter of an acre under Pirie's supervision.[136] At Georgetown, close by government wharf another shaduf was erected and an irrigated area of half and acre was prepared on an old rice paddy. The results reported in 1934 showed that irrigated farming was not quite as easy as expected, even using simple methods. At both sites it became apparent land preparation was needed using cow dung, while the land quickly alternated from being too wet and too dry. At Basse the water table was near the surface and the low evening temperatures of December and January made the soil cold and inhibited germination of rice, However, the results at Georgetown indicated it was good for rice and high yields per acre were recorded.[137] Meanwhile during 1934 Pirie searched for suitable sites elsewhere in the Provinces and supplied notes on layouts.

A note in The Gazette of 1933 proudly proclaimed that "Although irrigation has been discussed for the past 30 years, this is the first real attempt".[138] It was indeed a attempt but on such a puny scale and with such a limited budget as to be almost meaningless. And, in the long run it was the introduction of ox-ploughing which proved to be the most successful scheme. Yet the die had been cast for irrigated farming: the proposal first made by Parker, and then Dawe, for securing food by dry season irrigation was established as an integral part of the agricultural policy of The Gambia. These schemes born in the midst of adversity and out of dismay over the high levels of food imports were the pre-cursors of a succession of large-scale

---

[135] CO 89/18, Sessional Papers: Agricultural Department Report, 1932–33.
[136] Ibid.
[137] Ibid.
[138] GNA 47/7, Irrigation File, note 15th Feb. 1933.

irrigation schemes centred on the Georgetown area, which appeared after 1947 and which have experienced such a convoluted history and debatable usefulness. After the Second World War colonial development was construed in terms of large scale schemes based on western technology, and reflected the experience of the War and a commitment to planning espoused by the new government in London. The history of the first Gambian scheme is illuminating for what followed in this small colony and elsewhere in sub-Saharan Africa; and one is tempted to take the view 'plus ça change, plus la même chose'.

*Summary*

The post-1920 price-collapse of groundnut prices followed by de-monetization was a severe blow to The Gambian economy, in a period when commodity producers were facing stiff competition in international markets. The situation was exacerbated by the problem of the repayment of the 1919–20 government rice debt, which proved a particularly thorny issue for the Administration. In the end producer resistance and the fear of a collapse of the groundnut trade, especially if Strange Farmers could not be fed, led the government to cancel the debt. It was now abundantly clear the Gambian groundnut economy was heavily dependent on migrant labour and imported food, added to which there was the unreliability of the climate evidenced by the 1926 drought and 1927 floods. Once again the government had to resume rice distribution, although it was clearly recognized that border trading was something of a problem, for both food and groundnuts.

Notwithstanding these problems and occasional hiccoughs in production groundnut exports held up well during the period 1923–30, and while prices were fixed by the merchants, the reduction of the price of imported goods, especially rice, meant that the net barter terms of trade were not entirely disadvantageous to producers. The disenchantment of producers stemmed from the fact that the new Agricultural Department established in 1924, urged on by the merchants, was responsible for the introduction of measures to improve the quality of produce, yet because of price-fixing, Gambian farmers saw no returns for their increased labours. Arguably, the costs of sustaining the groundnut trade during this period were born by the increased efforts of the producers, while the merchants recouped some of their losses after the 1920 credit debacle.

Despite the government's policy initiatives the old pattern remained: it tried to manage events, but it couldn't always square a laissez-faire trading economy and its consequences with its own political objectives. Also, it was unfortunate that attempts to develop agricultural policies coincided with the trade depression, especially through the irrigation and mixed farming schemes. The irrigation scheme was almost doomed from the start because of the costs and the deterioration in economic conditions: the mixed farming and ox-ploughing scheme fared rather better. But these schemes were an interesting episode in government intervention, at times marked by acrimony and confusion among those involved as they confronted new idioms of agricultural development, compounded by the arrival of new technical experts. It was a glimpse of what was to come, both in The Gambia, and elsewhere in Africa.

## SUMMARY AND CONCLUSIONS

A major theme in the social and economic history of West Africa
is the region's change from a supplier of slaves to one of agricultural exports. The Gambian groundnut trade provides a particularly
early case of this shift to legitimate trade that was ultimately reinforced through colonial rule. How this occurred and with what consequences for local people has been the chief focus of this book. In
exploring the Gambian groundnut trade part of our intention has
been to temper theories which see imperial and colonial forces as
monolithic: rather we point to their interaction with a nexus of internal social and political dynamics, as well as the importance of environmental conditions. Thus the larger structural forces of metropolitan
capitalism and international trade were refracted through prisms of
local history, society and environment to produce specific contesta-
tions and outcomes.

The groundnut trade developed relatively quickly along the Gambia
river, as well as to the south in Casamance and to the north in the
lower Senegal valley. The cultivation of groundnuts for export was
launched upon the back of the commercial grain trade which formerly supplied the Atlantic slave trade, as well as being given momentum by the networks of legitimate trade which had co-existed with
slaving. In other words, there was not a simple shift from an external slave trade to legitimate trade, nor was this an area without previous experience of regional and international markets. There were
important pre-conditions in Senegambia, which allowed the trade to
develop rapidly and soften the process of adaptation. Initially chiefs
used slaves to grow groundnuts, but of particular importance was
the role of pioneer migrant farmers, known as the Strange Farmers
who worked on shared time contracts. These seasonal farmers were
also important in the diffusion of the exported variety of groundnut,
*arachis hypogeae*.

At the outset the British government's influence on the trade was
limited to two small colonial enclaves: it was the merchants and their
agents, especially the French who encouraged the trade as they penetrated the river and its hinterland, using gifts, persuasion and above
all goods on credit. The French connection was extremely important,

and France remained the chief market after partition in 1893 until the First World War. As elsewhere in Africa colonial boundaries created different legal, monetary and taxation systems, which encouraged border trading and population movement. The Gambia's boundaries became an increasingly intractable problem for the Administration as the 20th century progressed. In effect neither spheres of commercial influence, nor formal political boundaries inhibited movements of people and goods, and the social and economic hinterland of the river stretched well into present day Senegal, Mali and Guinea

The river itself was a major asset for the groundnut trade: it was a means of cheap transport; it facilitated the movement of food, and the commercial penetration of the interior by the merchants and their agents. And, both seasonal migrants and settlers were attracted to the river, as prices offered for groundnuts and the cost of imported wage goods were lower than inland. In particular this became true after the opening of the Suez Canal when Indian groundnuts increased competition in the European markets, which made the remoter locations of Senegambia less competitive. Thus regional economic disparities, together with the river with its better groundnut prices and access to imported goods became a magnet for migrants, who were crucial to the early development and further expansion of the groundnut trade.

After 1857 trade was increasingly specialized and the producer base widened such that groundnut farming was focused on the domestic production unit assisted by migrant workers, the Strange Farmers. Unlike tree crops, groundnuts are grown within a relatively short wet season, requiring substantial well timed labour inputs, and, labour was the limiting factor along the river, because of the low population densities. In addition, groundnuts as a wet season crop competed with local food production, which posed problems for feeding the growing number of seasonal migrants: by the second half of the 19th century The Gambia was importing rice to meet its food requirements. The further expansion of groundnut cultivation and increased production in the early 20th century was materially enhanced by a new inflow of migrants. This influx was fuelled by the transformation of societies throughout the western Sudan by a decline in domestic slavery, and the construction of the Dakar-Bamako railway.

By the early 20th century the Gambian was a migrant driven economy, and in 1910, it was estimated that at least 50% of the groundnuts grown were being cultivated by Strange Farmers. The influx of migrants can be explained as a result of both structure and agency: the regional economies of 19th century West Africa were profoundly changed by European interventions and markets, while individuals and certain groups responded to new opportunities. The presence of migrants also challenges assumptions that local populations were sufficient to support a flourishing export trade, while it modifies theses of agrarian change dependent on rising population levels.

Yet despite the dominance of the groundnut trade, The Gambia did not become a monoculture in the strictest sense, and the established systems of land use and farming techniques remained intact. Neither before, nor during colonial rule were existing social units shattered, but they were partially transformed and small producers were incorporated into Europe's economy to produce agricultural goods, as well as becoming consumers of new imported manufactures. One result of this incorporation was that local and regional merchant capital and their commercial networks were gradually overtaken by international merchant capital, which after 1870 became a dominant force. Thousands of producers became subject to the vagaries of the international market over which they exerted little influence, or of which they had little knowledge. And, the vagaries of the climate also played a part in the production and prices of groundnuts, as well as posing problems of local food supply in the specialized groundnut economy.

The mechanics of the shift into the export trade have been presented as resting on either African agency, or the larger structural forces of European capitalism and imperialism. The neo-liberal view is that the buoyant overseas demand for oilseeds, the incentive of wage goods and improved transport were the means of releasing local surpluses of land and labour, to develop an export economy based on domestic production and produce collection by European merchants. This process caused minimal disruption, required little technological innovation, and encouraged other sectors of the economy, notably local food specialization. Our investigation of the Gambian groundnut trade suggest that while the market was important, there were frequent problems associated with price fluctuations, as well as climatic irregularities, and cycles of indebtedness. In addition one cannot ignore the contribution of local agency, such as the role of pioneer migrants, while the increase in migration to provide sufficient labour led eventually to a dependency on imported food.

One issue we have frequently noted was the conflict of interest among those involved. The groundnut trade developed through collaboration and conflict among a number of interest groups, which included chiefs, farmers, migrant workers, African traders, European merchants and the colonial government. For example, chiefs were signatories to treaties on land and trade, while eventually they collaborated as tax collectors and salaried officials acting on behalf of the British. Producers and merchants clashed a number of times after 1880 over the f.o.b. prices offered and price fixing, which led to hold-ups, produce adulteration and occasional violence, which was particularly pronounced in the early 1920s. The merchants' agents also manipulated local prices of goods and rates of exchange for currency. There was also conflict among the producers, particular between Strange Farmers and local farmers over the instigation of hold-ups, which supports the view that migrant labour represents not only a flexible labour force for capital, but also a means of keeping the labour force under control and limiting the returns to labour.

But the merchants were not immune to disagreements among themselves, in particular between French and British; the former tried to stop the Anglo-French Convention of 1857 which gave the latter access to the river trade. Similarly there were disagreements over the use of barter trade and coinage, yet the firms did agree to form a Merchant Combine from 1900 to 1913. The European merchants also manipulated their African agents and traders, playing one off against the other, such that African agents never fully gained access to the import-export sector. Furthermore, African agents were frequently in debt to European merchants, who took them to court and secured their imprisonment. Yet all of these mercantile interests were capable of uniting at times, notably against the British government over the issue of the cession of The Gambia to France.

The European merchants on a number of occasions clashed with the government and were generally suspicious and resentful of interventions by the Administration and the government in London. One particular issue proved contentious, that of traders' licenses. The merchants motivated by profit and laissez faire economic liberalism saw licenses as a restriction of the liberty of the subject, and a restriction of free commerce. The colonial government viewed licenses and taxation in the broader context of economic policy and imperial ideology, and a necessity for ordered trade, good government and the protection of African people.

The government was certainly not unequivocally an arm of British capital: at times the merchant interest and that of the government converged, but in general it sought to mediate several interests involved in the trade. Usually that of the merchants prevailed because the government needed the revenues derived from exports, which were in the hands of the merchants. In essence, the government wanted the benefits of laissez-faire merchant capitalism, but frequently the consequences were at odds with its political objectives. Inevitably the Administration experienced its own internal conflicts, which we have frequently noted. Government officials, especially the Commissioners had divergent views about food importing, the treatment of Strange Farmers, and especially the distribution of rice and seeds on credit. By the 1920s the arrival of a number of agricultural experts in The Gambia also caused friction, and was representative of a wider concern by colonial administrators about the role of experts sent from London.

The colonial government's immediate objectives were to establish political control, boost the groundnut trade and introduce a formal taxation system that would make the colony financial independent. The role of colonial taxation has been much debated, and radical analyses have seen it as a key to cash crop development and associated labour migration. Certainly the Gambian government believed it was a stimulus to the extension of the groundnut industry, but it also seemed to have difficulty collecting taxes, while its main source of revenue was always import and export duties. Moreover, the groundnut trade pre-dates the colonial taxation system, while pioneer migrant farmers were initially attracted by the opportunities for groundnut farming combined with dry season trading. On the other hand, it is true that differential rates of taxation between French territories and The Gambia at times stimulated migration into the Gambia, as well as encouraging border trading.

Of greater significance than taxation was the erosion of domestic slavery in the early 20th century: combined with the economic marginalization of the interior it collectively stimulated the flow of migrant workers needed to expand the Gambian groundnut industry. The reduction of domestic slavery materially altered the relations of production within households, and released large numbers of workers who moved into new work relationships, creating a second wave of Strange Farmers. And, by the early 20th century migrant farmers also included young Gambian males, who left home for seasonal employment in other parts of The Gambia and beyond. It is also our contention that the use of credit by the merchants for both food and trade goods, together with the government distribution of food and seeds, especially at moments of environmental crisis were an important means whereby producers became firmly entrenched as export producers after 1857.

The colonial government made a number of interventions, and attempts at a policy to manage the groundnut trade, but most consistently they used food and seed distribution as a policy instrument, albeit often with reluctance. Food and seed distribution were designed to offset the worst effects of environmental hazards, as well as boosting the inflow of migrant workers whose contracts required their hosts to feed them. There was on these occasions a convergence of interest between government and producers, and it was at such times the government was prepared to override the merchant interest by distributing rice at lower cost, while in 1925 they cancelled the producers' rice debt The contingencies of climate and pestilence were a recurring problem for the Administration, but not only did drought, flood and ill-timed rainfall affect groundnut production, it also affected local food supplies, and so contributed to the volume of food imports needed to sustain the groundnut trade.

The rebuttal of arguments about the total evisceration of African economies still leaves a number of questions to be answered about dependency, especially with reference to external markets and the extent to which producers made gains from the groundnut trade. In the first half of the 19th century Gambian producers showed few signs of external dependency: generally the terms of trade were good and food suplusses were available in local markets. And, for example, in 1849 when French demand for groundnuts failed, producers retrenched output much to the concern of the merchants and the British authorities. However, in the second half of the 19th century the situation had altered. By 1857 local food surpluses chiefly from the South Bank could no longer cope with the degree of specialization that had taken place, and so production became more and more tied to the importing of rice.

As European credit using food and trade goods became common and widespread among producers, indebtedness increased, and they began to experience the social and economic effects of a dependency on international markets. Matters were not particularly bad while the terms of trade were satisfactory, but the Great Depression of the late 19th century exposed Gambian producers to the vicissitudes of the world market. No longer could producers easily curtail output when European markets were unfavourable, or when local f.o.b. prices were poor. And, this is why export production continued to expand in the face of the economic crises of the mid-1880s and during the early 20th century. Despite fluctuations in output related to the climate, wars, and market failures, in general producers kept producing in order to maintain the net income terms of trade to satisfy their material needs, and to service their debts. Their responses to price changes were limited as they had little knowledge of European markets; the merchants being the only source of information prior to the planting season, while the prices received could vary significantly during, as well as between seasons.

When farmers tried to implement hold-ups, they were berated by the government and undercut by the substantial numbers of Strange Farmers who wanted to sell and move on. Resistance to low prices took other forms, notably moving groundnuts into Senegal, or mixing foreign matter with the groundnuts, but usually the merchants won in the long run. The government frequently asserted that people didn't live within their means, yet it proved impossible to do so without credit as many farmers lived from one season to the next. The Merchant Combine attempted to operate without credit from 1903–1913, but this was a brief interlude, which was followed by a surge in credit, first after the 1913 drought and then during the 1914–18 War when groundnut prices reached all time highs. In 1921 prices collapsed and there was a credit crisis and widespread indebtedness.

The post-war price collapse was compounded by de-monetization in 1922, a particularly depressing episode marked by government incompetence and merchant opportunism at the expense of producers. These events and the general state of the commodity markets steered the government towards replacing *ad hoc* management with an Agricultural Department. In West Africa after 1900 the state became more concerned about its role as an agent of development, particularly by recognizing the need to improve communications in order to assist commercial development and the penetration of capital, as well as on strategic grounds and the establishment of political control. In the 1920s, colonial governments had to confront the aftermath of the Great War, and some of the failings of the markets and the re-structuring of merchant capital. They did so by a number of initiatives such as quality control and mixed farming schemes, to allow individual territories to compete on better terms. In The Gambia improved transport was not a priority, but the improvement of the quality of groundnuts was necessary to increase Gambia's competitiveness in an increasingly difficult trading climate. This was a particular moment of conflict between the producers on the one side, and the government and merchants on the other. And, it was the producers who bore the brunt of improved quality as prices were maintained at low levels. In another sphere aimed at improvement to the trade, the help of 'scientific management' was sought, which introduced a number of innovations such as agricultural surveys, mixed farming and ox-ploughing, and not least plans for an irrigation scheme in the hope of solving the need to import food.

The problem for the Agricultural Department, and the government was that the attempts to improve the groundnut economy coincided with the world trade depression. The price collapse of 1921 marked a reduction in commodity prices, which had surged during wartime. However, from 1922–30 oil seeds fared better than other commodities; prices stabilized; imported rice was cheaper and the net income terms of trade were improved. During this period the output of groundnuts was maintained not only by the stable terms of trade, but by farmers who were now dependent on the crop for the reproduction of their households, as well as meeting other payments for food, debts and taxes. Output was also sustained by the continued influx of Strange Farmers, and of particular significance was the cancellation in 1925 of the government rice debt. But by 1931 groundnut prices slumped in real terms, as the trade depression entered a new phase. Groundnut output fell, as well as the number of Strange Farmers coming into The Gambia. In such circumstances hopes for the much discussed irrigation scheme faded, and the Agricultural Department was retrenched and then suspended: meanwhile the government sought an increase in taxation to maintain its financial position. Matters did not improve after 1934 as the Second World War exacerbated the trade depression, and Gambian groundnut production showed a sustained decline, sinking to 20,000 tons for the 1943–44 season, the lowest since 1897.

The production of Gambian groundnuts during the period 1834–1934 described an upward but undulating trajectory. But who were the 'winners' and 'losers' during this period? Among the Gambian people probably the chiefs, large farmers and some African traders benefited for much of the time: chiefs became salaried officials, and they had privileged access to seeds and rice when distributed by the government. Their clients and other large farmers benefited too, such that the groundnut trade introduced new kinds of social and economic differentiation. As for smaller producers, they suffered the worst effects of the ups and downs of the trade, while having their economic and social dependency increased through debts and a reliance on groundnuts. And, there were those miserable episodes associated with the contingencies of drought, flood and pestilence mediated through a variety of social and political structures, when food was scarce and costly. It was the sheer uncertainty of the trade that characterized the lot of many groundnut producers.

Overall, a majority of Gambians did not secure any striking benefits from the actions of the colonial state, in terms of government expenditure from revenues so closely dependent on the groundnut trade. Because of the river, roads received little investment, while expenditure on agriculture, health and education was minimal. Given the size of the country and its heavy dependency on one crop it was run on a shoe-string: in general the Administration was concerned with tight budgets and balancing revenue and expenditure, in the face of such events as de-monetization and the write-off of seed and rice debts. The colonial state in The Gambia provided a context for the operation of merchant capital, even if it did not always approve of the actions of the merchants, or directly support them. Unsurprisingly it was the merchant interest that gained most from the groundnut trade, although it is difficult to make accurate assessments of the profitability of their operations, as the government found on several occasions when the firms refused details of their businesses. Given what we know, the differences between prices received for groundnuts by producers and those offered in Europe at times seems to have been substantial, especially under price-fixing by the merchants. And, in common with other mercantile operations in West Africa, it was the importing of goods—including food, and their use as credits that was particularly profitable

The Strange Farmers comprised a special category of producer, and their composition and contracts changed over time. Strange Farmers were probably less vulnerable than other wage labourers, because they had some bargaining power over their contract, while over time many developed special relationships with their hosts. Strange Farmers were able to enhance their incomes by dry season jobs too, as well as taking trade goods back home, which they sold at a profit. And by the 20th century as many Strange Farmers were ex-slaves, arguably the groundnut trade had opened-up new social and economic niches for them. Like their hosts, they were subject to the vicissitudes of the world markets and local f.o.b. prices, and these events were transmitted back to their households in the remoter areas which had become labour reserves as part of the changing regional political economies of West Africa. Yet the migrants were fed during the wet season, which was a material gain for their families back home who could offset this against the loss of their labour.

In The Gambia groundnut cultivation was never as intensive as in parts of Senegal, but as the trade grew, so more land was cleared for cultivation. The removal of bush may have altered rainfall patterns and it may have allowed the spread and proliferation of pests and diseases, which were held firmly in check by continuous belts of un-cleared land. But as we have already noted, Gambians did not abandon their farming techniques and their crop rotations combined with animal manures, which were capable of providing sustainable cultivation systems. Yet over a long period of time they had become reliant on imported food and credit because of the dependence on groundnuts, which fundamentally affected household reproduction. The groundnut trade in The Gambia not only comprises a long time span, it also provides a window through which we can observe how merchant credit, European markets, African farmers, migrant workers, colonial administrators, food importing and environmental circumstances were interwoven, to produce economic and social patterns generated by structure, agency and contingency.

# INDEX